W9-ASG-075

# From Crossbow
# to H-Bomb

U 27
B 76

Brodie, Bernard

# From Crossbow
# to H-Bomb

REVISED AND ENLARGED EDITION

# Bernard and Fawn M. Brodie

INDIANA UNIVERSITY PRESS
Bloomington & London

JUN 2 6 1975

188098

First Midland Edition, 1973

Copyright © 1962 by Bernard and Fawn M. Brodie
Revised and enlarged edition,
Copyright © 1973 by Indiana University Press
All rights reserved

No part of this book may be reproduced or utilized in any
form or by any means, electronic or mechanical, including
photocopying and recording, or by any information storage
and retrieval system, without permission in writing from
the publisher. The Association of American University
Presses' Resolution on Permissions constitutes the only ex-
ception to this prohibition.

Published in Canada by Fitzhenry & Whiteside Limited,
Don Mills, Ontario
Library of Congress catalog card number: 72-90408
ISBN: (cloth) 0-253-32490-4
        (paper) 0-253-20161-6
Manufactured in the United States of America

# Contents

# Introduction

This book is about the history of the application of science to war. We use the word "crossbow" in
the title to suggest a point of beginning long ago. Actually,
we go back not to the crossbow of medieval times but to
the giant crossbow or "ballista" of antiquity; but the precise
time of beginning or the choice of a single weapon to
launch the story is an arbitrary matter. The reader will find
that a single chapter takes him through antiquity and into
the Middle Ages. In contrast to our own times, the equipment of war changed very slowly in those days, and what
changes occurred usually had little to do with science.

If we use the term "science" in the sense that the scientist himself uses it, then we must say that the application of
science to war is new, because science itself is new. Apart
from mathematics, we can find little science in antiquity
and in the Middle Ages that looks respectable by modern
standards. The scientist is concerned with basic principles
describing nature, these principles being subject to verifica-
tion by repeated experimentation or other appropriate observation. The growth of science is thus an inductive
process, where new increments of knowledge round out or
modify existing principles. The application of science to
machines, on the other hand, is a deductive process; it begins
with a principle and proceeds to a mechanism.

It is obvious, therefore, that if we attempted in this book
to stay within the austere definition of the word "science"
that the scientist might expect of us, we should not be start-

ing with anything so antique as the crossbow; but we are concerned also with the work of craftsmen, or intuitive inventors, who were able to accomplish wonderful things for reasons that were often unknown to them. Gunpowder, for example, was known and used in Europe at least from the early part of the fourteenth century, but the purpose served by the nitrate in it, which is to provide oxygen for the quick combustion of the other components, was not fully understood until nearly five centuries later.

Therefore, when we speak in the following pages about the application of science to war, we shall be using the word at different times in different senses—though we hope it will be clear in each case what we mean—all having in common the connotation of insight and experimentation being used to invent new military weapons or to improve existing ones. The scientist will thus get his due, but so will the imaginative engineer and craftsman. However, we shall not be insensitive to the importance of the special meaning of the word science as we have described it above, nor to the revolutionary results which were likely to follow whenever it did make its appearance.

The slowness of weapons progress prior to the nineteenth and especially the twentieth centuries requires, nevertheless, still other explanations. What science there was, and what talent there was for invention, seem often to have been dedicated to other pursuits than new weapons, and in fact to have avoided that field. We propose in these introductory pages to suggest some of the reasons for this avoidance, but we must first acknowledge the limitations of our understanding of these matters, mostly because of the anonymity in times past of the great majority of men who were responsible for advances in what we now call "the state of the art." To be sure, this tends to be true also today, but more because of the large numbers of people involved than because it is difficult to trace their individual contributions. Certainly the names of the inventors of the ingenious contrivances of antiquity and the middle ages—the complicated ballistae, the moving towers, the siege catapults, the early hand guns and cannon—are lost to us. Many inventions

were devised by soldiers to provide for the immediate neces-
sities of the battle; others were by-products of the peacetime application of new developments in arts like metallurgy.

It is noteworthy, incidentally, that most of the advances
in hand guns until quite recent times were in weapons
intended for hunting animals instead of man. The hunter
was usually a gentleman and aristocrat, far richer than the
soldier and more highly regarded by society. The prince
who hunted with artful and costly wheel-lock guns had no
thought of arming his own soldiers with anything but the
cheap and less efficient matchlocks, which dominated European infantry war for generations.

Scientists will appreciate the further fact that their precursors tended to be disdainful of inventions that did not
represent pure science. Archimedes, for example, perhaps
the greatest mathematician of antiquity, turned his inventive genius toward war only when his own city, Syracuse,
was besieged by the Romans in 215 B.C. As Plutarch tells
the story, Archimedes designed a super-catapult which
hurled 1,800-pound stones at the Roman galleys with such
success that Marcellus, the Roman commander, was moved
to admit that "Archimedes really outdoes the hundred-
handed giants of mythology." The capture of Syracuse was
actually delayed for three years, and when it came Archimedes was one of those who fell. But it is said that until his
death he consistently depreciated his war machines, which
were merely inventions, demonstrating but not creating any
new principles of natural law. He was more proud of his
discoveries in mathematics, in which respect he was entirely
at one with the modern scientist, who always values the discovery of new principles far above the application, however
clever, of known principles to machines.

This attitude is observed even when no moral feelings are
involved, but the latter, too, have played a part. In our own
time we have seen certain nuclear scientists staring appalled
at the weapons which their own talents had spawned, and
striving first to control and then to disassociate themselves
from their creations. The atomic bomb, to be sure, is an

instrument of very special destructiveness, but there is always the matter of perspective. There have been many new weapons which looked excessively deadly in their time, but the intellectual ancestors of the modern scientists tended to be more obedient, or at least more vocal about obedience, to moral and Christian principles.

Roger Bacon, who speculated about flying machines, mechanically propelled ships, and circumnavigation of the globe 250 years before Columbus discovered America, devised in 1248 a workable formula for gunpowder, but he chose to hide his formula in a cryptogram. Leonardo da Vinci was clearly troubled by the destructive nature of many of the instruments which he designed or suggested, as he made clear when writing about his submarine design, part of which he deliberately kept secret. "This I do not divulge," he wrote, "on account of the evil nature of men, who would practice assassinations at the bottom of the seas by breaking the ships in their lowest parts and sinking them together with the crews who are in them."

Niccoló Tartaglia, the father of modern ballistics, had similar hesitations. He at first kept secret the results of his calculations concerning gunshot trajectories because he had decided that "it was a thing blameworthy, shameful and barbarous, worthy of severe punishment before God and man, to wish to bring to perfection an art damageable to one's neighbor and destructive to the human race," and that to concern oneself with such matters was a "grave sin and shipwreck of the soul." When an invasion of Italy by the infidel Turks became imminent, however, he changed his mind. "Today . . . ," he wrote, "in the sight of the ferocious wolf preparing to set on our flock, and of our pastors united for the common defense, it does not seem to me any longer proper to hold these things hid, and I have resolved to publish them . . . so that all should be in a better state whether to attack the common enemy or to defend themselves against him."

And Cervantes, whose left hand was maimed in the bloody naval battle of Lepanto, put in the mouth of Don Quixote a sentiment which is not obviously mad: "Blessed be those happy ages, that were stranger to the dreadful fury of these devilish instruments of artillery, whose inventor, I am satisfied, is now in hell, receiving the reward of his cursed invention."

Similarly, the Scottish mathematician John Napier, who invented logarithms, was induced to turn his mind to the invention of war machines at the time the Spanish Armada was threatening to invade England, because as a devout Calvinist he could not bear the thought of Protestant England falling to a Catholic monarch. But once the Spanish threat collapsed, he did his best to keep his various inventions secret. When pressed on his deathbed to reveal them, he is reported to have protested that "for the ruin and overthrow of man, there were too many devices already framed, which if he could make to be fewer, he would with all his might endeavour to do so; and that therefore seeing the malice and rancour rooted in the heart of mankind will not suffer them to diminish, by any new conceit of his the number of them should never be increased."

Are we to suppose from this that over the centuries the progress of armaments has been materially slowed down by such sentiments? Probably not, because recent developments owe too much to modern science. But the prevalence of views like those expressed by Leonardo, Tartaglia, and Napier no doubt accounts in some part for a certain absence of invention in the military arts. After all, men of inventive talent and imagination are relatively scarce in any age, and a full accounting has to be made of them.

One other factor is even harder for the modern mind to grasp. Today we have a passion for putting things in what we conceive to be their proper places, and certainly the place for art, in the aesthetic sense of the term, is not on the battlefield. But that was not the view of the renaissance gentleman, who combined art and armament in what he considered an essential partnership. The beautiful and expensively wrought armor, guns, and swords which can easily be seen today in any of the appropriate museums bear out the point. It would be difficult to judge, and no doubt easy to exaggerate, the inhibiting influence on technological progress of the renaissance preoccupation with beauty, but it certainly affected cost, and cost has always been a limiting factor. We can at any rate rejoice that in this day of burdensome military budgets we are not paying extra for sculpturing on the missiles.

To finish our introductory remarks with something that is clearly important, we come to the proverbial old "cake of custom," the invisible but powerful force that makes men unwilling to part with accustomed ways and accustomed thoughts. Generals have been particularly blamed for their conservatism, but that is often unjust. Sometimes, as we shall see in the following pages, they have had good reasons for opposing a change which a later age was to consider a landmark of progress. Sometimes they have been merely fools, but even here their record is not noticeably worse than that of other professions, as is clear, for example, from the history of medicine.

Today we are confronted with a special situation. The choice of strategies and of weapons systems is not only immensely more difficult than it has ever been before, but also involves questions that are deeply and essentially baffling, even to the ablest minds. As Captain B. H. Liddell Hart put it in 1935, in a world far simpler strategically than the one we know today, "It is not that generals and admirals are incompetent, but that the task has passed beyond their competence. Their limitations are due not to a congenital stupidity—as a disillusioned public is so apt to assume—but to the growth of science, which has upset the foundations of their technique . . . a scientific habit of thought is the last thing that military education and training have fostered. Perhaps that is an unalterable condition, for the services might hardly survive if they parted company with sentiment." This was a marvelously perceptive as well as foresighted statement, because sentiment is the very stuff of leadership and dedication, which are what most military histories are all about.

Our own effort which follows is at the opposite end of the spectrum of military history. It has to do not with sentiment, even in that grand sense in which we apply it to the great generals of history, but with the application strictly of intelligence to the problem of war—of intelligence not as it sometimes expresses itself on the battlefield, but in quiet studies or laboratories far removed.

# 1. Antiquity

In the history of the technology of war great inventive achievements have sometimes been used only once, or perhaps a score of times, and then abandoned or forgotten. The super-catapults and grappling cranes devised by Archimedes seem not to have been used elsewhere, though inferior ballistae were used throughout Europe. One of the greatest military feats in antiquity was the bridging of the Hellespont (the ancient name for the Dardanelles) by a gifted Greek engineer, Harpalus, who chose to place his talent at the service of the invading Persian enemy, Xerxes. In 481 B.C. Harpalus designed two floating roadways made of covered fifty-oared galleys. They were linked by six cables, two of flax and four of papyrus. The western bridge had 314 ships, the eastern 360. The bridges, which would be impressive even by modern standards, solved a major logistics problem for Xerxes and made possible the invasion of Greece. No comparable engineering feat of this magnitude would even be attempted till modern times.

Greek fire, an ingenious chemical weapon, the napalm of its day, was used with deadly effect, but on rare occasions only, and then abandoned. It was invented, apparently, by a Syrian architect named Kallinokos of Heliopolis, who gave the secret formula—a mixture of sulphur, pitch, niter, petroleum, and probably quicklime—to the Emperor Constantine Pogonatus when Constantinople was being besieged by the Saracens in 673. Constantine fitted out his galleys with projecting tubes which squirted the Greek fire into hostile vessels. It clung to whatever it hit and burned fiercely, soon winning the reputation of being inextinguishable, which doubtless greatly enhanced its efficiency as a terror weapon, though actually it could be put out, or so the story has it, by vinegar or wine, with sand.

The Moslems used the same weapon against the Christians over 500 years later in the siege of Acre (1190), when a Damascene engineer burned all the siege machines of the Crusaders by having jars of Greek fire flung against the moving towers the Franks had reared against the city walls. At Mansura the Saracens flung it from great arbalests. The French chronicler Joinville says the missile was "like a big tun, and had a tail of the length of a large spear: the noise which it made resembled thunder, and it appeared like a great fiery dragon flying through the air, giving such a light that we could see in our camp as clearly as in broad day." When it fell, scattering the liquid everywhere, the trails of flame set fire to everything they touched.

Why this terrifying incendiary weapon was not more extensively used, and why the secret of its making was lost or abandoned for centuries is not known. But its story does dramatize the absolute lack of any well-defined body of knowledge about the most primitive chemistry, and the failure of communication of the secrets of well-tried devices from one generation to another even in the same community or state.

There were other isolated instances of chemical warfare. The Greeks used a gas attack with sulphur fumes at the siege of Delium in 424 B.C. And of course there was fairly frequent use of simple incendiary materials dating back almost to pre-history—blazing arrows, pots of boiling oil, and naphtha. In fact, liquid fire is represented on the bas-reliefs of the Assyrians. But until quite recent times the science of chemistry, except as it related to metallurgy, was so primitive as scarcely to deserve the name. The chemical formula of the gunpowder used in Europe in 1600 or even that used in the United States in 1860 was not very different from that employed by the Chinese in their primitive rockets for battling with the Tartars in 1232.

In metallurgy there was a good deal of continuity and considerably more science than in chemistry. Throughout antiquity metallurgy seems to have been entirely developed by craftsmen. Their secrets were transmitted by word of mouth, from master to apprentice. Innovations and improvements sometimes spread quickly, sometimes not at all. Many inventions were perfected independently of each other in various parts of the world. Development and progress in weapons and armor were extremely slow, and there were long periods of stagnation. In fact if one studies a stone sculpture in the Louvre, the Stele of the Vultures, in which Eannatum, King of Ur, commemorated a victory over a neighboring city in about 2550 B.C., one can see remarkably little difference between these helmeted Babylonian spearmen, protecting themselves with square shields held edge to edge, and the Greek phalanx or the Roman legion of nearly 3,000 years later.

The Chaldeans and Assyrians, the earliest warriors of history of whom we have detailed knowledge, were armed with spears, battle-axes, maces, swords, and shields, as well as bows and arrows. Their defensive armor was light but tough. The Assyrians devised a scale armor, composed of many small metal plates sewn on a leather jacket so that the rows overlapped, a kind of armor that would persist till the time of Oliver Cromwell. Even the earliest Chaldeans used horses and fought from chariots, though fighting from a mounted horse came much later. But throughout antiquity the infantry was paramount in war. Lightly armed, disciplined and toughened, the foot-soldier could perform extraordinary feats of valor and endurance. Alexander's soldiers could march 400 miles in two weeks, and once made 135 miles in three consecutive days.

The Greek infantryman, or hoplite, carried a ten-foot spear, a short cut-and-thrust sword, and a round shield. His armor and weapons weighed about seventy pounds, the chief burden of which was borne by a slave, who also foraged for food (Fig. 1). The Roman used the pilum, a seven-foot throwing and thrusting spear, and the gladius, a twenty-inch cut-and-thrust sword with a heavy broad blade (Fig. 2). Both weapons were superior to the weapons of the

Fig. 1. Greek Hoplite

past. Battles were generally fought without any attempt at secrecy or surprise. The cavalry took its position on the wings; the infantry was massed in squares at the center, and the chariots were drawn up behind. Archers began the contest, and the battle followed as a great collision of infantry, with the cavalry doing its best to outflank the enemy.

The horse was used primarily for fighting with chariots; mounted cavalry was never the primary fighting arm in antiquity. Since no efficient harness was designed till the tenth century, the horse could not be used efficiently for

Fig. 2. Roman Legionary and Centurion

drawing loads. Slaves bore the burdens instead. Horses were considered nobler objects in any case. Cicero, debating in his *On Duty* whether one should lighten a ship in a storm by casting over a favorite horse or slaves, decided on the slaves.

The metal workers who devised and improved the early weapons worked by rule of thumb, empirically. Eventually they discovered that a metal usually becomes harder when it is beaten, and they learned that it was best to beat the bronze metal of a sword while cold, and then to temper it afterward to remove the brittleness. This was a technique they employed for thousands of years, and they perfected the art till the bronze swords had edges almost as hard as steel. No one could know why beating hardened the metal until the modern discovery of X-rays, which made it clear that the beating rearranges the crystals.

The secret of making wrought iron was discovered as early as 2500 B.C., but for more than a thousand years it remained only a curiosity. Then about 1400 B.C. the tribe of Chalybes in the Armenian mountains discovered how to heat wrought iron in a charcoal fire and give it a steel facing by hammering. The result was a core of wrought iron surrounded by steel. This carburization or cementation gave iron hardness and thus real utility. Additional techniques—slagging the iron ore, that is, adding limestone to liquefy the slag in the furnace, the handling of a bloom, the quenching and annealing—were all learned eventually. The Hittites spread the techniques of the new iron-making when they were driven out of their own kingdom and scattered throughout the Near East in 1200 B.C., so that iron knives, scissors, axes, weapons, and plows rapidly came within the reach of everyone. The Hindus became renowned as the best temperers of steel in the world.

On the American continents, though some of the aborigines had used copper and bronze, they had never developed wrought iron or steel for weapons, and stone arrowheads and spearheads continued to be used till after the time of Columbus. Even in the old world, the use of stone did not disappear as completely as one might have expected, for the Normans in France were using stone arrowheads and lanceheads as late as the eighth century A.D.

The only sciences which made a real impact on the technology of war in antiquity were mathematics and physics, or more properly, theoretical mechanics. Some of the latter, as well as a vast deal of ingenious craftsmanship, went into the design and invention of the siege weapons used in attacking fortified cities. Many of the fortifications of antiquity were impressive by any standards, including those of our own day. Nineveh, constructed in 2000 B.C., had stone walls 50 miles long, 120 feet high and 30 feet thick. The Great Wall of China, built in 200 B.C., was twenty feet high and continued for 1,400 miles. These outclassed even the greatest works of the Romans.

The Assyrians were skillful in the art of attacking as well as of building fortified cities. By the tenth century B.C. they already had a disciplined mobile army, complete with battering rams which were mounted in wheeled wooden towers and protected in front by metal plates. The Babylonians used as battering rams immense metal-tipped spears mounted on wheels. The Old Testament King Uzziah, of the eighth century B.C., seems to have used catapults which he placed "on the towers and upon the bulwarks to shoot arrows and great stones withal."

But it was the Greeks and Romans who developed the astonishing siege machines capable of destroying some of the most impressive fortifications of antiquity. In addition to battering rams, which consisted of a whole tree trunk suspended from a roofed framework and tipped with an iron head, there were movable towers topped with drawbridges which made it possible to mount the highest city walls (Fig. 3). Then there was the ancient artillery, comprising ballistae, onagers, and catapults.

The Greek ballista was an immense crossbow using, like the small medieval crossbow, the principle of tension (Fig. 4). It was used with particular success by Dionysius of Syracuse in his wars with Carthage in 400 B.C. The power of the tension crossbow was limited by the elastic strength of the bow itself. It could carry fire to houses or forts; it could even breach walls. Curiously its development preceded that of the hand crossbow by centuries.

The later Roman ballista, like the catapult, was powered by torsion, the energy being stored in two thick skeins of twisted cords (Fig. 5). The onager, meaning wild ass—its rear end kicked up when the stone was discharged—was a much simpler device. It too used a thick skein of cords twisted to great strain by geared winches, and suddenly released a projectile (Fig. 6). Modern replicas have been

Fig. 3. Fighting Towers, Showing Battering Ram

unable to recapture the secret of preserving the elasticity of these cords.

The mangonel, which employed a series of levers, winches, and counterweights, could hurl a sixty-pound rock about 500 yards with some degree of accuracy. As Edwin

Fig. 4. Greek Ballista

Tunis has pointed out in his attractive pictorial history of weapons, "an American Revolutionary naval cannon had little more than twice that range and little better accuracy with a shot weighing half as much." The smaller catapults usually shot short javelins weighing about six pounds and were fairly accurate.

Greek and Roman engineers thoroughly understood the principles of the lever and the wedge, and could use the screw to exert pressure. Fighting towers were moved into place by hundreds of men working levers. At the siege of Rhodes, fourteen years after Alexander's death, the largest fighting tower required 3,400 men to move it up to the walls. Another thousand men wielded a battering ram 180 feet long. Rhodes held out, however, for six years, and was finally relieved by allies who came to her aid by sea.

In the development of their siege weapons and fortifications, as well as of their architecture in general, the Romans were indebted not only to Hellenistic geometry but also to the unique outpouring of pure science which re-

Fig. 5. Roman Ballista

sulted from the great concentration of scientific talent at the academy of sciences and arts founded by Alexander the Great in 332 B.C. at Alexandria. Here for several centuries the Egyptian sovereigns concentrated the most brilliant minds of the time and, for experimentation, provided huge laboratories, a zoo, botanical gardens, and a hospital. A library was developed which at the time of its destruction contained 400,000 manuscripts.

In this extraordinary citadel of learning, astronomy, mathematics and medicine flourished. Hero of Alexandria made the first important discoveries in theoretical mechanics, and there was no real improvement on his theories for more than a thousand years. Many of the theories advanced came from the study of machines that were already more than a thousand years old, for the Egyptians had been using the balance with unequal arms in their shadoofs for raising water, and the lever and screw in their oil and wine presses. Many new machines were invented and the theoretical concepts of their working discovered. There were force pumps, trains of gearing, piston weights, water wheels, windmills, rotary grinders, flap valves, even a reaction steam turbine. Automatic slot machines were invented and put to use selling holy water in the Serapeum. Actually most of the machines, though sometimes masterpieces of precision mechanics, were designed to produce motion rather than to do work, and few were adapted for productive uses.

One impressive device was the Pharos, a special lighthouse constructed by Sostratus of Cnidus in the reign of Ptolemy II, 283-247 B.C. It consisted of a 500-foot tower with a fire on top and a special mirror which projected the light of the fire thirty miles across the Mediterranean. The tower remained intact until 1375 A.D., when an earthquake toppled it.

Some work seems to have been done directly on engines of war. Dionysius of Alexandria constructed a polybolos, the equivalent of a machine gun, which fired a succession of arrows. The bow was bent by turning a wheel and released by an endless chain, which at the same time reloaded the bow. Ctesibius, an engineer in the same city, succeeded in gearing to the bow arms of catapults pistons working in cylinders filled with compressed air. But neither of these machines seems to have seen combat service.

Archimedes worked with the scientists of Alexandria through correspondence, particularly, it seems, with the successors of Euclid. Using the mathematics of the time with as much theoretical maturity as any modern mathematician, he developed his treatises on statics and hydrostatics. It would be 2,000 years before his invention of the driven helical screw—with reversed action to make it push rather than be pushed—would move ships across the seas.

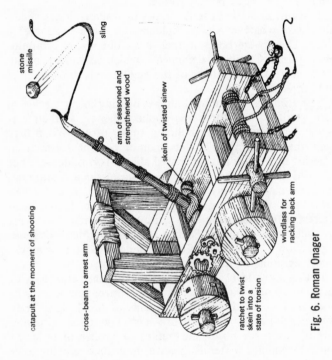

stone
missile

sling

catapult at the moment of shooting

arm of seasoned and
strengthened wood

skein of twisted sinew

cross-beam to arrest arm

windlass for
racking back arm

ratchet to twist
skein into a
state of torsion

Fig. 6. Roman Onager

But his theory explaining the lever was of enormous practical value at the time he lived. It enabled engineers of all kinds, including the military, to calculate the dimensions of levers needed for particular tasks. This saved time and prevented accidents. His theory would not be improved upon until 1586 A.D. Curiously, the researches of his followers seem to have been largely sterile.

It seems clear that the inventors of war machines generally used whatever design calculations were available to them. There were hosts of ancient handbooks on catapults, among them Ctesibius' *Belopoeica,* which contained formulas to correlate the caliber of the engine with the weight of the projectile.

The Romans contributed almost nothing to pure science; their great natural forte was applied science, as their stupendous achievements in building amply prove. When they built the Pantheon they hit upon a cement formula so superior that it has already lasted almost two millennia, but they did not know the exact proportions of silica, aluminum, and iron oxide which went into the mixture. There is evidence that the best of the Roman engineers had a keen interest in mathematics. The writings of Marcus Vitruvius on architecture and of Sextus Julius Frontinus on aqueducts show a conscious effort to understand the scientific theory implicit in their engineering activity. The Romans used the water level, plummet, surveying instruments with accurate sights, water wheels, and bronze pumps as efficient as those of the fire departments of the 1800's. They even developed a primitive fire-control system, using the guts of cattle for hoses and pumps of bronze in order to douse incendiary materials heaped upon their moving towers. They copied the great Alexandrian lighthouse, building two like it at Carthage and Ostia.

When it came to war engines they were amazingly skillful in utilizing all the devices of antiquity. In addition to ballistae, catapults (Fig. 7), and onagers, they employed mantelets, penthouses, towers, mounds, terraces, the ram, the bore, and the mine. At the siege of Carthage 6,000 men were employed to build a single emplacement and penthouse, for one enormous ram. By the fourth century the Roman legions had a ratio of one siege engine to every hundred men in the infantry; Napoleon's divisions would have three pieces of artillery for every thousand men at best.

Fig. 7. Roman Catapult

Certainly the efficiency and ingenuity of the Roman weapons were directly related to the relatively advanced state of the mathematics and mechanics of the time. Caesar was without a rival in the art of fortification and siege work. It should be pointed out, however, that in his time no less than in later periods a good deal of credit was due the simple art of digging. At the siege of Alesia in 52 B.C., Caesar's men shifted two million cubic meters of earth from trenches. Another Roman general, Crassus, dug a trench fifteen feet deep, fifteen feet broad and thirty-four miles long across the toe of Italy.

With the fall of the Roman Empire the fine theory and engineering techniques of the Romans fell into disuse, and for several centuries were lost to western Europe altogether.

# 2. The Middle Ages

Western Europe entered upon a period of barbarism and anarchy. Even the technology of Rome was largely forgotten, to say nothing of the science, and war reverted to its most primitive beginnings. For a time even the techniques of fortification and siege warfare were lost. The invaders from the north wrought an improved weapon here and there; the francisca of the Franks, a single-bladed axe with a heavy head deeply hollowed in the interior, could shear through the stoutest Roman shield or helmet. But the weapon the invaders used to greatest advantage against the Romans and against each other was the horse.

The Romans had relied chiefly on their infantry, which enjoyed an extraordinary mobility as a result of the network of Roman roads. The road system, as Hilaire Belloc put it, "struck like a lash across the conquered provinces." After their legions were overwhelmed at Adrianople in 378 by the cavalry of the Goths, the Romans belatedly tried to strengthen their cavalry arm. But the northerners, perhaps because of their better pastures, seem to have had superior horses, and used them to better advantage even before the invention of the stirrup.

This invention came surprisingly late in history, considering the fact that the bridle had been in use since the Age of Bronze. The Greeks and Romans had never designed an efficient harness, always attaching the load to be drawn much too high on the collar, and had failed to invent iron horseshoes. The Chinese had made an efficient curved saddle about 200 B.C., but nothing resembling it was known in Europe till the fourth century A.D. The stirrup, also a Chinese invention, came about 600 A.D. It resulted in a vastly increased military efficiency among the Mongolian nomads, from whom it spread quickly to Europe. The stirrup made it possible for a man in armor to assault on horseback; without it he could not easily withstand the shock of combat.

With the deterioration of the Roman roads the armored knight came to replace the Roman footsoldier as the symbol of power and the arbiter of justice. Since the Roman system of regular pay for soldiers was not used by the northern chieftains, and fighting men were rewarded out of the loot they could save for themselves, the chief aim of the soldier became plunder rather than conquest. Tactics and strategy degenerated. As C. W. C. Oman, the great historian of war in the Middle Ages, described it, "By the sixth century the last survivals of Roman military skill had disappeared in the West. No traces remained of it but the clumsily patched walls of the great cities." The art of fortification degenerated; most chieftains were content with earthworks or crude wooden palisading; only a few of the old Roman walled cities were kept in good repair—Verona, Rome, Narbonne.

The Byzantines, on the other hand, with a stable government contrasting strongly with the anarchy of the west, continued to build fortifications of stone, and the Turks and Saracens developed it to a high art. Byzantine war theory, a remarkable combination of sophistication and good sense, was codified in two great military textbooks, the *Strategicon* of Emperor Maurice (562-602) and the *Tactica* of Leo the Wise (886-911). Battles were avoided if the odds were considered too high; cunning was considered a part of good generalship, and useless sacrifice of lives was deplored. Above all, war was considered practical and not heroic.

In the west, as feudal traditions became more universal, fighting became extremely localized. Fighting was organized around the heavily armored mounted lancer, and the fate of the dismounted men serving him depended upon the fate of the knight. The infantry, armed with pikes and bows, was generally despised, the important part of the battle being the clash between the men-at-arms, knights or potential knights. Although defeated footsoldiers were likely to be cut to pieces by the vanquishing party, the knights were held for ransom. Eventually ransom came to play a leading role in medieval warfare, influencing both causes and tactics. As Theodore Ropp described it, "Everyone preferred live prisoners who could be ransomed to dead men whose relatives or friends might take revenge."

Battles were almost never fought in winter, and the art of war became ever more stylized. The great masses of the common people, though heavily taxed to build the fortified cities and castles, and subject to the banditry of the unemployed soldiers in the winter, managed to escape the brutalizing effects of warfare altogether for long periods. The Catholic Church strongly discouraged Christians fighting Christians. It partially succeeded in barring warfare on or near church property, as well as attacks on pilgrims, peasants, merchants, women, and all men and women associated with clerical orders. This meant immunity for a large proportion of the population.

The exceptions to the extreme localization of war were, of course, the Crusades, when religious zeal overrode local jealousies, and the church sanctioned the fighting. But even these immense upheavals, requiring considerable co-ordinated military effort, resulted in very little change in the strategy and tactics of war. As Oman has pointed out, the Crusaders came back with some new ideas on fortification and armor, but they failed to employ after their return the most significant strategic lesson of the Crusades. The greatest successes in the wars with the Turks had been the result of the proper combination of infantry and cavalry. Those generals who failed to utilize the foot soldier had always failed disastrously. But as late as the twelfth and thirteenth centuries, fighting in Europe continued to consist mostly of clashes between armored knights. The mailed man on the horse continued to be supreme, and the man on foot a despised and relatively helpless member of his entourage.

The Crusades did, however, immensely stimulate a revival of military architecture, which had been neglected for five centuries. Architects and soldiers alike were impressed

Fig. 8. Morning Star

by the great walled cities of Nicaea, Antioch, Jerusalem and Constantinople, against which their siege weapons had proved so futile. Richard Coeur de Lion, an original military engineer of no mean talent, brought back ideas from the Near East and improved upon them in building his own castles. Wood was replaced by stone; the square tower, or keep, was surrounded by outer defenses, and these supplemented by ditching and hedging. Castle building, which saw tremendous growth in the twelfth century, was brought to perfection in the thirteenth. Old fortifications like the Tower of London and Carcassonne were remodeled into concentric castles of prodigious strength.

Every town fortified itself with a ring wall; and by 1300 defense was so superior to offense that the only certain weapon in siegecraft was famine. Moreover, invading armies, interested chiefly in plunder, could seldom be persuaded to conduct a year-long siege, so great was the doubt of its success.

The decline and stagnation of science throughout this long period needs no documentation here. The attitude of the Catholic Church was inimical to science; the authority of the theologian and the occasional scholar of antiquity remained supreme. Even in medicine, where observation and experimentation would have had immediate practical value, learning in the universities was entirely by rote. The successors of Galen taught anatomy for 1,200 years before it was discovered that the dissections he described were of monkeys rather than of men. It was the rare anatomist who dared to point out that men did not, in fact, have one less rib than women. As J. G. Crowther has wryly pointed out, few intellectuals were prepared to go to the stake for their opinions, since the intellect is cool and does not nerve a man for martyrdom.

Even the medieval cathedral architects reached their magnificent achievements by experience rather than analysis. Improvements were entirely empirical. When the builders of the cathedral at Beauvais tried to surpass all others in the height of their vaulting arches, they paid for their daring in two successive collapses of their structure, which as a consequence was never brought to completion.

The gifted practical technicians and builders of the Middle Ages passed on many valuable methods, but not the spirit of scientific inquiry. For a time Greek science was preserved and taught in the Byzantine Empire, but eventually the hostility of the church sent the non-orthodox scientists fleeing to the Near East where they handed on the Greek heritage in centers like Haran, Baghdad, and Gunde-Shapur. Arab universities arose in Basra, Kufa, Cairo, Toledo, and Cordoba. The Arabs salvaged mathematics from the wreck of the Roman Empire and added to it the Arabic notation and algebraic form of thought, much of which had come to them from India. Specifically, it was the Arabian scientist Mohammed ibn-Musa Abu al-Khowari-zimi, the librarian of al-Mamun at Baghdad, who in 830 wrote the famous *Al-jebr Wa'l-muqâbalah,* which gave the science of algebra its name and became the medium by which the Indian numerals and decimal system were eventually transmitted to Europe.

The Arabs learned from India the art of making crucible steel, and founded metallurgical centers in Damascus and Toledo. The "damascened" blades from these cities are still famous. Al-Kindi wrote a series of treatises on producing iron and steel for weapons. The Arabs developed the windmill, an invention the Crusaders admired and took back to Europe. They were using the compass in the Mediterranean and Indian Oceans when it was looked upon as a mere curiosity in Europe.

Arab science, mathematics, and astronomy found their way into Europe through Moorish Spain and northern Africa. Moors, Jews, and Spaniards in Toledo knew both Arabic and Latin. The library in Cordoba, Spain, had 600,000 manuscripts as early as 900. In 1300 the library of the king of France would number no more than 400.

The full impact of Arab science was not felt in Europe till the twelfth century. Then it became popular to study particularly the works of Euclid and Archimedes. By the thirteenth century the Arab chemists had mastered cupellation, the separation of gold and silver by nitric acid, the extraction of silver by amalgamation with mercury, and the quantitative analysis of alloys of gold and silver. But when this chemistry got to Europe it became alchemy, where any further advance was stifled by superstition and fraud. As Albert Rupert Hall puts it, "the most remarkable feature of all alchemical writings is that their authors prove themselves utterly incapable of distinguishing true from false." It would not be till the seventeenth century that chemistry would see any real advance.

The alchemist considered himself professionally above experimenting with mere iron, and all the developments in the metallurgy of this useful element were left to the lowly blacksmith, who did surprisingly well considering his lack of status and the natural limitations of his craft. By 1300 the European blacksmith had mastered the art of casting iron, that is, he could make iron flow into clay molds by heating it to a very high temperature. Wrought iron continued to be produced and so did crucible steel. For power the smith used the water-mill, which also ground grain and moved the carpenter's saw. Without power from the mill to supply blast air for his bellows he couldn't have made cast iron.

The thirteenth century saw an enormous growth of interest in the study of mechanics. Streams of manuals on engineering and metallurgy appeared, with instructions on the making of all sorts of primitive machines. The crank was invented, and cams and gears were greatly improved. Many of the metallurgical techniques developed during the late middle ages would be utilized right up to the nineteenth century.

The great medieval inventions were few in number, but were not without significant consequences. The foremost, of course, was printing. Two others were immensely important for mankind in general and for the art of war in particular—the hinged rudder, and the mariner's compass. Columbus was dependent upon both for his discovery of America, as well as upon the improved but far from reliable methods of calculating longitude based on Moslem astronomy and trigonometry. A primitive astrolabe was used in Europe from the third century onward, but it was not perfected until the renaissance. The compass was slow to be adopted in the west, for it was widely believed that there were magnetic mountains which would draw to destruction any ship fitted with iron nails and carrying a compass.

All through the middle ages there was very little advance in weapons or in methods of attack, though the art of fortification flourished. The smith and armorer, the supreme craftsmen of the period, remained paramount in the development of war weapons, but their genius was not highly inventive. The siege weapons used in 1300 were not notably different from those employed 2,000 years earlier. Since Roman times there had been only one truly new development; this was the trebuchet, developed about 1100, a device which depended for its power not on torsion or tension but on the sudden release of heavy weights by counterpoises. It consisted of a long pole balanced on a pivot supported by uprights. The longer part was pulled to the ground and a missile attached. This was held down by ropes or wooden catches worked by a winch. Meanwhile the shorter end of the pole was loaded with heavy weights. When the pole was released, the stone flew off to a considerable distance (Fig. 9). By the end of the thirteenth century several kinds were in use.

Perhaps the most significant weapon introduced in medieval times was the hand crossbow. Developed independently

Fig. 9. Trebuchet

in the tenth century, it was actually a small version of one of the siege ballista developed by the Greeks. At first the bow was made of horn, sinew and wood. It was bent by holding its nose to the ground, with one foot placed in a stirrup at the front end of the stock, while the cord was pulled by a hook on the archer's belt. The Italians, who were the first to use it extensively, became famous for their skill with this weapon. The great advantage was that it could be drawn ahead of time and kept drawn without physical strain to the archer while being aimed. Then too, unlike the bow, it could be used effectively by relatively unskilled men. It was quickly adapted to naval warfare and to the uses of cavalry.

The crossbow was so lethal a weapon that a dismayed Pope, Innocent II, in 1139 forbade its use, denouncing it as

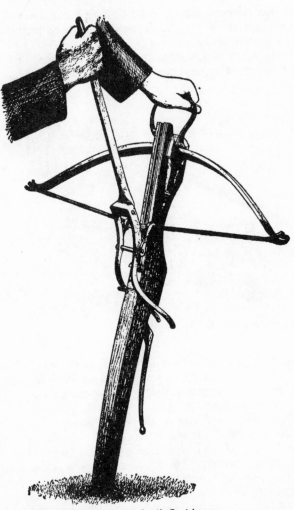

Fig. 10. Military Crossbow with Goat's-Foot Lever

"hateful to God and unfit for Christians." Later this edict was modified; Christians were permitted to use it against Mohammedans, and shortly thereafter they used it freely against each other. Richard Coeur de Lion died of gangrene from a wound inflicted by a crossbow bolt.

By 1370 the crossbow was fitted out with a stout steel bow, which could be bent mechanically by a goat's-foot lever (Fig. 10), windlass, or cranequin. The lock of the crossbow was cleverly designed, requiring only a simple trigger to release it. These improvements made the steel crossbow the most powerful weapon of war for a century, until it began to be displaced by the hand gun between 1460 and 1470. Its chief disadvantages were that it was heavy and the firing was slow.

The pike, especially as used tactically by the Swiss infantry, also became a useful weapon against the armored knight. The Swiss would place their pike shafts in the ground, thus providing an obstacle against oncoming cavalry which was formidable, and not unlike a modern tank barrier. Against dismounted knights the pike was held at the shoulder with the point slightly down. But even in combination, the crossbow and the pike were not enough to cost the armored horseman his preferred place in the medieval war games.

The knight adapted himself by shifting from mail to armored plate, and by using the crossbow himself. As his armor became heavier, the demand increased for bigger and stronger horses. But the horse too was vulnerable, and had to be given armor plate as well as the rider; this meant still bigger horses. Meanwhile the knight became so heavily armored that he was helpless in fighting except when mounted (Fig. 11). Eventually the whole development became a gigantic absurdity, which was fully recognized by many. James I of England was later to say ironically that armor provided double protection—first it kept a knight from being injured, and second, it kept him from injuring anybody else.

The first serious threat to the supremacy of the armored and mounted knight came not from the invention of the gun, as is commonly believed, but from a simple improvement in the design of the bow that had been used for centuries. The superior longbow was developed in Wales as a hunting weapon, but it was Edward III who first saw its possibilities as a military weapon and trained companies of longbowmen in preparation for his invasion of France

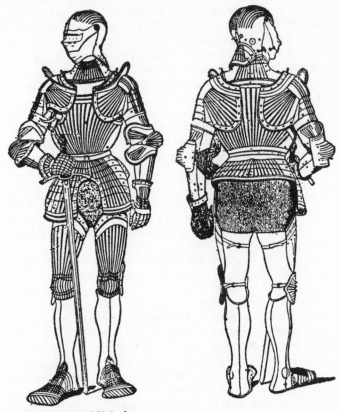

Fig. 11. Suit of Plate Armor

in 1337. The longbow, intended to be "as tall as a man," varied from six feet to six feet, seven inches, and was generally made of yew. The wood was tapered with extreme care; the cord was made of hemp carefully whipped with light linen cord. The virtue of the longbow was in its long draw, and thus its long thrust. A strong man wielding the bow could shoot a 37-inch arrow that would pierce chain mail or kill a horse at two hundred yards. At closer range he could make an arrow penetrate ordinary plate armor, two layers of mail armor, or a stout oaken door. Though not as heavy in its pull, the longbow outranged the crossbow, and had four or five times the rate of fire.

The longbow proved its superiority in the first battle of the Hundred Years' War, when the Earl of Derby landed in Flanders on St. Martin's Eve, 1337, and forced his army ashore under the cover of a rain of arrows which drove off the shorter-ranged Flemish crossbowmen who had lined the quays to oppose them. But the French refused to be really impressed by the longbow until the Battle of Crécy, August 26, 1346. They were superior in numbers to the English by more than two to one, having 12,000 men-at-arms, 6,000 crossbowmen, and 20,000 militiamen against 3,900 men-at-arms, 11,000 archers and 5,000 Welsh light troops.

The Genoese crossbowmen, the best trained in all of Europe, descended into the valley after a thunderstorm, cheering and shouting defiance at the English men-at-arms, who were dismounted and massed on the opposite slope. They were divided into three divisions, or "battles," flanked on both sides by the longbowmen. With the sun shining brightly in their eyes the crossbowmen let fly at the English, but their arrows fell a few yards short. The English longbowmen (Fig. 19) replied with a murderous volley that laid low the whole front line of the Genoese formation.

The crossbowmen reeled back up the slope, only to be trampled by their own horsemen, who came charging down the slope in a fury at what seemed to be the cowardice of their own infantry. Early chroniclers reported the contemptuous cry of the Count of Alençon: "Away with these faint-hearted rabble. They do but block our advance."

Then the English bowmen let fly at the mounted warriors. As one participant put it, ". . . every arrow told on horse or man, piercing head, or arm, or leg among the riders and sending the horses mad." The French seemed unable or unwilling to realize that their men and horses were being cut down by the archers, and concentrated futilely on the English knights, who presented a formidable concentrated mass of spears to the oncoming horses. There were altogether sixteen such separate and successive reckless and ill-ordered charges. By midnight, when the battle ended, the French had lost 1,542 lords and knights, and a number of those "not of gentle blood" estimated at over 10,000. The English had lost two knights, one squire, forty men-at-arms and archers, and "a few dozen Welsh."

The French seem to have learned from this decisive battle to copy the English by dismounting their knights and sending their horses to the rear. However, they missed the real significance of the victory, a basically new tactical combination. Edward III had learned to combine archery fire and steady spearmanship efficiently. From this day forward—and especially after the English archer's victory at Poitiers and Agincourt—the infantry regained the old importance it had lost with the disintegration of the Roman legions.

# 3. The Impact of Gunpowder

**Although in our day it is a cliché that the** invention of gunpowder hastened the end of feudalism and revolutionized the art of warfare, one forgets how slowly this revolution took place. The old weapons and defensive body armor held on tenaciously. Although many gunpowder siege weapons and several kinds of hand guns were in use during the fifteenth century, the making of body-plate armor during this period, far from being abandoned, developed into an extraordinary art. Beauty, what Prof. John U. Nef has called "the claims of delight," was as important to the renaissance craftsmen as utility.

In the navies, warships and their sails and banners were richly decorated. Until the middle of the seventeenth century flagships were ornamented with bas-reliefs and covered with gildings and paintings. Fortifications were designed to be pleasing to the eye as well as impregnable. The renaissance swordsman was interested in the elegance of the hilt of his weapon as well as in the quality of the steel. Heavy body armor (Fig. 12) was designed well into the seventeenth century, partly as a last desperate defense against musket fire, but partly also because armor, being very costly, was a badge of status, and the aristocracy was loath to abandon it even after the writing of *Don Quixote*.

The sword and lance outlasted armor, one persisting as a status symbol, and both as special weapons of the cavalry. As late as 1937 official manuals for the British Army had a section on "the use of the sword in war," and devoted twenty-three pages to sword and lance exercises. It is debatable which is the more extraordinary, that these manuals should still emphasize weapons that had been dead for fifty

Fig. 12. Armor for Man and Horse. South Germany, 1475.

years, or that the lance and sword managed to hold their own as respectable weapons 450 years after the first serious use of gunpowder in war.

The early primitive gunpowder weapons were themselves slow to give way to improvements. The transition from touchholes to matchlocks, then to wheel locks, then to flintlocks, and then to percussion caps, took centuries. There was no radical change in the design of cannon from the time of the first cast-bronze tube of the late fifteenth century to about the middle of the nineteenth century.

The basic metallurgical discoveries in copper and iron leading to the widespread use of firearms were made before 1490. Medieval Europe had developed the use of water-driven machinery to an extent unknown among the Greeks and Romans. In the eleventh century it was used for grinding grain and fulling cloth. During the late twelfth and thirteenth centuries the use of water power spread to metallurgy. In central Europe water power drove the bellows and hammers which converted ore directly into wrought iron in the style of the ancient craftsmen. The hammers and bellows became larger, and finally in the fourteenth century a heart-shaped bellows was invented which generated so fierce a flame that it melted iron ore. It was now possible to transfer the techniques for casting bronze to casting iron. Since iron was cheaper it was soon extensively used. The use of copper also greatly increased in the fourteenth century, particularly after 1450, when Johannsen Funcken discovered how to separate silver from argentiferous copper ores with the help of lead.

Although the new improvements in copper and iron had their widespread use in firearms, the development of these weapons as instruments of war efficient enough to supplant the bow, lance, and sword could not—or would not—be hurried in advance of the general development of scientific and military technology. For a long time the early gunpowder weapons had mostly a nuisance or terror value, depending on the type of gun.

Moreover, the pressure for improvements was seldom insistent. The soldier was tolerably well satisfied with the weapons he had, and he feared innovation. Monarchs were reluctant to increase their military expenditures, and were generally appalled at the cost of new weapons. The tradition that it is ignoble to kill a man from a great distance continued to influence tactics for a surprisingly long time.

The first people to develop gunpowder were the Chinese, who used it chiefly for incendiary and display purposes. They did, however, develop a primitive rocket early in the thirteenth century, and are said to have used it in fighting the Tartars in 1232. The idea of the rocket spread quickly into Mongolia, India, and Arabia, and thence to western Europe. The Italians are said to have experimented with rockets as early as 1281 at Forli (now Emilia); there are reports of rockets at Ghent in 1314, at Metz in 1324, and in England in 1327. The Mongol conqueror Tamerlane is said to have used them successfully in the Battle of Delhi in 1399. But the primitive rocket was inherently uncontrollable, inaccurate, and dangerous, and it was shortly displaced by the gun everywhere except in India, where it continued to be used spasmodically up to the nineteenth century.

The first "cannon" was probably the Arabian madfaa, a deep wooden bowl holding powder, with the cannon ball balanced on the muzzle-top and popped off by the explosion. The French improved on this with their pot-de-fer, the first drawing of which appears in an illuminated manuscript of 1326 now in Christ Church, Oxford. Edward III is said to have used it in Scotland in 1327. The pot-de-fer was an iron bottle containing saltpeter and sulphur, with an iron arrow wedged into the neck with leather. A red-hot wire thrust through a touchhole at the bottom set off the explosion.

A true cannon, invented later, was made of wooden pipes closed at one end. It fired stone or lead balls an inch or so in diameter, or crossbow bolts. There were no gun carriages; the cannon was laid on a heap of earth with the muzzle pointed up. Virtually useless in this small size, it was quickly replaced by very much larger bombards which hurled big stones. Short-barreled bombards were smaller at the breech than at the muzzle end; longer-barreled bombards were constructed of parallel iron bars bound with hoops, like a modern beer barrel (Fig. 13).

The famous Mons Meg gun, built at Edinburgh, had the hoops welded together, and was lengthened by having several sections screwed together. The frequent shattering of the stones as they were fired was remedied in part by hav-

Fig. 13. Short-Barreled Bombard

ing the stones themselves bound with iron hoops. It is said that the Germans used guns of some kind at the siege of Cividale in Italy in 1331; there is also some evidence that the English brought a few guns to the battlefield of Crécy in 1346. Siege guns mounted on wheels were introduced by John Zizka in the Hussite wars, 1419-1424.

The invention of the bombards brought to an end the relative invulnerability of the isolated medieval castle, though it was a long time before the fortifications of larger cities were considered useless. Naturally, the countries with an advanced metallurgical technology had an advantage. As Winston Churchill put it in his *History of the English*

*Speaking Peoples,* describing the conquest of Ireland by the British under Henry VII, "The cannons spoke to Irish castles in a language readily understood. But the cannons came from England. The Irish would use but could not make them. Here for a time was the key to English control over Irish affairs far beyond the outlook of Henry VII."

Fig. 14. Froissart's Gun, 1390

The most dramatic test of the efficiency of the bombards came with the siege of Constantinople by Mohammed II, who had become sultan of the Ottoman empire in 1451 and was determined to capture the last great Christian stronghold in the Near East. Constantinople was surrounded by towering walls and great natural fortifications. Mohammed II, who at twenty-one had the reputation only for being a sadist and pervert, would here prove himself, as James R. Newman has said, "a great, studious and stubborn tactician."

Using the genius of an Hungarian ordnance engineer, Urban, who had deserted to him after being ill-treated by the Byzantines, Mohammed II supervised the building of an immense siege train. There were fifty-six cannon and twelve great bombards, including one super-bombard called Basilica which was made of hooped iron and measured thirty-six inches at the bore; it was so heavy it required two hundred men and sixty oxen to move it. Its ball weighed 1,600 pounds and could travel for more than a mile. The

Basilica took more than an hour to load, and was expected to fire no more than seven times a day. After the first few shots, which struck terror to the garrison, the Basilica fell apart. But the smaller cannon did better.

Constantine Paleologus, the Emperor, mounted on the city walls his own guns, which were much inferior, but he

Fig. 15. The Dardanelles Gun of 1453

found that the shock of the recoil weakened and occasionally demolished the walls. During the frontal assault, which failed twice, a few Turks made their way past a badly defended gate in the rear. Though the Turks were in fact killed, word that they were in the city brought panic to the defenders. Mohammed, aware of the demoralization, flogged his assaulting troops into a third attempt; they succeeded in scaling the battered walls. Constantine was killed, and the Turks massacred 2,000 inhabitants and sold 60,000 of the city's 100,000 as slaves.

The Turks were justly proud of the bombards, which had played no minor role in the final collapse of the Byzantine empire, and kept their monster fieldpieces in the captured city. Some of them were used against a British squadron in 1807, some 354 years later. A 700-pound stone shot cut the mainmast of Admiral J. T. Duckworth's flagship, and a second shot killed or wounded sixty men (Fig. 15).

The bombards were so obviously superior to the medieval catapults that they pushed them out of the siege trains altogether by the end of the fourteenth century. It was a long time, however, before the bombard entirely supplanted the trebuchet, the rock-thrower of the Middle Ages. Less costly to build, and having a faster rate of fire, the trebuchet was retained in use for another two hundred years.

Early in the fourteenth century it was discovered that the same method used for casting church bells could also be used for casting guns. Liquid metal made from tin and copper could be run into the form of a hollow cylinder to make bronze cannon. As John U. Nef described it sadly, "The early founders, whose task had been to fashion bells which tolled the message of eternal peace from Sweden and Poland to Spain, and from Ireland to the Balkans, contributed unintentionally to the discovery of one of man's most terrible weapons." The inventor of the first cast-iron mortar was Merklin Gast. He also produced the first good hand-firearm, and helped make Augsburg famous for its guns.

Actually the technique of gun casting did not advance much beyond the skill of the bell-founder. The bell-maker had a special mold for each bell, which he destroyed after using it only once, and the gun-founders did the same. This wasteful practice would continue for two hundred years, after which it was belatedly realized that a whole series of cannon could be produced from the same mold, and that all the cannon would then be able to use the same size ball —a very great advantage.

Although metallurgy was much studied by early scientists, practical metallurgy was an empirical art of the metal workers. There was no such thing as a scientific explanation for the reduction of ores to metal, the formation of alloys, or the conversion of cast iron into wrought iron and steel. Even the works of Roger Bacon, Albertus Magnus, Raymond Lully, and Vincent de Beauvais, who were renowned as chemists, were not so much innovations as the rewriting of the works of Arabian chemists.

The great German scholar Georgius Agricola (1494-1555) called "the father of mineralogy," gathered his materials for his famous *De Re Metallica* (1556) mostly by touring through central Europe and observing what was being done by miners, metallurgists, and glassmakers. He gave massively detailed accounts of geological formations, mining machinery, and chemical processes, and devoted many years to the study of ores and the preparation of metals and salts. He recorded his experiments on the amalgamation process of extracting gold and on flame tests for various metals. Although primarily a compiler rather than an innovator, Agricola was remarkable as a true scientist in an age when alchemy was the toy of magicians and monarchs.

The making of guns continued to be a highly skilled craft. Most cannon were cast hollow in a single big block, exactly like a kitchen kettle. There was no standardization; every cannon was an individual, and many were treated as pieces of bronze sculpture, finished with the same lavish ornamentation as a suit of armor. An extraordinary piece of cannon-sculpture, probably exceptional even for the renaissance, can be seen today in the Bargello Museum in Florence (Fig. 16).

Between three and four tons of bronze went into the biggest cannon. The gun carriages, though made of wood, had bands of iron, heavy iron bolts, and a chain and stout iron hook above the axle to keep the cannon from slipping downhill. The iron in the gun carriage weighed almost as much as the bronze of the gun, more than two tons. Some cannon were named after saints, and the gunners adopted Saint Barbara as their patroness. The gunners were hired at high wages and were responsible only to their own masters, not to the warring prince. They became an independent lot, interested primarily in saving their guns if the fighting became tough. Some princes resorted to hiring foot soldiers to stand by to keep the gunners from running away.

In primitive artillery the fuses were unreliable and the projectiles unpredictable. The recoil bounced the cannon out of position, a fault that was not to be corrected until the end of the nineteenth century. Rain was ruinous to firing. Cannon were expensive to build and difficult to move and aim, as Ferdinand and Isabella found when their commanders tried to use clumsy guns made of iron bars held together by iron bolts and rings to hurl balls of marble. Still, the cannon were more effective than the old siege engines, and castles all over Europe fell before their onslaught. Charles VII of France, relying on artillery, recon-

Fig. 16. Cannon Named after St. Paul

quered Normandy in 1449-50. He chalked up sixty successful siege operations in sixteen months. In England the Wars
of the Roses saw the gun become master of the stoutest
fortifications.

Cannon acquired immensely more force in the middle of
the fifteenth century when the French brothers Bureau introduced iron cannon balls, which fitted the cannon bores
more tightly than stones. Missiles now were actually shot
rather than tossed. Powder became better as purer saltpeter
was produced. Since the bombards themselves occasionally
blew up, a trend toward smaller cannon with thicker walls
resulted. The Germans perfected the casting of iron balls,
which became as large as a man's head. They also invented
a primitive shell, a hollow iron ball filled with gunpowder,
but a century passed before a method was devised to shoot
it without having it explode prematurely within the gun.

Just before the end of the fifteenth century, guns were
given carriages which could be drawn by horses and for the
first time achieved real mobility. The great French com-
mander-king, Charles VIII, used long horse-drawn artillery
trains in invading Italy in 1494-95. His was the first modern
army. The gunners fired iron cannon balls instead of bronze
or lead shot, and for the first time managed to keep up
with the infantry and to fire relatively rapidly. Before this
time the old brass or iron bombards had fired so slowly
that defenders could often repair fortifications between
shots. Now cities and castles fell before his new siegecraft,
and it was shown that even the greatest fortifications of antiquity and the Middle Ages were vulnerable. Machiavelli wrote that Charles VIII "seized Italy with chalk in
hand"—that is, his gunners took every spot he marked on
the map with chalk.

The new maneuverability, though still inferior to that
of the Roman legions, meant an immense change in the
strategy and tactics of war. C. W. C. Oman has described
warfare in the fifteenth century as "shut up in many water-
tight compartments . . . separate stories, having few and
infrequent cross-relations with each other." In the sixteenth century war grew into one immense complex. The

new tactics, which were to continue for a hundred years, were demonstrated in the Battle of Pavia in 1525. The artillery opened the way; the pike protected the musketeers, and the musketeers cleared the way for the pikemen, the mounted swordsmen, and the lancers.

In 1520 it was discovered that if powder was "corned" into coarse grains instead of ground to the consistency of meal, fire would ignite the whole charge more quickly. This increased the effectiveness of the artillery. Though the design of the gun remained unchanged, techniques of casting and boring large guns greatly improved. Inventors still failed to solve the problem of locking a breechblock tight, so breech-loading was generally abandoned in favor of muzzle-loading. Breech-loading would not be used with artillery again until the late nineteenth century, when new techniques of forging and machining steel permitted "obturators" to be developed which sealed in the gases formed by the explosion.

The first iron gun made of a single casting was produced in England. Henry VIII, lacking the money to import foreign brass, in 1543 imported a French metallurgist, Peter Baude, and sent him to the Sussex iron foundry where round shot were being cast. Baude apparently used the casting technique described by Vannoccio Biringuccio in his *De la Pirotechnia* (1540), which had described in detail a blast furnace and a bronze and iron foundry. It was Baude who succeeded in casting the first iron gun, thereby founding what was to become the great English ordnance industry.

Actually the iron guns were not in the beginning superior to the brass, being inclined to blow up more often, but the invention was nonetheless significant. Dominance in the art of metallurgy for the first time shifted to England, where it remained until the end of the nineteenth century. The Sussex iron industry became of immense economic and political significance. It placed a powerful source of military strength in the hands of the commercial Protestant powers; it gave Englishmen their first sense of industrial importance. Elizabeth took a benevolent interest in the new developments, hoping to see England become self-sufficient in brass and iron.

The output of iron in Germany, Bohemia, Hungary, the Low Countries, France, and Spain also leaped forward. Although the percentage of expansion was prodigious, the actual output by later standards was small. The annual production of iron and steel in western Europe from 1530 to 1540 was between 100,000 and 150,000 tons; in 1910 it would be 60,000,000.

During the sixteenth century even the biggest guns became mobile, though some required as many as forty horses to move them. The Germans invented the short, thick-walled mortars, built to drop shot on an enemy by throwing it at a steep angle. The Dutch developed the technique of shooting bombs from mortars, the bomb being a hollow metal ball filled with powder and having a narrow hole drilled in it for a fuse. There were many accidents.

One of the most surprising characteristics of artillery in the sixteenth century was the continued lack of standardization. Henry II, King of France from 1547 to 1559, tried to lessen the chaos in gun sizes by cutting the number to six; the Spanish used twelve sizes, the English sixteen, ranging from the four-ton cannon royal, which fired a 74-pound shot, to the 300-pound rabinet, which fired a five-ounce ball. The word "cannon," now used for all large artillery, was then a gun of definite size and type used mainly as a siege weapon. The British guns were called cannon royal, cannon, cannon serpentine, bastard cannon, demi-cannon, pedrero, culverin (which in the fifteenth century had been a small gun), basilisk, demi-culverin, bastard culverin (Fig. 17), saker, minion, falcon, falconet, serpentine, and rabinet.

In England the design and manufacturing of these guns were largely left to the experience and ingenuity of the iron-founders. Government officials ordering the guns asked only that the new ones be as good as those already in service. Occasionally a distinguished ordnance expert enjoyed the special patronage of the king, especially if he was imported from the continent. It was not till the time of

Charles II that British experts were employed on a large scale and given royal favor.

Insofar as science was supported at all by royal patronage, as it came to be in the seventeenth century, it was usually the chemist who was singled out for favors. The

Fig. 17. Bastard Culverin of Brass

man who promised more powerful explosives and more terrorizing incendiary materials always had a better audience than the ballistician who offered simply greater accuracy.

## DEVELOPMENT OF THE HAND GUN

The first "hand gonne" was simply a small iron tube, lashed to a round wooden stock, which shot lead· balls. It was cradled under the right arm and fired by applying a slow-burning match to powder in the touchhole. First mentioned in 1364, it was adopted in 1391 in Italy, and used largely as a weapon of defense behind fortifications. Some horse soldiers used it, with difficulty, by mounting it on a forked rest fitted to the saddlebow. A truly satisfactory hand gun, which could easily be carried into battle and fired with some confidence of success, was not, in fact, developed for another hundred years.

The Spanish seem to have contributed the first basic improvement—a device to make a gun shoot like an arbalest, by squeezing a trigger. Their matchlock, or arquebus, developed in the late fifteenth century, was soon adopted throughout Europe. Like the older gun, the matchlock had a touchhole and a priming pan. To this was added a movable clamp known as a serpentine—having the same function as the modern gun's hammer—which held the slow match on the gun. When the trigger was pressed, the smoldering match was dipped into the powder in the pan. The advantage was that the arquebusier could focus on the target instead of looking for the touchhole.

Early matchlocks were extremely complicated to fire, requiring what some have counted as ninety-six separate motions. Powder was measured and poured down the muzzle; next the lead ball was dropped in with a wad of rag on top. Then the priming pan was uncovered and fine-grained priming powder poured in and the cover closed. The match was adjusted in the serpentine, the pan cover was opened, and then the trigger squeezed. Sometimes nothing came of it but the "flash in the pan." The gun had to be cleaned between shots, and was obviously useless in wet weather.

The arquebusier carried in addition to his gun and sword a big flask of regular gunpowder, a smaller one of priming powder, a ramrod, scrapers, bullet extractors, cleaning rags, bullet lead and a brass mold for casting it, and flint and steel for relighting matches. It was no wonder that he needed and usually had a helper, who carried some of the equipment and tended a small fire. The Spaniards fired the arquebus from the shoulder; other Europeans in the beginning fired it from the chest.

The musket, a larger and longer version of the arquebus, was developed as a weapon to puncture armor at long range. It was so heavy it required a forked rest, which the musketeer carried along with the rest of his already formidable load of equipment (Fig. 18).

In the beginning the arquebus was certainly not as accurate as either the crossbow or the longbow, but it was more frightening, and when the aim was true it was likely to be more deadly against the armored knight. One late-fifteenth-century Italian commander, Gian Paolo Vitelli, was so incensed that lowborn arquebusiers had killed some of his nobles that he gave an order that all captured gunners should have their hands cut off and eyes plucked out.

Fig. 18. Musketeer

The Spaniards brought matchlocks to America, both the ten-pound, .72-caliber arquebus—which shot a .66-caliber ball, the difference allowing for irregularities in the ball—and the twenty-pound musket with a 10- or 8-gauge barrel. These weapons would see service in America for nearly a century and a half before being replaced by the better designed flintlock. Useful as they were as a terror weapon against the Indians, the matchlocks and even the Spanish crossbows were slower than the simple, light Indian bow, and the Indians, in addition to using poisoned arrows,

Fig. 19. English Archers Using the Longbow

had a wholly different fighting technique. One of De Soto's men complained bitterly in his journal: "They never stand still, but are alwaies running and traversing from one place

to another: by reason whereof neither crossebow nor arcu-
buse can aime at them: and before one crossebowman can
make one shot, an Indian will discharge three or foure
arrows; and he seldom misseth what he shooteth at."

Nevertheless the gun proved decisive in the conquest of
both North and South America. Even though the Indian
managed later to acquire the gun himself, chiefly by barter-
ing beaver skins, the white man had an inestimable advantage; he controlled the sources of manufacture.

The Spaniards were the first in Europe to use large numbers of hand guns in their infantry. During the early Italian
wars about a sixth of the Spaniards carried guns—either
arquebus or musket—and fought alongside the crossbowmen and pikemen. Since the slow-firing arquebusiers were
extremely vulnerable to the fast-riding cavalry, the pikemen
usually protected them against the mounted knights with
a solid wall of pikes. But the pikemen were themselves vulnerable to the swordsmen, who infiltrated their ranks once
the pikes were entangled, and slaughtered with great skill.
Machiavelli, in his *Art of War* (1521), was greatly impressed by the Spanish swordsmen. Astute as he was, particularly in judging the growing importance of infantry in
war, he missed the chance to predict a great future for the
new gunpowder weapons. He chose the opposite course,
holding that the art of war would be technically improved
if commanders returned to the tactics and weapons of the
Roman legions. Though greatly interested in the new firearms, he was more impressed by their inefficiency than by
their potentialities.

The need for a gun that could make its own fire was met
by the Germans of Nuremberg in 1515, when they invented
the wheel lock. This had a roughened steel wheel which
was wound up like a clock with a "spanner" or key. When
the trigger released the wheel it rotated against a stone and
spurted sparks which ignited the primary charge. This was
a great improvement over the matchlock, but it was costly,
and hard to repair. It was never adopted by the colonists in
America, who clung to the matchlock until the flintlock
finally became available a century later.

The first practical pistols were wheel locks. They were eagerly adopted by the cavalry in Europe, for the matchlock could be used from horseback only with great difficulty. The man on the horse had had to abandon part of his armor in order to retain his capacity to fight at all; by acquiring a pistol as a supplement to his lance and saber, he regained some of the old offensive power he had lost when the two-ounce musket ball began to smash armor and disable horses at 300 yards.

There were early experiments with repeaters. In 1339 there appeared the ribaudequin, or orgues de bombardes, a primitive mitrailleuse consisting of several small iron tubes so arranged that they could be fired simultaneously. One constructed in Verona in 1387 had 144 barrels, permitting twelve separate discharges of twelve balls. It required four horses to draw this machine. In the Battle of Ravenna in 1512, Pedro Navarro, a Spanish military engineer, placed thirty carts mounted with multiple arquebuses in front of his infantry. But the repeaters presented too many problems for the primitive technology of the time, and went into the discard along with the early breechloaders.

The battles of the sixteenth century thus became lethal games with a fantastic variety and combination of weapons —guns, pikes, swords, lances, and artillery of every shape and description. The logistics problems became enormously complicated. In one sense the invention of gunpowder had vastly increased the maneuverability of European armies, for as the medieval fortifications fell before the onslaught of the new artillery, war could no longer be compartmentalized and contained within one or several small feudal states. Tactically, however, the new guns meant less maneuverability than that enjoyed by the Roman infantry. Whereas the Roman soldier had carried a short sword, shield, helmet, breastplate, stake, spade, javelin, and two weeks' rations (altogether about 80 pounds), the Spanish soldier of the sixteenth century could carry almost no food. His musket, sword, rest, ramrod, and ammunition were much heavier than Roman weapons; his defensive armor alone—helmet, breast and backplates—weighed almost as much as the total Roman supplies. The Spaniard was inevitably tied to the pack train.

Where the Roman soldier or blacksmith repaired or manufactured his arrows and javelins on the spot, the Spaniard had to be provided with shot and powder by a central authority. The Spanish commander had to worry about the safety of his artillery trains, magazines, and food convoys. And when the Spanish Hapsburg lines extended from northern Italy to the Netherlands, the single matter of keeping these lines intact became a major strategic problem. The land route could be imperiled by a French offensive anywhere from Milan to Flanders; the sea route could not be kept open without the friendship of either England or France.

Fighting in the sixteenth century was complicated by the fact that armies were still not national but combinations of recruits from many sources. At St. Quentin in 1557, in the biggest battle of the sixteenth century, Philip II had but 9,000 Spaniards in an army of 53,000. Mutiny and desertions of whole regiments were common. Commanders had a perpetual problem in maintaining the loyalties of the mercenary armies, and had to face the logistics problems imposed by the thousands of noncombatants who followed the armies. Wives and grown daughters often accompanied their husbands and fathers; it was said that there was a woman and a boy for every soldier.

Later, in the seventeenth century, when Europe was convulsed by the Thirty Years' War, the number of noncombatants would increase to four and five for every soldier. If these hordes were not fed regularly, the civilian populations and the armies themselves suffered the consequences. Many of the frightful atrocities and casualties of the period can be laid to starvation and famine as much as to the greater ferocity of the weapons.

As the sixteenth century progressed, the proportions of men with hand guns increased in all the armies. The English had abandoned the arbalest by 1535; after 1550 the longbow was considered obsolete, though an expert archer could still outshoot any gunner in accuracy and speed of fire. Slowly the musket came to replace the arquebus. In the 1560's the Duke of Alva had fifteen musketeers to every one hundred arquebusiers. Skillfully trained, they mowed down the Dutch citizen soldiers, though often outnumbered ten to one. Like his contemporary, the artillery gunner, the musketeer had become a trained specialist. He was inter-

Fig. 20. Head of Halberd

ested only in firing and avoided, if he could, close combat involving pikes and swords. In 1600 it still took ten to fifteen minutes to load and fire an arquebus.

The Swiss retained the pike and halberd (Fig. 20) the longest; these were weapons with which they had had conspicuous success for many years. The Portuguese and Spanish were the last to abandon body armor, which was generally detested by the common soldiers, who hated to have the cost of it deducted from their pay, and who found it oppressively heavy and hot, and an encumbrance to fighting in any case.

Swords evolved in the direction of thinness and lightness. By 1500 the old bulky rigid blade of the armored knight was being replaced by rapier types, and by short, heavy-bladed weapons like the Italian malchus and cinquedea. It would not be until the seventeenth century, however, that the sword and gun were finally combined in one weapon with the introduction of the bayonet, and not till after 1740, with the wars of Frederick the Great, that the bayonet was used extensively as a weapon of attack.

## NAVAL POWER, THE SAILING SHIP AND THE GUN

In the development of naval weapons up to 1600 the role of the scientist was much the same as in the evolution of weapons of land warfare—that is, sporadic or non-existent. We have already noted that Leonardo da Vinci made drawings of a submarine. His notebooks mention a small bomb which divers could plant on the hulls of ships to explode them. Though neither was developed, an explosive mine and floating battery were actually put to use by a contemporary of Leonardo's, Pedro Navarro (1460-1528). A Spaniard who began his career as a common sailor, Navarro fought in the wars between the Genoese corsairs and Mohammedans of North Africa, and won the reputation of being not only a tough mercenary but also one of the best military engineers of his time. His mining operations against the castles of Naples, held by French garrisons in 1503 and his successful conquest of Velez de Gomera in 1508 by means of his floating battery won him temporary fortune and lasting fame. Because of the extremely slow development of the science of chemistry, the explosive he developed in his mine was not much improved upon for almost four hundred years.

Inventions like Navarro's, however ingenious, were relatively unimportant. The great revolution in naval warfare came slowly, waiting first upon the development of the sailing ship, and second upon the evolution of gunpowder weapons. Just as the opening of men's minds had to wait upon the invention and widespread use of printing, so the great developments in sea power had to wait upon the opening of the oceans to navigation.

In the history of printing the genius of Gutenberg towers above his contemporaries. So, too, in the history of the conquest of the sea, one sees looming early above the rest Henry the Navigator, King of Portugal from 1433 to 1460. Though not himself a scientist, Henry surrounded himself with mathematicians, astronomers, cosmographers, chartmakers, physicians, and instrument-makers. Until his time systematic voyaging was largely confined to the Mediterranean and coastal waters. Mariners had had the compass in general use for about a century. The astrolabe for determining latitude—invented by the Greeks and said to be the oldest scientific instrument in the world—had long been in the hands of the ordinary sailor. Exact but unpublished maps, made largely by sailors for sailors, were available in the portolan charts.

In Lisbon, and in his academy at Sagres, Henry's scientists and technicians, among them Arab and Jewish mathematicians, greatly improved the art of map making, the science of navigation, and the design of ships. An observatory was built at Sagres to make more accurate tables of the declination of the sun. Most important, Henry brought his captains and pilots to his academy for instruction in the new discoveries. The impetus to exploration and discovery was tremendous; Henry made voyaging a national passion.

This concentration of scientific talent dissolved with Henry's death in 1460; it was unique for its time and for generations afterward. One result among many during Henry's lifetime was that Portuguese caravels became the best sailing ships afloat. Instead of one big mast and one large sail, these ships had three masts and five or six adroitly designed sails, which made possible the art of sailing close to the wind. Without the development of this art, which inaugurated the sailing ship, long ocean voyages would have been impossible. Commercial power shifted decisively to the ocean-going nations, as the passion for exploration spread swiftly to Spain, France, and England. A single century—1425-1525—saw the maritime exploration of more than half the globe and the three greatest voyages in human history, those of Vasco da Gama, Columbus, and Magellan.

Even by itself, the development of the sailing ship would have altered the strategy and tactics of naval warfare, which had remained relatively unchanged in the Mediterranean from the days of Actium to the fall of Constantinople in 1453. But the revolution in navigation and sailing happened also to coincide with the development of gun-powder.

The galley, with auxiliary sail power, had dominated naval warfare from antiquity. But a vessel driven primarily by oars had to be light, and the 200-ton renaissance galley was little different from that used by the Greeks 2,000 years earlier. The galley was doomed by the big gun, for she could not mount it, and she had no defense against it. Nevertheless, although the larger and thicker-walled sailing ships quickly proved themselves superior in firepower, range, and protection, the galley was retained for a remarkably long time. Colbert revived it in France during the reign of Louis XIV, though there was no good reason for doing so except possibly its superior maneuverability in close coastal waters.

In the Battle of La Rochelle in 1372, hand guns used by the French and Spanish played a decisive role in winning a victory over a smaller British squadron. Small guns designed to kill men rather than to damage ships were mounted on a British ship, *Christopher of the Tower,* in 1410. Cannon were first mounted by the French in 1494, and they were used in a skirmish with the British in 1512. But the end of the usefulness of the galley was not clearly demonstrated till the Battle of Preveza, when Venetian galleons assaulted a division of Turkish galleys, raked the rowers with primitive guns, and blew the galleys apart like matchboxes. At Lepanto, in 1571, the lesson was repeated.

Lepanto was the last great battle dominated by oar-propelled vessels. Here Christian forces coming from Venice, Genoa, the Papal States, and Spain, decisively defeated the Turks and crushed Moslem power in the western Mediterranean. Each side had about 300 ships: the Turks had 250 galleys, manned in part by 15,000 Christian slaves; the Christians had 208 galleys and 8 galleasses (heavier oar-manned ships mounting heavy guns). One of the bloodiest naval battles of all time, Lepanto saw 8,000 Christians killed and 25,000 Turks, with unnumbered wounded on both sides, among them Cervantes, whose arm was crippled in combat.

The prodigious rise in Portuguese and Spanish sea power was matched in the second half of the sixteenth century by that of the British. Henry VIII took a keen interest in the fleet, and it grew rapidly under his patronage and later that of Elizabeth. Henry VIII was responsible for the first ships designed exclusively as warships, the earliest of them being

Fig. 21. Heavy Broadside Cannon

*The Mary Rose.* Heavy guns were mounted on the lower decks with holes cut through the sides for firing. These guns were intended to damage the hulls and rigging of the enemy ships as well as the men aboard them.

The standard fighting ship in the British Navy became the galleon, a two- or three-decked ship with main batteries in the broadside (Fig. 21) and lighter, quick-firing pieces fore and aft. Armed merchant ships of 300 tons and over, called greatships, supplemented the galleons. They too mounted culverins and demi-cannon. The sixteenth-century culverin, ancestor to the long eighteenth-century gun, had a range of well over a mile. The smaller demi-cannon, with a nine-foot barrel and six-inch bore, threw a 32-pound shot which was effective to at least 500 yards.

The Spanish retained many galleys in their fleet. They looked formidable, with their sinister bronze rams and their forecastles crowded with smaller cannon; actually they could not risk ramming the heavier sailing ships and were dangerous only to other galleys. As Garret Mattingly described it in his superb study *The Armada,* "Any one of Drake's seven heaviest ships could throw more metal in a single broadside than all Don Pedro's galleys put together, and throw it a good deal farther (Fig.. 22)."

It was inevitable that the two greatest naval powers in the Atlantic would one day test their strength in battle. Elizabeth managed artfully to delay it many years. But in 1580 Philip II annexed Portugal and thereby acquired not

Fig. 22. Destroying a Straggler from the Armada. From a painting by C. M. Padday.

only the ocean-going Portuguese galleons, but also the services of the Portuguese shipbuilders, who were skilled in constructing ships to fight in the South Atlantic rather than the Mediterranean. Still, when compared with the British ships, the Spanish galleons were unwieldy and overmasted, and had a tendency to drift in a high wind because of their flat bottoms.

The Armada which finally sailed against England in 1588 had 130 ships carrying 2,500 guns and 30,000 men, two-thirds of them soldiers. There were twenty galleons, forty-four armed merchantmen, eight Mediterranean galleys, and an assortment of smaller craft. The Spanish commander, the Duke of Medina Sedonia, was prepared to follow the age-old Mediterranean tactic of grappling the enemy ships and gaining victory by boarding. His fleet concentrated on heavy short-range cannon, and had few long-distance culverins.

The British shipbuilders, concentrating on seaworthiness and speed, had cut down the castles which towered above the galleon decks, and had deepened the keels. John Hawkins had developed the revolutionary tactical theory that cannon should not be considered "an ignoble arm" fit only for an opening salvo, but should be used to batter the enemy ships to pieces. The warship was no longer a fort with a garrison of soldiers but an arsenal of guns. The whole psychology of British fighting was accordingly altered.

The Queen's warships numbered only thirty-four, but they had a formidable armament of long-range culverins. In addition, one hundred and sixty privately owned vessels were hastily collected to help cope with the Spanish fleet, but half of these were too small to be of any use.

The Spanish commanders were perfectly aware of the superiority of the British ships and guns. They had had a bitter lesson in 1587 when Drake took four ships into the harbor at Cadiz and defeated a whole fleet of Spanish galleons with the broadside fire of his heavy guns. It was not surprising, then, that one of them wryly described his battle expectations to a neutral observer as follows: "It is well known that we fight in God's cause. So, when we meet the English, God will surely arrange matters so that we can grapple and board them, either by sending some strange freak of weather, or, more likely, just by depriving the English of their wits. If we can come to close quarters, Spanish valor and Spanish steel—and the great mass of soldiers we shall have on board—will make our victory certain. But unless God helps us by a miracle, the English, who have faster guns and handier ships than ours, and many more long-range guns, and who know their advantage just as well as we do, will never close with us at all, but stand aloof and knock us to pieces with their culverins, without our being able to do them any serious hurt. . . . So we are sailing against England in the confident hope of a miracle."

As it turned out, the battle was not too decisive a test of the success of the new British tactics. The shot of a sixteenth-century culverin or demi-culverin at a range of 300 to 700 yards either failed to pierce the hull of the galleon or greatship, or it made only a small hole which could be quickly caulked by a quick-working crew. The gunnery on both sides was extremely bad because of the inexperience of the gun crews and the imperfections of the guns. The Spanish spent much of their stock of cannonballs futilely, and were reduced to using up the powder they had hoped to save for the actual landings on British soil. The British, who also ran out of ammunition, had the inestimable advantage of being able to replenish their supplies from nearby ports, so that when the fleets did come within closer range, they were able to pour a murderous fire on the Spanish ships.

The actual tangling of the fleets was in part the result of Spanish panic over the supposed presence among the English of a "magician-scientist" whose reputation was not unlike that of Archimedes. Federigo Giambelli, an Italian military engineer, had made himself famous in 1584 during the siege of Antwerp by loading two ships with incendiary materials and blowing them up at the sea-entrance to the city. The explosion of his "hellburners" killed more than 1,000 Spanish soldiers and very nearly succeeded in breaking the siege. But Antwerp was finally forced to surrender to the Duke of Parma, and Giambelli fled to England. When the Spanish invasion of England threatened, Elizabeth hired him to devise fortifications to block the Thames. Though his presence in London was supposed to be a war secret, it was common gossip on the Armada that Giambelli had been hired by the Queen to devise some new and devilish instrument of warfare.

When the Spanish fleet was anchored off Calais Roads, the British managed one night to send eight fireships into the harbor, their decks aflame with incendiary matter and their guns exploding. Convinced that the "hellburners of

Antwerp" were upon them, the Spanish commanders pan-
icked, cut their cables and made for the open sea. In the
ensuing desperate eight-hour fight the British won a decisive
victory, but because their ammunition ran short at a critical moment two-thirds of the Spanish ships escaped.

Already terribly battered by the English cannonade, the
Spanish galleons now faced a devastating storm. But by
extraordinary seamanship they managed to get most of the
fleet around the tip of Scotland, back down past the Irish
coast—where 5,000 soldiers were massacred when they
went ashore for water—and back to Spanish harbors.

For a time the battle was thought to be indecisive; Queen
Elizabeth like many others was disturbed that there had
been no real destruction by ramming and boarding, no
really close-in fighting. No English ship had been seriously
damaged, and only a score or two of seamen killed. But
gradually, as news of the magnitude of the Spanish casualties and the disaster to the Spanish fleet trickled into England, it became clear that Hawkins' revolutionary tactics
had been decisive. The ancient ramming and boarding tactics associated with the galley were gone for good; the
supremacy of heavy artillery, sailing ships and line-ahead
tactics was unmistakable.

The waste involved in the useless cannonading early in
the battle left an imprint on British tactics. Cannonading
had come to stay, but not yet at long ranges. Sir Walter
Raleigh forbade any gunner under his command to shoot
his gun at any range but point-blank—which is to say with
gun barrels at the horizontal instead of elevated—and the
tradition of close, brutal engagement continued into the
nineteenth century. This was due partly to the continued
inefficiency of the guns at any other than point-blank range,
but mostly to the gross inaccuracy of the firing.

There are many extraordinary things about the Spanish
Armada battle, not the least being the prodigious myth
which grew up afterward that the British had fought against
great odds. The British had better ships, more homogeneous
and better trained crews, and better guns, and were fighting where they could without too much difficulty replenish

their ammunition. Still, the battle became for the British, as Mattingly has put it, "a heroic apologue of the defense of freedom against tyranny, an eternal myth of the victory of the weak over the strong, of the triumph of David over Goliath."

Somewhat less surprisingly, the battle seems to have contributed to another myth, which came to be widely held in the seventeenth century—the myth that the invention of gunpowder had made war less horrible. After all, the British had lost no ships and fewer than a hundred men, and the difference between these casualties and those of the equally decisive Lepanto was, in truth, phenomenal. John Donne, the famous British poet and divine, speaking in praise of reason at St. Paul's Cathedral, said on Christmas Day, 1621:

"So by the benefit of this light of reason, they have found out Artillery, by which warres come to quicker ends than heretofore, and the great expence of bloud is avoyded; for the numbers of men slain now, since the invention of Artillery, are much lesse than before, when the sword was the executioner."

This kind of thinking made it possible for many men to believe, as they did well into the eighteenth century, that of all the ingenious inventions of history the three most beneficial to mankind had been the compass, printing, and the invention of the gun.

## THE RISE OF THE MILITARY ENGINEER

During the late renaissance the word engineer meant military engineer, just as the word architect meant civil engineer. There were many kinds of military engineers, ranging from men like Niccoló Tartaglia, the genius of theory, to men like Pedro Navarro, the practical soldier-inventor. Moreover, the term engineer included artists, for example, Albrecht Dürer, who published a book on fortification in 1527.

Adding to our confusion is the fact that the "natural philosophers," who were not military engineers in any practical sense, were enormously interested in ballistic theory. Today we consider ballistics a highly specialized science dealing with the motion of projectiles. The renaissance ballistic theoreticians considered it a natural bridge between mathematics and "natural philosophy." Usually they had nothing to do with guns.

By 1500 military engineering had become one of the few truly technical professions of the renaissance. The technological problems of war had become so numerous and so complex that every ruler had to have at least one member of the profession. He was expected to know explosives and ballistics, military architecture and sapping—that is, the art of undermining a fortification—and to be in addition a master craftsman. The most celebrated were likely to be those who chose to work with incendiaries and explosives, like Giambelli of Antwerp, for their exploits were bound to win more admiration from the public than less spectacular work on fortification and design.

Leonardo da Vinci, as we have noted, called himself a military engineer and held a post with that title under the Duke of Milan for eighteen years. Certainly his sketches for tanks, breechloading cannon, rifled firearms, wheel-locked pistols, rapid-fire catapults, steam cannon, parachutes, and an arsenal foundry—to say nothing of submarines, balloons and flying machines—would supremely justify his right to the title. He also did work on fortifications, with projects and drawings of moat protection, masonry cupolas, and bastions. His tank was designed to hold eight men, who were to move it by crank handles attached to horizontal trundle wheels. These wheels were designed to turn the circular spindles of pin wheels, which in turn would drive the wheels of the car. It was to be an armored car with holes for the guns and an opening in the top for ventilation.

Leonardo was a great scientist, and widely versed in the science of the past. He knew the work of Albert of Saxony on gravitation, of Jordanus on levers, and of Roger Bacon on optics and flight. He knew the architecture of Vitruvius and Alberti, and the writings of Archimedes. Had he organized and published the material in his own notebooks, the history of modern science would probably have begun much earlier. Actually, his manuscripts were not wholly lost to the world for 300 years, as is commonly believed, for much that he wrote filtered anonymously into seventeenth-century scientific literature, chiefly through the writings of a few men who plagiarized him. Jerome Cardan's treatise on hydraulics and dynamics, published by Castelli in 1621, is an example. But the war machines of Leonardo were entirely still-born, and most of his devices were actually inappropriate to the technology of his time; a contemporary smith or carpenter might have pointed out insuperable difficulties in their manufacture. Nevertheless, they have given us invaluable glimpses into a mind that combined the rarest gifts of invention and of theory.

Another great military engineer of the renaissance, Niccoló Tartaglia (1500-1557), was also a theoretician. Though he holds an unchallenged position as the father of modern gunnery, he was actually, as Albert Rupert Hall has pointed out, "without experience of artillery except that which he gained in talk." Tartaglia, a mathematics teacher in Verona, was the first writer who tried to compute the ranges of cannon by means of tables derived from a theory of dynamics. In this he was not as successful as Galileo in the next century, but he did make a useful application of the impetus theory to ballistics. And though he had little to do with guns, he wrote two books on artillery, and one on fortification, and he devised the useful gunner's quadrant— a tool for measuring true angle of elevation—which was widely adopted after his death.

After Tartaglia, European primers in artillery firing were published in every tongue, beginning with the rudiments of arithmetic and geometry, continuing through elementary surveying to the use of proportions and to the theory of gunnery. Notable among these books was Konrad Keyser's *Bellefortis*. Ballistic theory still had very little to do with the art of gun-making. An artillery school had been established in Venice in 1506, and a few years later at Burgos in Spain. The so-called "gunnery experts" who followed in

Tartaglia's footsteps, primarily academicians in the schools, busily weighed and measured charges, angles, and distances over several generations, but scarcely added an important datum. They were incapable of correcting Tartaglian mathematical theory where it was wrong, and their theoretical speculation was largely divorced from the actual art of shooting cannon at long ranges. Certainly it was divorced from the art of the gun-founders.

Badly needed standardization in gun-making seems to have been imposed primarily by the monarchs. Emperor Maximilian I ordered the standardization of his artillery according to the weight of the cannon ball, and Prince Maurice of Orange standardized the caliber of hand guns by the number of balls contained in a pound—which is the basis of the "gauge" still used in the modern American or British shotgun.

Perhaps the best example of the successful military engineer of the time was Vannoccio Biringuccio of Siena, who served under several Italian princes. Starting out with a post in the army of Siena, he advanced to become head of the foundry and director of munitions for Paul III. That he was a skillful businessman as well as administrator he demonstrated by his personal monopoly of the saltpeter production in the area. But he also felt an obligation as a scholar, as his great *Pirotechnica,* published in Venice the year after his death in 1540, amply demonstrates.

The seventeenth century would see a few genuinely distinguished scientists, like Simon Stevin and Otto von Guericke, among the professional military engineers. But these men for the most part held only temporary posts in war or else came finally to abandon the profession altogether for the more beguiling one of pure science.

# 4. War and Science in the Seventeenth Century

War in Europe in the late sixteenth and almost the whole of the seventeenth century was less a succession of campaigns and battles than a way of life. European civilization was in effect a military civilization, in which the prevalence of war was taken completely for granted. If philosophers concerned themselves with the causes of war, it was only to debate among themselves which wars were just and which were unjust. The masses of people ordered their lives as best they could to minimize the impact of practically continuous conflict. Peace was always temporary, whether imposed by force or the result of exhaustion and anarchy.

The emerging scientists—of which there was a great galaxy in the seventeenth century—paid little heed to the plundering and slaughter and almost none to the slowly improving technology of war. Among the military engineers, on the other hand, there was increasing awareness of the importance of such sciences as astronomy, ballistics, and chemistry, and there were some awkward, belated, and usually futile efforts to utilize the emerging scientific theory of the time. Governments began to recognize the usefulness of schools for military research and training, and actually founded some.

By the end of the century it was generally recognized that the problems of logistics, armament, and fortification were of such complexity as to demand some standardization of equipment. Many changes in the nature of war derived from this standardization, as well as from the strengthening of the nation-state. This century of almost incessant warfare pressed heavily upon the industrial resources of western Europe. National self-sufficiency in armaments became a preoccupation of the statesmen of every important country, and many of them began to look to the emerging sciences for assistance in the discovery of new processes and in the substitution of native commodities for those normally imported from elsewhere. The economic doctrines which we call "mercantilism" reflected from beginning to end a concern with national power.

War at the end of the seventeenth century was very different from war at the beginning. The Thirty Years' War (1616-1648) has been aptly described as "collisions of communities," but war as conducted by Louis XIV at the turn of the century meant the use of disciplined armies controlled by a complex military hierarchy and using improved gunpowder weapons on land and sea. It is difficult to say whether war technology had improved because of the continuous battling or in spite of it, for the kind of industrial progress so essential to the real improvement of weapon development had been made impossible in large parts of Europe by the hideous devastation of the Thirty Years' War.

This conflict, whatever the complexities of religious and political issues, was for the common soldier, and his victims—the humble farmer, shopkeeper, and artisan—essentially a war of plunder. Both Catholics and Protestants levied taxes to pay the soldiers, but there was no developed bureaucracy to collect them, and the unpaid and unfed soldiers took to wholesale and systematic pillaging. Soon it became clear that the great armies led by such generals as Tilly and Wallenstein were often governed not by political or military considerations but by the single problem of food. Their men descended on a prosperous section of the countryside, devoured it like a swarm of locusts, and then moved on. Wallenstein managed more efficiently than most; his exactions were so systematic and the products he took by force so efficiently used that he fed 50,000 on what others took to feed 20,000. A skillful general took pains to winter his army in an area that had not already been mulcted.

The result on the strategy of the war was extraordinary. As Carl Friedrich has pointed out, "Anyone looking at the map of the campaigns of the Thirty Years' War is puzzled at first that the armies were to be found anywhere except in the country for which they were presumably fighting. Most princes were anxious to keep armies away from their dominions at all costs. Recurrently, the generals would be forbidden to move into the home country."

Except for pikes, arquebuses, pistols, and ammunition, soldiers were expected to supply all their own equipment—including clothing, for uniforms were neither supplied nor standardized. French, Spanish, Austrian, and Swedish armies used Belgium, Austria, Bohemia and most of Germany as a battleground. In the last stages of the war the Bavarian army, numbering 30,000, was accompanied by 130,000 hangers-on—men, women, and children. All but 6,000 of 35,000 Bohemian villages were destroyed, and the population of Germany dropped from sixteen million to under six million. Religious bigotry contributed to the casualties; the Bishop of Wurzburg put 9,000 to death as witches and wizards in 1627 and 1628. Massacre was common and the burning of cities routine. At the siege of Magdeburg 30,000 died in the flames. The whole central European area, which had been leading in industrial progress, remained for the better part of a century "in the stillness of exhaustion."

Nevertheless, the Thirty Years' War did see changes in the tactics and technology of war, and these can in large measure be ascribed to the genius of the King of Sweden, Gustavus Adolphus. Gustavus was a gifted tactician, an imaginative administrator, and a leader with prodigious personal magnetism. He took a keen interest in the technology of armaments, and under his stimulation the Swedish gun industry, which began about 1618, soon rivaled the British. He curbed the power of his own nobles, established a centralized government, and encouraged a productive industrial economy.

Many things contributed to his success in battle, the most important being the professional character of his army. At least half of his men were Swedish and Finnish yeomen, organized through a kind of national draft. All were paid good wages and given superior guns and artillery. He reduced the length of the pike from eighteen to eleven feet, and used a lighter, improved musket, a wheel lock instead of the old matchlock. Instead of carrying into battle the awkward flasks, or bandoleers, of gunpowder, his men carried paper cartridges containing both powder and shot, which speeded up the loading. Instead of massing his infantry in solid squares, he used small squares interspersed with cavalry, which made for much greater flexibility in battle.

Gustavus standardized cannon by their shot weights and bore diameters, and kept his guns light. Queen Elizabeth's army had used 30-pounder culverins weighing more than two tons; Gustavus used cannon as small as 4-pounders weighing 500 pounds, which could be handled by four men or a single horse. Before his time most armies had had one heavy cannon for every thousand men; he had six 9-pounder demi-culverins and two 4-pounders for every thousand. His field guns, generally made of cast iron, could be maneuvered into position by two horses and three men. Instead of restricting cannon to use against fortifications, he massed them directly against soldiers. Sometimes his artillerymen fired case shot, or canister—musket balls or scrap metal in cans.

Unlike many commanders of the time, he was disturbed by casualties among his own soldiers, and he devised tactics to lessen them. In the siege of Riga he made his soldiers dig trenches and traverses to approach close to the walls, and he dug enthusiastically along with his men. As a result the morale of his army was superb. He took such pains with proper planning of transport and supply that he was the first commander in modern Europe to fight winter campaigns with success.

But like the other war leaders of his time he took it for granted that his soldiers had every right to be fed by whatever country they conquered. "It must make no difference that the peasantry complain," he wrote, "for We do not attach so much importance to the well-being of the country as to the need for succoring and providing for the soldiers who by faithful service have assisted to conquer it; which you shall look to by all manner of means, not caring if the peasant squeal . . ." Yet it should also be recorded that he seems genuinely to have deplored the horrors of war, though he regarded them as inevitable.

Gustavus fell to an untimely death on the battlefield near Lützen on November 6, 1632, but his victories did much to preserve Protestantism in northern Europe. Eventually the military lessons he taught were utilized throughout the armies of Europe. With the increasing centralization of the European states, the armies became more disciplined. Mercenaries were no longer hired from contractors but were recruited, paid, equipped, and managed by the states. France took over the control of the manufacturing of all her artillery. Cromwell issued regular uniforms in 1640 to distinguish his soldiers from those of Charles I, though these were not the first seen in England, for Henry VIII had prescribed red and blue coats for his regular troops and "a sad green color" for those who took part in forest fighting. Plunder and massacre gradually lessened, though they certainly did not disappear.

Maurice of Nassau developed a dependable standing army, insisting on long-term enlistments and strict discipline. Believing less in pitched battles than in maneuver, he taught his Dutch infantry to move with surprising speed, and saw to it that his musketeers continued to fire during combat. He learned the art of concentrating his artillery, and developed an able corps of military engineers. The standing army became a permanent fixture on the European scene; the hangers-on disappeared, and the soldier became completely divorced from any kind of family life. Armies became bigger. Louis XIV attacked the Spanish Netherlands in 1667 with 73,000 men, and at the end of the second

war in 1678 he had 279,000. Still, as the military writer
Jacques de Guibert wryly put it, all that had happened was
that "small armies carrying out large operations had suddenly been replaced by large armies performing small
tasks."

The standing army was not, however, as yet a national
army. The Dutch maintained English, Scottish, and French
regiments; Louis XIV had English, Scottish, Irish, German,
Spanish, and Swiss units. Sometimes auxiliary troops in
ready-made formations were hired out by one government
to another, and according to the international law of the
time this did not involve the former state in war. Mass
desertions were still common. In 1671 it was reported that
10,000 soldiers who had been expected to invade the Low
Countries, deserted the service of Louis XIV. Helpless before such mass action, he "published a general pardon."

Long before the end of his reign, however, Louis XIV
made the authority of the king over the army supreme.
François Louvois, his great war minister, centralized the
military administration and improved the status of the
infantry as well as the quality of their weapons. In Russia,
Peter the Great, copying the West with furious haste, built
up a field army of 100,000 men by 1716. This was as big
as the Austrian army and larger than the army either of
Sweden or Prussia. Like Gustavus Adolphus three-quarters
of a century earlier, he studied mathematics, fortification,
navigation, shipbuilding and gunnery. The whole of Europe
would later feel the impact of the scientific learning of this
one great monarch.

## IMPROVEMENTS IN THE HAND GUN

The hand gun in the early part of the seventeenth century
continued the development it had seen in the late sixteenth.
The first successful rifle (from the German word *riffeln*, to
groove) was invented either by Gaspard Koller, a gunmaker
of Vienna, or August Kotter, an armorer of Nuremberg.
Guns with grooves had appeared in the late 1400's; the
grooves, however, had not been intended to spin the bullet,

but to serve as a reservoir for the powder ash. The new rifling introduced the principle that was to make the gun at last an accurate weapon. But, apart from the difficulty of cutting the grooves, there was the problem of combining rifling with muzzleloading. Even with successful rifles the lead ball had to be driven down the barrel with a ramrod and mallet. Loading continued to be such a laborious process that the rifle was largely confined to target shooting and hunting until the late eighteenth century.

The basic hand gun of the seventeenth century was not the rifle at all but the smoothbore flintlock. There were five or six kinds of primitive flintlocks. As early as 1615 a French inventor substituted flint for pyrites in the wheel lock, making the gun less complex and more manageable. The snaphaunce, developed in Scandinavia and the Low Countries, operated much like the wheel lock. The name came from the Dutch *snap-haan*, meaning "snapping cock," or "pecking fowl," for the cock snapped into the flint and the sparks ignited the powder in the priming pan. Other early flintlocks were called frizzens, miquelet locks, Scandinavian snaplocks, and dog locks. Finally the inventors perfected a flintlock where the falling cock uncovered the priming pan and struck the necessary sparks simultaneously.

The flintlock was much lighter than the old matchlock, and was enthusiastically preferred by the settlers—and the Indians—in North and South America. Not the least remarkable thing about this gun was that once it was adopted over the western world—its use was widespread by 1650— it held undisputed sway for 200 years. Its range and accuracy remained relatively unchanged, and armorers continued their efforts to make body armor impervious to its shot, though the weight of the plates was extremely heavy. Small arms ballistics were completely ignored by seventeenth-century scientists and ballistics experts, who were interested only in artillery, and what improvements were made came from the inventive fertility of the gunsmiths themselves.

The flintlock was not immediately adopted by armies because it often missed fire and was expensive to manufacture. The English formally introduced the flintlock into their infantry in 1682. The famous "Brown Bess" musket, an improved gun, soon followed and remained the standard infantry arm in Britain for 160 years (Fig. 23). Its name came from the fact that its stock was walnut and its barrel artificially browned by rusting with acid. It was not rifled,

Fig. 23. Brown Bess, a Flintlock

but accuracy of fire was considered less important at the time than volume of fire. It was not a handy gun—it took forty seconds for a well-trained soldier to load and fire a single shot—and it weighed ten pounds. Its accuracy, and those of related guns on the continent, was appallingly bad at any but short ranges. At forty yards it could hit a foot-square target almost every time, but at three hundred yards only one bullet out of twenty would hit a target eighteen feet square.

Infantry tactics remained relatively static. The training of troops in marksmanship was considered relatively unimportant; a soldier was lucky to have fired five rounds before going into battle. Training consisted of dry runs and physical hardening. The Marechal de Saxe put it succinctly when he wrote: "All the mystery of maneuvers and combat is in the legs."

Soldiers were taught to advance in battle shoulder to shoulder, generally two or three lines deep, at eighty steps a minute. Because of the ineffectiveness of their weapons at long ranges, they were taught to hold their fire until the last minute. Then the side which fired first had to reload while the enemy fired from a still closer range. At Blenheim in 1704 the French waited till the leading British brigadier struck the barricades with his sword only thirty feet away. With this kind of fighting the casualties were likely to be fearful, and only iron discipline kept soldiers reloading and firing amid the dead and writhing bodies of their comrades.

The only significant change in infantry tactics came toward the end of the seventeenth century as a result of the invention of the bayonet. There is some dispute about the origin of the word; apparently it was derived from the French town, Bayonne, where a short dagger called the

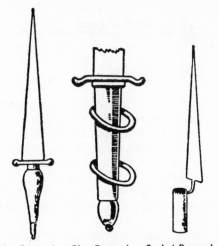

Fig. 24. Plug Bayonet    Ring Bayonet    Socket Bayonet

*bayonette* was being manufactured at the end of the fifteenth century. At first it was only a plug bayonet, a steel dagger fitted into the muzzle of the musket. These were issued to a regiment of French fusiliers in 1671 and to an English dragoon regiment in 1672. The obvious disadvantage was that use of the bayonet meant the end of the firing.

A ring bayonet was invented in 1678, and a tubular socket followed (Fig. 24). Louis XIV was suspicious of the improved zigzag bayonet, and it was therefore not adopted by the French till 1703, though the Germans and British officially adopted it and abandoned the pike in 1697. Sir John Moore greatly improved the bayonet by introducing a spring clip for fastening it to the musket; this remained in standard use in the British Army till it was replaced by

the sword bayonet, which could be used as a sword or dagger apart from the rifle. This was used during World War I.
The bayonet meant the final doom of the pikeman and the
final fusion of the two major infantry arms into one. This
fusion was a major step in standardization and simplification. Toward the end of the seventeenth century the grenade
was introduced. Used at first only in siegecraft, it had made
its way by 1704 into the infantry, and the grenadier became
a new name in the armies of western Europe.

## ARTILLERY CHANGES, 1600-1700

Except for the tactical improvement in maneuverability resulting from the lighter field guns produced under Gustavus
Adolphus, seventeenth-century artillery showed less improvement in design than the hand gun. The scale of cannon
increased, especially on the warships, but there was no
great improvement in accuracy in the big gun until well
into the nineteenth century. As Albert Rupert Hall has said,
"The guns of Queen Victoria's wooden ships were capable
of little more accurate practice than those of Drake's fleet
which defeated the Armada." Gunners were now using the
Tartaglia quadrant as a means of accurately setting the
angle of elevation with reference to the horizon rather than
the ship's deck. But there were no sights on the cannon;
the quadrant was simply put into the bore and the angle
read from the position of a plumb line on a protractor
scale. More modern quadrants, designed to be placed on
top of the gun, use a bubble level rather than a plumb line.

One notable new invention was the coehorn, a mortar
devised by a Dutch fighting engineer and soon adopted
everywhere. This was a small gun with a barrel only about
twice as long as the bore diameter; it was the ancestor of the
howitzer. The coehorn used a greatly improved fuse, which
lessened the casualties among the gunners, who had too
often been killed by their own fire.

It may seem curious that although war was almost continuous in Europe from 1540 to 1721, the basic design of
the big guns remained relatively static. One reason was

simply the absence of pressure for change. Field and naval guns were so expensive relative to the military budgets of the times that they were expected to last many years, and the most that the masters of ordnance demanded of their foundrymen was that the guns be as good as those already in service. Moreover ammunition was so scarce that it could not be lightly wasted in practice. The shortage of saltpeter, derived largely from barnyards and pigeon lofts, was acute until the Dutch East India Company found a supply in India after 1750. And despite that find, good supply of saltpeter and gunpowder was to remain a major military problem as late as the French Revolution.

The standard book on artillery at the end of the century was *Mémoires d'artillerie* by Surirey de Saint Rémy (1650-1716), who had co-ordinated French munition manufacture and supply. It was the principal guide to munitions manufacturers for other countries as well as France until well into the eighteenth century. Saint Rémy's three volumes indicate a preoccupation with the permanence of existing weapons rather than with replacement and improvement through new invention and metallurgical change.

All through the seventeenth century ammunition remained technically imperfect, and artillery ranges remained about the same as those of medieval siege warfare. The great developments in artillery had to wait upon three things: first, the science of ballistics, which developed slowly and quite independently of the art of war in the researches of Galileo, Descartes, Newton, and their followers; second, the science of chemistry, which would not really be born till the eighteenth century; and third, the technological developments in manufacturing which could come only with the industrial revolution.

### SEVENTEENTH-CENTURY SCIENCE

The development of truly superior guns was impossible without a correct ballistic theory. Neither Tartaglia nor his followers had supplied it; it took the genius of Galileo to start the necessary revolution. The full impact of this great innovator on all of science needs no emphasis here. He was the first to carry experimental and mathematical methods into physics, particularly dynamics. After him there was no return to the old mythologies.

Galileo, like the natural philosophers before him, was fascinated with the theory of projectiles. As a young man he had read Archimedes, and he went on to study the artillery pieces of his time, not because he had any real interest in improving military technology, but because the gun was the best instrument yet devised for testing his mathematical theories. When he examined the physical principles of the ballistics experts, he found them to be incapable of mathematical expression, so he looked for new laws. His parabolic theory, as propounded in 1638, was a truly revolutionary advance, but it had no effect whatever on either the designing or the shooting of seventeenth-century cannon. Tartaglian theories remained unchanged till 1674, thirty-two years after Galileo's death, when Robert Anderson succeeded in popularizing the theory of parabolic ballistics in England with his *Genuine Use and Effects of the Gunne.*

The importance of Galileo's mathematical discoveries impressed scientists of the time and influenced a whole galaxy of followers. The great Dutch physicist Christian Huygens tried to improve on the parabolic theory, which he recognized to be inexact. Leibniz, Jean and Jacques Bernouilli, James Gregory, and finally Isaac Newton all wrestled with ballistic theory and greatly altered it, though Galileo's faulty original theory was considered scientific truth till well into the eighteenth century. Robert Boyle, the great British chemist, was the first in England to use the word ballistics in print; he classed it, with pneumatics and hydraulics, as a mixed science.

Isaac Newton knew nothing of guns, carried out no experiments in gunnery, and had only the slightest interest in the technological application of the great mathematical discoveries recorded in his *Mathematical Principles of Natural Philosophy*, published in 1687. None of these men investigated the technology of the ordnance industry, which was actually so inferior that it could not have served as a good scientific laboratory, so great were the irregularities of the guns of the day.

This is not to say that these great mathematicians were not themselves highly talented technicians. Galileo, after hearing of the invention of the telescope by the Dutch optician Johan Lippershey, at once made one of his own. From his first telescope of three-fold magnifying power he went on to attain a power of thirty-two. Galileo's pupil Evangelista Torricelli (1608-1647), who also had a happy talent for applying mathematical analysis to physical problems, invented the barometer in 1643, though it would not be until 1660 that anyone would point out the correlation between barometric pressure and climatic conditions. Gottfried Wilhelm Leibniz, one of the inventors of differential calculus, designed a calculating machine for multiplying, dividing, and extracting roots. James Gregory, the Scottish mathematician and astronomer, invented the reflector telescope, ancestor of the modern giant at Mount Palomar.

One mathematician, the Frenchman Gérard Desargues (1593-1662), lent his talents to military science for a time; the others seem to have kept aloof from it altogether. Christian Huygens, engaged by the French Academy of Science at its foundation in 1666, worked with gunpowder, but he was interested only in the possibility of using it as motive power for a combustion engine. René Descartes (1596-1650) was a volunteer in the army of Prince Maurice in the Thirty Years' War, but seems to have seen no real soldiering. Even during his years in battle-torn Germany, pure mathematics dominated his activities rather than war. Finally he retired to Holland, where he invented co-ordinate geometry and did much writing in physics and philosophy.

Otto von Guericke, military engineer at the siege of Magdeburg, his home city, eventually turned away from designing fortifications and armament toward a more peaceful science. He constructed the first electrostatic generator. This primitive generator consisted of a large ball of sulphur which could be rotated on a horizontal iron axis by a crank; electrification was produced when a hand was held on the rotating sulphur. He experimented with vacuums in copper casks, inventing the first air pump to produce a vacuum, a technical invention that proved important as a means of investigating gases.

By 1654 he was able to demonstrate before the Imperial Diet at Ratisbon an experiment that became famous as the Magdeburg hemispheres. He fitted two hollow bronze hemispheres carefully together and removed the air with his brass pump. The external atmospheric pressure held the two halves together so tightly that eight horses could not pull them apart. When he admitted air through a stopcock the two hemispheres fell apart.

The discoveries and writings of all these men would influence the military technology of the future, but the lag was considerable. Though Newton's discoveries provoked many essays in ballistics, they belong to the eighteenth, not the seventeenth century. In fact, as Albert Rupert Hall has pointed out in his excellent study *Ballistics in the Seventeenth Century,* the sophistication and ingenuity of the engineers of the gun factories would not really catch up with Newton until the nineteenth century. The true stagnation was not in science but in engineering and manufacturing.

During the seventeenth century the new enthusiasm for mathematics spread quickly to the artillerists. Louis XIV founded an artillery school at Douai in 1679, and his great minister, Jean Baptiste Colbert, was able to attract to it the finest gun-founders in Europe. Spain had had artillery training schools since before the end of the sixteenth century. In all these schools a good deal of lip service was given to mathematics, particularly since mortar bombardment had become increasingly important in war. However, as centers of research and training, the military departments in the new academies were poor makeshifts. In artillery, France had a slight technical superiority over her enemies, but it was not decisive in the wars of Louis XIV.

Manuals in mathematics were written for use in many technical fields. Surveyors, merchants, seamen, and architects studied them as well as soldiers. The diarist Samuel Pepys, at twenty-nine, hired the mate of the *Royal Charles*

to instruct him in mathematics, beginning with the multiplication tables. In architecture, a study of the strength of
materials became a new branch of mechanics. The techniques of shipbuilding were re-examined when it was realized that the shape of the hull and the disposition of the
rigging could be improved by mathematical analysis. Merchants relegated the abacus to the nurseries of their children
and did their sums on paper. The general use of mathematics was further stimulated by John Napier's invention of
logarithms, certainly the most universally useful mathematical discovery of the seventeenth century.

Numerous scientific societies were founded. The first
important one, established in Rome in 1603, included Galileo in its membership. The two Medici brothers Ferdinand
II and Leopold founded an influential physical laboratory
in Florence in 1657. They provided money to buy the
services of the finest instrument makers, equipped the
laboratories with barometers, thermometers, and time-meas-
uring devices, and staffed them with able men, some of
them students of Galileo. This school did much to shape
the course of experimental science elsewhere in Europe,
but it lasted for only ten years. When Leopold Medici became a cardinal the academy was dissolved.

There was a continuous tradition of scientific gatherings
in Paris, ultimately centralized in 1666 in the *Académie
Royale des Sciences*. In London the Royal Society for the
Promotion of Natural Knowledge received its charter in
1663. It was granted no royal patronage, however, and remained impoverished and badly housed, though it sheltered
some of Britain's most celebrated scientists. In Berlin, the
first scientific academy was founded in 1700.

A few great scientific names loom large above the rest,
in addition to those we have already mentioned. William
Harvey (1578-1657) made one of the most fundamental
discoveries in all the history of science, the circulation of
the blood. The science of physiology, based on accurate observation rather than the heavy weight of authority, properly began with the publication of his *Anatomical Disser-
tation Concerning the Motion of the Heart and Blood in*

*Animals.* William Gilbert (1540-1603), who belongs more to the sixteenth than to the seventeenth century, made a fundamental study of magnetism and electricity at a time when both forces were obscured in a maze of superstition. It was he who introduced the word electricity into the language. His *De Magnete,* published in 1600, was far in advance of his time. Experimentation in electricity remained spasmodic—as in the work of Otto von Guericke, for example—till late in the eighteenth century.

Chemistry in the seventeenth century was slower in developing than physics. The old preoccupation of the alchemists persisted; some of Newton's most distinguished contemporaries tried to change base metals into gold, and Newton himself is said to have taken a long look at their recipes. By the middle of the century most chemists knew the common metals, their alloys, and their salts, but little more. There was no theory of chemistry except the atomic hypothesis advanced centuries earlier by Democritus and the Ionian Greeks.

The father of modern chemistry, the Englishman Robert Boyle (1627-1691), improved on the air pump of Otto von Guericke, began experimenting with gases, and evolved the concept that air is an elastic medium. In 1660 he published his *New Experiments Physico-Mechanicall Touching the Spring of the Air.* A year later he published the results of his chemical experiments in *The Skeptical Chymist.* Newton showed that Boyle's celebrated law connecting pressure and volume of a gas could be deduced mathematically if the gas consisted of particles, and the ancient atomic hypothesis of Democritus became a truly scientific theory—though the concept of molecules as distinct from atoms was not yet grasped. For the first time chemistry was provided an essential theoretical foundation.

Boyle also did the science of chemistry much service by helping to break down the barrier between the gentleman and the craftsman. Most of his contemporary scientists were wealthy amateurs, generally contemptuous of social inferiors. Boyle, who had gained much of his technical information from craftsmen, derided the men who disdained them, saying, "he deserves not the knowledge of nature, that scorns to converse even with mean persons, that have the opportunity to be very conversant with her."

The budding chemistry of the seventeenth century was a very long way from influencing the technology of war. Powder and explosives remained remarkably unchanged. Boyle himself made clear that he thought no learned man should contribute to the "hellish machines" of destruction, and showered bounties upon one scientist who had invented a new explosive to keep him from selling it.

The century did see, however, an enormous preoccupation with machines, especially pumps and mills. Ramelli's *The Various and Ingenious Machines,* published early in the century, in 1616, described a hundred kinds of pumps and 24 kinds of mills, with jacks, bridges, and derricks of all kinds. Edward Somerset's *Century of Inventions,* published in 1663, gives a picture of the extraordinary number of inventions that had been added in 57 years.

Toward the end of the century the first steam engines were produced. Back in 130 B.C., Hero of Alexandria in the *Pneumatica* had described a primitive steam reaction turbine and another device which was a prototype of the pressure engine. Now, finally, in 1663 a patent for a workable steam engine was granted to the Marquess of Worcester. Thomas Savery patented the first commercially successful one in 1698. It was, in fact, simply the reduction to a workable form of the ancient scientific toy. But an effective steam engine would not be built in England until early in the eighteenth century, and the industrial revolution would have to wait until the end of the eighteenth century before it felt the impact of the genius of James Watt.

The most powerful prime mover in the seventeenth century was the waterworks for the fountains of Versailles, considered one of the great wonders of the age. By harnessing the Seine, it developed 100 horse power and could raise a million gallons a day 502 feet. But the most fabulously intricate of all the machines were certainly the clocks. Lewis Mumford in his *Technics and Civilization* has designated the clock rather than the steam engine the key machine of the modern industrial age, insisting that it has consistently out-paced all the other mechanisms of modern times. The inventors and improvers of the seventeenth-century clocks are largely unknown, but their craftsmanship is certainly astonishing. For accuracy of measurement and fineness of articulation they would meet the most exacting standards of the modern scientific laboratory. This development was a response less to a need than to an enthusiasm, for Europe went crazy over the clock.

## SEVENTEENTH-CENTURY FORTIFICATION

We have seen that the medieval fortress was doomed by the development of artillery; it seemed for a long period too that the walled city was equally vulnerable before sustained attack. The necessity of building new fortifications which would withstand cannonballs became the preoccupation of all military engineers, and even excited the imaginations of the greatest intellects and artists of the renaissance, Leonardo, Michelangelo, Machiavelli, and Dürer. Dürer's projects, published in 1527, were too massive and too costly for practical execution, but some of his designs, including the first practical gun casemates, were taken over by the engineers of the time.

The Italian engineers in the sixteenth century were the first to design real improvements in fortification. As early as the siege of Padua in 1509, Emperor Maximilian's artillerymen were nonplussed by the new wet ditches, ramparts, and bastions. But the biggest strides were made by the French in the seventeenth century. The first lesson learned was that in order to protect the old walls earthen bulwarks must be placed in front with advanced gun positions. The second lesson was that all new fortifications should be low, preferably with the walls sunk into a ditch. Behind the walls were ramparts—banked earth thrown up out of the ditch—upon which the guns were placed. Counterforts were buttresses built inward from the wall into the rampart; they strengthened the wall and made breaches more difficult. Bastions were extensions outward from the main fortification, with flanks attached to the main wall. Improvements in artillery made it possible to cover all areas in front of the fortification.

A fine example of the complete bastion system was Paciotto's citadel of Antwerp, built in 1568. Had the Dutch been able to duplicate this citadel everywhere, they would have done better in their valiant efforts to throw off the hated Spanish yoke. As it was, Dutch methods of fortification acquired a formidable reputation, particularly their use of "wet ditches." The Dutch vastly expanded their canal system and used great quantities of palisading, chiefly from the timbers of old ships. Discovering, however, that a frozen canal immediately became a highway, they had to devise means of draining the canals or ditches at will. To resolve this and other problems they enlisted the services of a great mathematician.

Simon Stevin (1548-1620) had been responsible for the introduction of the decimal system of fractions. Actually the decimal system had been known for five centuries, but it took Stevin to bring it into the life of the common shopkeeper. He urged with less success the adoption of decimal coinage, weights, and measures, but that was not to come to Europe till the French Revolution. Stevin willingly went to the aid of his monarch. He introduced and elaborated a system of sluices which could be emptied or filled as needed, and designed the whole line of river fortifications for Maurice of Nassau.

Most of the improvements in the seventeenth-century fortifications came not from mathematicians but from the non-theoretical military engineers. Geometrician Gérard Desargues was for a time an army officer in the engineering section at the siege of La Rochelle. Daniel Speckle, who published a treatise with many new ideas on how to make forts more defensible, was an architect for the city of Strasbourg. But most of the names in fortification were those of professional soldiers.

The new fortifications did much to stabilize warfare in the seventeenth century. Even the more primitive improvements could mean a great increase in the casualties of the attacker and a prolongation of the period of siege. The Venetians, holding Candia in Crete against the Turkish assault of 1667, managed to delay its capture for two years. Though the enceinte, designed by Italian engineers, was already obsolete, it cost the Turks 100,000 men to capture it. The Venetians lost 30,000. Among the military engineers fighting at the siege of Candia was George Rimpler. In 1683 he published his first-hand observations and suggestions in *Fortifications with General Bastions,* a book that exercised a great influence on the military engineers of his own and subsequent generations.

The most prominent name in the siege warfare of the seventeenth century was that of a professional soldier and military engineer, Sébastien le Prestre, Marquis de Vauban It is difficult to say which he influenced more during his lifetime, the art of attacking fortifications, or the art of designing them to withstand attack. Orphaned at ten and very poor, Vauban became a soldier at eighteen and devoted the rest of his life to war and preparations for war. He took part in forty-eight sieges, forty of which he directed as chief engineer without a single failure. His phenomenal success in attack—for in only one of these forty was he on the defense—was largely due to his method and thorough organization. His preparation for his career included a careful self-training in mathematics. In his method there was a deadly certainty that left nothing to chance.

Having been a common soldier, he had a regard for the lives of his soldiers. He believed that most of the casualties incurred in taking a fortification resulted from the use of the frontal assault. Although the soldier usually disliked digging, Vauban insisted on it. His sappers made a slow but methodical progress toward the fort, past the outworks, across the ditch, and up to the breach, in a series of trenches and traverses, all designed according to plan. Thanks largely to his phenomenal success, the idea took hold that it was impossible to arrest such an attack however complicated the outworks of a fort. Finally it became an honored military custom to abandon a fort if the enemy advanced far enough to make the defenders believe they could no longer hold it. If the garrison surrendered without putting the attackers to the necessity of a frontal assault, they were generally well treated; if, on the other hand, the defenders held out valiantly to the end, they could expect a wholesale massacre. The rewards were definitely on the side of being reasonable.

Later a famous French revolutionary leader, Lazare Carnot, would write contemptuously that "what was taught in the military schools was no longer the art of defending strong places, but that of surrendering them honorably, after certain conventional formalities." It would not be until the Crimean War that the idea would take hold that true defense was offensive action outside the fort—going out to meet the besieger with counter-trench and counter-mine.

Vauban was honored by being made Marshal of France in 1703, after which he took no more part in sieges but did a good deal of writing. His early treatise, *Mémoire pour Servir à l'Instruction dans la Conduite des Sièges,* had been published in 1669; his *Traite de l'Attaque des Places* and *De la Défense des Places* appeared after he ceased active fighting.

During his lifetime Vauban was famous not only for his skill in attack but also as a designer of fortifications. He repaired or constructed more than a hundred and sixty. Actually he made few revolutionary innovations, but refined and perfected with great skill the ideas he had inherited. Though military historians have described his innovations in terms of "systems," he was in fact contemptuous of systems and simply utilized his practical genius for devising the best construction for the site—the real test of the engineer. Sometimes he used the straight flank, sometimes the curved flank with an orillon—a projection at the shoulder of the bastion. Almost always he employed the ravelin—a detached work with two embankments—whose fire protected the salients and near faces of the neighboring bastions. Ditches eighteen feet deep and parapets eighteen feet thick were typical of Vauban.

Vauban's bastioned system was the best contemporary solution for the seventeenth-century fortification problem.

The artillery and musketry of the day were of too short range and too slow fire for an effective frontal defense. The problem was how best to flank the essential ditch and how to protect the flanking arrangements. The late seventeenth century saw an immense outpouring of literature on

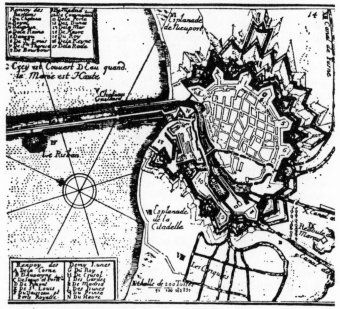

Fig. 25. Vauban's Reconstruction of Dunkirk

the theory of fortification, much of it written by men who had no practical knowledge of the subject. Theorists vied with each other in proposing new "systems," mazes of gates, sally ports, ravelins, demilunes, hornworks, and bastions. Vauban's writings superseded all of these and became military gospel (Fig. 25, 26). In the end this proved to be unfortunate, for so great was his prestige that his authority paralyzed French military thought on the subject of fortifications during the eighteenth and most of the nineteenth century.

Marc René, Marquis de Montalembert (1714-1800), an eighteenth-century military engineer and writer of very great talent, tried to introduce into the French army improvements in the art of fortification which were of signal value, but he could not withstand the hostility of the Vauban worshippers. He was forbidden to publish his method or to build extensively. Drawing from the tenaille system popular in Sweden and Prussia, which stemmed from the principles of Dürer, Speckle and Rimpler and was considered simpler than the bastion system of Vauban, he devised a fort that consisted simply of an immense battery so constructed that the defender could bring an overwhelming fire to bear on the attackers. The essence of his polygonal system was its simplicity (Fig. 26). He was one of the first to see the coming necessity for detached forts; he designed one which, with its straight or slightly broken exterior sides, could be used on any sort of ground.

Toward the end of his life he was permitted to publish *La Fortification Perpendiculaire* and other works, and after a temporary exile during the Revolution he was given the rank of general and consulted often by Carnot on military affairs. The Germans read Montalembert with enthusiasm and used his ideas with much success in the nineteenth century.

### SEVENTEENTH-CENTURY NAVAL WARFARE

The seventeenth century saw almost continuous naval warfare and profound changes in the power alignments of western Europe. There was often no clear line between war and peace. Great powers could be at peace with each other at home, but at war abroad with their trading companies. In 1639 Spanish sea power, a hollow giant, collapsed for good with the defeat of the Spanish fleet by the brilliant Dutch Admiral Tromp. Driven to take shelter in English neutral waters, the Spaniards were annihilated by the Dutch, who ignored English protests. Seventy of the seventy-seven Spanish ships were sunk or captured.

James I had let his fleet disintegrate, and for a time the

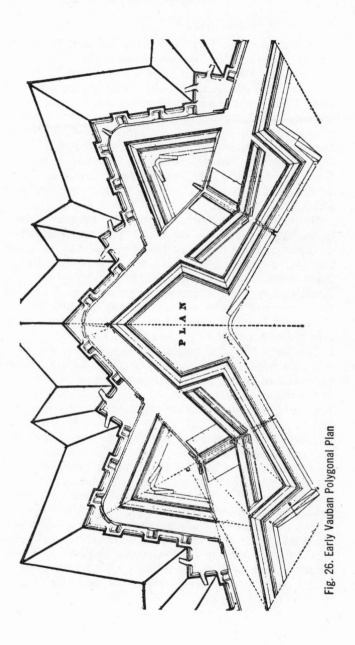

Fig. 26. Early Vauban Polygonal Plan

Dutch almost drove the English from the seas. But under the Commonwealth and also under Charles II, the fleet was brought to a high degree of efficiency. The English fought two wars with the Dutch, leaving the Dutch exhausted in 1674. Then, when Louis XIV threatened to take the Flemish ports, the Dutch and English, who were then fighting a third war, joined hands and destroyed the French fleet in 1689 at the battles of Barfleur and Cape La Hogue. After years of further warfare, the French Toulon fleet was defeated off Malaga (1704) and the English captured Gibraltar and held it. Now England was firmly entrenched as a Mediterranean power.

During this century there was very little advance in naval technology, though there were some important administrative changes. After the Anglo-Dutch war of 1653-54, which saw twelve desperate sea fights, the great admiral Robert Blake concluded that the merchant fleets supplementing the English navy were untrustworthy in action. Thereafter Parliament built its own warships and supplied their officers. Piracy was largely suppressed in the Mediterranean; maritime law was better defined and better enforced.

The Royal Navy had bigger ships than before, with more and heavier guns. A few inventions were adopted, like the bell-mouthed blunderbuss, which used an enormous load of buckshot and cut a deadly swath over a wide area at close range. It proved excellent for repelling boarders in battle. But from the Armada to Napoleon there were few basic improvements in the construction or handling of ships.

Naval tactics were stereotyped; a single line ahead was considered the most effective formation for broadside firing. Ships fought yardarm to yardarm until one was so weakened she could be taken by boarding. England's success in naval warfare, according to Albert Rupert Hall, "owed less to any advantages of technique or skill than to sheer persistence in battle. Out-maneuvered by the Dutch, out-sailed by the French in many a campaign, the English commander disdained exchanges of shot at long ranges, relying upon the brutal destruction of the enemy's crew and hull at close quarters to win the day."

There were hints of great forthcoming changes, the most intriguing being experimentation with the idea of a submarine. From the time of Leonardo men had occasionally toyed with submarine drawings. In 1578 William Browne, an English mathematician and gunner, made a drawing of a submarine which was supposed to be rowed under water. The sides were to be contracted by hand vises, thus causing submergence. The drawing was published in his *Inventions and Devises,* but no working model was ever built. In 1620, however, a crude submarine was actually built and launched by the Dutch mechanic and chemist Cornelius Drebbel. Propulsion was achieved by rowers sitting in a kind of diving bell covered with greased leather. When James I watched a demonstration of this machine on the Thames, he was astonished to see it traveling twelve or fifteen feet below the surface of the river.

John Wilkins, an imaginative British divine and scientist, wrote at considerable length about submarines in his *Mathematicall Magick,* published in 1648. By 1727 fourteen types of submarines had been patented in England. None, of course, was practicable.

More important from the long view was the establishment of naval academies and centers of naval research. In France under Colbert the best naval architects worked out problems of design and ordnance for the new French warships. This great minister reorganized the navy, raising it from twenty warships in 1661 to a hundred and ninety-six in 1671 and to two hundred and seventy in 1677. He renovated old harbors and arsenals and modernized the French ports. Training academies were established at Rochefort, Dieppe and Saint-Malo. This was truly a foretaste of things to come, when the resources of several great European states would be harnessed to the building up of immense military establishments.

# 5. The Eighteenth Century and Napoleonic Wars

By the beginning of the eighteenth century the western world was so closely knit that every local question ran into every other and the contest for power dominated them all. The mannered formalities of late seventeenth-century warfare began to break down; the emphasis on defense and fortification gave way—particularly under the influence of the Duke of Marlborough—to an offensive strategy that foreshadowed Frederick the Great and Napoleon. Russia wrested the hegemony of the North from Sweden, conquered the Ukraine, and gained a foothold in eastern Europe. By the close of his reign in 1725, Peter the Great had a regular army of 210,000 men and a fleet of forty-eight ships of the line.

For a time the civilized traditions of moderation in war persisted. The French general and military writer Maurice de Saxe (1696-1750) wrote: "I am not in favor of giving battle, especially at the outset of a war. I am even convinced that a clever general can live his whole life without being compelled to do so." It was not that the generals abhorred the bloody battle but rather the unfavorable or indecisive battle. They were extremely skeptical of pitched battles between fairly evenly matched armies.

The numerous peace treaties written over the century generally reflect the understanding that moderation would reconcile an undestroyed opponent to defeat. Louis XV is said to have refused to permit the French armies to adopt a newly perfected gunpowder on the grounds that it was "too destructive of human life."

War continued to be waged by rigid rules, with tactics largely a chess-game affair. Even the changes wrought by the greatest military innovator of the mid-century, Frederick II of Prussia, were largely technical and tactical rather than strategic. Frederick improved the training of his infantry, drilling his men to secure a rapid, steady musket fire at very close ranges, between fifty and one hundred yards. Where the best that his enemies could deliver was two volleys a minute, his men could deliver five, and they were taught to lay down a barrage to prepare their own advance.

Frederick also increased the mobility of his artillery. In most armies of the time cannon were hauled to the field of combat by civilian contractors who then withdrew their horses from the line of fire. Frederick employed army horses and trained his soldiers to use them, with the result that his light horse-drawn guns could move with almost the same speed as his cavalry. When the artillery were close to the opposing infantry the gunners changed from solid shot to grape shot—fifty or sixty iron balls about an inch in diameter—which sprayed out from the muzzles with devastating effect. Frederick experimented with massing his field howitzers, gathering together as many as forty-five in one great battery in the Battle of Burkersdorf. Most important, by inaugurating limited conscription he tapped the manpower resources of his nation as no European monarch had done up to his time. Where France had one soldier for every 150 citizens, Frederick had one for every twenty-five. Before his death he had established Prussia as one of the great powers of Europe, and had given her a military tradition of victory through conquest which the Germans, unfortunately, would not forget.

The eighteenth century was the first to see widespread acceptance of the national standing army. Mercenary armies largely disappeared, and if foreign soldiers were employed at all they usually entered as individuals. This meant greater uniformity in training and less desertion. Still, the soldier's life was a dismal one, and desertion and death remained common. In Prussia, a tenth of Frederick's army escaped each year and another tenth died. Moreover, war for the common soldier was a much bloodier business than it had been in the late seventeenth century, thanks to improved muskets, greater mobility, and reliance on frontal attack. At the Battle of Zorndorf the Russians presented a wall of flesh against Frederick's troops; the results were casualties of 38 per cent for the Prussians and 50 per cent for the Russians, with a high proportion dead. This battle Voltaire bitterly satirized in *Candide,* calling it "heroic butchery."

There was still no special reason for training in marksmanship, for ammunition remained costly and muskets inaccurate. The weaknesses of the "command volley" tactics, which so often resulted in little else but mass slaughter on both sides, were slow to be recognized by the military. In 1770 the brilliant twenty-seven-year-old Comte Jacques de Guibert (1743-1790) published his *Essai Général de Tactique,* which vigorously attacked the conventional practices. He advocated firing at will in a kind of lightning warfare that concentrated troops and artillery at the point where the enemy's position was meant to be forced and created the illusion of such attack at other points. He believed in using the column for maneuver and approach, and the line for fighting. Napoleon was much influenced by Guibert.

The weaknesses of the old tactics were further undermined by the new improvements in artillery, though this was not at first grasped. In France, when Jean de Gribeauval (1715-1789) was appointed Inspector-General of Artillery in 1776, he reorganized the artillery from top to bottom. Having fought against Frederick he had a profound respect for Prussian artillery and was determined to make the French superior. He restricted field artillery to 4-pounder regimental guns, and reserve or divisional artillery to 8- and 12-pounder guns and 6-inch howitzers. For garrison and siege work he adopted 16- and 12-pounder guns, 8-inch howitzers and 10-inch mortars. He made the parts interchangeable as far as possible, improved gunsights, and ordered the ball and charge packed into cartridges. He invented the barbette carriage, which allowed cannon to shoot over a parapet instead of through openings in it. It was now theoretically possible for the French field artillery to be massed within 350 yards of an enemy and batter a battalion to pieces, though it would not be till Napoleon's time that the impact of Gribeauval's reorganization and improvements would be fully felt in war.

The artillery used during the American Revolution was fairly primitive. Washington's army had guns of thirteen different sizes ranging from 3-pounders to 24-pounders. Every iron founder with a water wheel was put to work casting cannon for Washington's army. Civilian drivers still hauled the cannon to the field and then fled before the battle; from that point forward it was the muscles of the gun crews that provided the traction.

Benjamin Robins (1707-1751), a distinguished British mathematician, was the first to put gunnery on a truly scientific basis. He did outstanding work in both exterior ballistics, which concerns the flight of projectiles after they leave the gun, and interior ballistics, which concerns their motion inside the gun, always checking his theories with rigorous experiments in the field. He soon discovered many errors in the ballistic theories of Galileo, Newton, and their followers. He also worked with terminal ballistics, which concerns the effect of projectiles at the target. He used the ballistic pendulum, which had been invented by M. Cassini in 1707, an instrument enabling the gunner to measure the velocity of a projectile. He was the first to prove that air currents affect the flight of a cannon ball.

Robins was one of the first scientists who could combine, with a good conscience, speculative scientific work and gunnery engineering; his Quaker background seems never to have deterred him. His *New Principles of Gunnery*, published in 1742, was translated into German and French and had great influence. He strongly urged the adoption of a breechloading rifle and musket, but these were not to be perfected and in general use for many years.

Even the muzzleloading rifle, which until the invention of the expanding bullet remained difficult to load, was not popular till the middle of the eighteenth century, when German and Swiss gunmakers improved it. Barrels became

Fig. 27. The Kentucky Rifle, a Flintlock

slenderer and longer, the popular standard bore finally becoming stabilized at 42 inches; but otherwise it continued to be true that no two rifles were alike. In Europe the rifle remained largely a hunting weapon throughout most of the century.

In America the "Kentucky" rifle (Fig. 27), actually made in Pennsylvania, was used in the wilderness for fighting as well as hunting. It differed from the German rifle in being longer but lighter, with a smaller bore. The gun-maker forged it by hand, wrapping a strip of hot iron spirally around a rod, then heating and hammering it till it was welded into a rough tube. He made the barrels in two lengths which had to be welded together. Then he rifled the interior by hand, a most delicate process, and polished it with emery powder. Every gun was provided with a special mold for making the exact size bullets to fit it. The bullet, or ball, slightly smaller than the bore, was wrapped in a patch of greased linen and hammered home with a thin hickory ramrod. The patch provided a gas seal around the ball and also fastened into the rifling to give the shot a twist. But the fit had to be tight.

The rifle as a fighting weapon remained unpopular in America wherever the field tactics of the British regulars were accepted military doctrine. Not till the American Revolution, particularly in the Battle of King Mountain and the

Second Battle of Saratoga, would the British learn that the only effective answer to an American rifle was a British rifle. The slowness of its acceptance, even as a specialized weapon, is surprising in view of its far greater accuracy than the smoothbore musket, though it had, to be sure, important shortcomings in military use, above all its longer loading time.

The American revolutionists fought mostly with smoothbores, two shiploads of which came from France. Most were Charleville .69-caliber guns, costing about five dollars each. Almost all the powder had to be imported. European tactics prevailed through the earlier battles, and the badly trained American militiamen suffered severely in fighting the well-trained British regulars. Washington taught his men, however, to pick their targets and to aim rather than to fire volleys in the general direction of the enemy.

The success of this was clearly demonstrated in the Battle of Trenton, December 26, 1776, the turning point of the Revolution. Washington successfully crossed the Delaware River at night with 2,400 men in the hope of surprising the Hessian garrison. When General Sullivan sent him word that the muskets were wet and would not fire, he replied, "Tell General Sullivan to use the bayonet. I am resolved to take Trenton."

The Hessians, taken by surprise, went into the streets disorganized, and were further demoralized by the fact that they could not fire their muskets in the rain. Washington's men concealed themselves inside the houses, from which they took careful aim and with great deliberation shot down the Hessian officers—thereby grossly violating a sacred tenet of eighteenth-century fighting etiquette, which opposed musketmen's picking off officers. The three Hessian regiments, surrounded, outnumbered, and virtually without officers, quickly surrendered. The victory cost Washington four wounded and no dead.

Lafayette did his best to introduce the skirmishing tactics of the Americans into the French revolutionary armies, and succeeded in getting a rifle company in each battalion. The lessons in marksmanship and in taking cover, which he introduced, had a measurable effect, but the rifle would not replace the musket in the French armies till 1830. And the new tactics of the American revolutionary armies would meet with prolonged resistance before general adoption in Europe.

## THE FRENCH REVOLUTION AND THE NAPOLEONIC WARS

It has been said with some justice that the most momentous change in the military history of the eighteenth century was not a new weapon or new tactics but the innovation of universal conscription, adopted by the revolutionary government of France on August 23, 1793. As Lynn Montross has put it, "Thus with a few strokes of the pen the entire military past was abolished. All the faults and virtues of eighteenth-century warfare, the moderation along with the cynicism, the humanity as well as the greed, were swept into the discard of history. The modern nation-in-arms, half god and half monster, had been evoked to dominate the battlefields of Europe down to the present day." Universal conscription increased the French Army to nearly 750,000, the greatest "horde" seen in Europe since the days of the barbarian migrations. Skillful utilization of this horde was possible because Europe had more food, more metals, better transportation—and in addition more science—than ever before.

The French Revolution saw the first real attempt to mobilize the scientific talent of a nation. This was largely due to the imagination and organizing genius of the revolutionary minister of war, Lazare Carnot. Before the revolution he had been a military engineer; he was also a talented mathematician and able executive who believed in harnessing science to the war effort. He believed passionately in the idea of a national army—he would organize fourteen armies totaling a million men—and in the appointment of men of talent to high office.

To solve the desperate need for small arms, Carnot, together with the Committee of Public Safety, directed a large-scale program of economic mobilization. Special arms committees were organized which drafted cabinet-makers and metal-workers by the hundreds. They were set to work manufacturing guns in hundreds of publicly owned musket shops set up in the Paris parks and gardens. By 1794 Paris was producing 750 muskets a day, a faster rate of manufacture than in all the rest of Europe at the time.

Directions for the gathering of saltpeter were printed and sent all over France. The prescribed recipe for saltpeter, charcoal, and sulphur was dispatched to the flour mills, and the powder was ground according to simple specifications. Each district was directed to send two citizens to Paris for a month's course in the casting of bronze and iron and in new methods for the manufacture of powder.

The government in 1795 offered a prize of 12,000 francs for the discovery of a practical method of food preservation. This was finally won in 1809 by a Parisian confectioner, Nicolas Appert, who had learned to preserve certain foods in specially made glass bottles by prolonged immersion in boiling water. Appert won the title of the father of the modern canning industry, but his method was based on trial and error, and the development of a theory to account for his success would have to await the birth of the science of bacteriology. Tin-coated metal cans would not come into use till after 1839, when they were invented in America by Peter Durand.

During the revolution the French Academy of Science offered a prize to anyone who could work out a method for making cheap alkali. This was won in 1790 by Nicolas Leblanc, who treated salt with sulphuric acid to obtain salt cake or sodium sulphate. He roasted the salt cake with limestone to produce "black ash"—sodium carbonate and calcium sulphide—then dissolved the sodium carbonate in water to crystallize it. His work was extremely important for the soap and textile industries, and led to ever more complicated experimentation in chemistry.

The revolutionary government founded the École Polytechnique in 1794 as a place where military engineering and mathematics could be taught to artillery officers. Gaspard Monge (1746-1818), the founder of descriptive geometry, took an active part in this school. Monge had been a military engineer in his youth, and had won great respect by his use of geometrical rather than arithmetical principles in designing fortifications. Monge was entrusted with drawing up plans for the defense of France against invasion, and later became minister of the navy. Thus for the first time in history two men with high executive authority in a nation's armed forces were also distinguished scientists. The same brilliance that went into solving problems of distribution and supply showed in their works on fortification. Discarding the sacrosanct traditions of Vauban and drawing heavily upon the theories of Montalembert, they shifted to the new theory of active defense, advocating a heavy concentration of artillery fire upon advancing troops. Carnot's great book on fortification, *De la Défense des Places Fortes,* published in 1810, played a significant role in the rise of modern fortification.

Carnot's military strategy was very different from that of Maurice de Saxe. "Act offensively and in masses," he instructed his generals. "Use the bayonet at every opportunity. Fight great battles and pursue the enemy till he is utterly destroyed." This was fundamentally the strategy adopted by Napoleon.

In 1797 Carnot was forced to flee to Switzerland, as the revolutionists began devouring their own heroes, but he returned in 1799 and became minister of war in 1800. Opposing Napoleon's increasing despotism, however, he retired to write on mathematics and fortification, and the young emperor was deprived of Carnot's great talents.

As for Napoleon himself, it can be said that though he was a genius as a general and a political innovator of no mean imagination, he was remarkably uninterested in the relation of science to war. He had read with profit Robins' book on gunnery, and had derived from Guibert the idea of the supreme value of mobility and fluidity of force, as well as the value of self-contained divisions. Nevertheless, as Liddell Hart has pointed out in his *Thoughts on War,* Napoleon was "curiously indifferent to the opportunity of introducing new weapons, and his era of warfare was notably unproductive, though it coincided with the spring tide of the Industrial Revolution."

Part of his success came from such simple improvements in tactics as doubling the step of his men from the orthodox seventy paces a minute to a hundred and twenty. In his own phrase, he "multiplied mass by velocity." He learned to use the cavalry to screen his own movements and as a surprise-assault arm. His cavalry charged the infantry with great success at Eylau, Dresden, and Leipzig; at Waterloo it failed signally. By using field guns in masses, firing salvos of case shot from point blank range, he had little trouble in blasting breaches in whatever front opposed him. *"Le feu est tout,"* he said, and the result was carnage by fire-power.

In improving his communications he made use of Chappe's signal telegraph system, but he rejected military balloons. The first successful balloon had been built in France in 1783, when two brothers, Jacques and Joseph Montgolfier, manufactured one of paper, filled it with hot air and sailed it to 1,000 feet over Annonay. In Paris in the same year physicist Jacques A. C. Charles and the two Robert brothers utilized the discovery of the solubility of rubber to construct a balloon of taffeta impregnated with rubber. They filled it with hydrogen gas (which had been isolated by Henry Cavendish in 1766), and launched it from the Champ de Mars in Paris, whereupon it rose to 3,000 feet and sailed for fifteen miles. When it landed, the superstitious villagers filled it full of bullet holes, tore it to pieces with their scythes, and tied it to the tail of a horse. The government of France was forced to spread the scientific explanation far and wide lest the incident be repeated elsewhere.

Balloon making had continued to improve during the decade and gave great promise for reconnaissance in war. In 1785 one carried two men across the English Channel. The French revolutionists even organized a balloon company in 1794. When Manberg was under siege, they sent over a thirty-foot hydrogen balloon which so demoralized the Dutch and Austrian attackers they abandoned the siege. The balloon figured prominently in several subsequent victories. Napoleon sent up several hot air balloons in Cairo to impress the crowds with the military prowess of France, but seems to have had no real appreciation of their military potential. In 1799 he disbanded the two balloon companies then functioning in the French army. As we shall see, he also rejected Robert Fulton's submarine.

Napoleon continued the revolutionary tradition of harnessing a whole nation to the business of fighting. But he also returned to the older tradition of plunder, which had largely disappeared with the ravages of the Thirty Years' War. As commander-in-chief at twenty-six he said to his men in Italy: "Soldiers, you are hungry and naked; the Republic owes you much, but she has not the means to pay her debts. I am come to lead you into the most fertile plains the sun beholds. Rich provinces, opulent cities—all shall be at your disposal if you arrive where I direct and follow me where I shall lead."

The Napoleonic banditry continued for many years. In the beginning it gave him an advantage in mobility over his enemies, who were hampered by long supply columns. The military code of the Austrian and Prussian armies forbade plunder or seizure of private property; after their defeat by Napoleon at Jena, the Prussians endured bitter cold rather than confiscate wood which was privately owned.

It has been said that Napoleon's cavalier attitude toward the profoundly important problems of supply proved his undoing. "Supplies?" he said, "don't talk to me about them. Twenty thousand men can live in a desert." The result was that during the Peninsular Campaign in Spain and Portugal he lost 25,000 men, of whom only 2,000 fell in action. In the arid wastes of Russia his logistics failure led to a catastrophe beyond compare. He crossed the Russian border with an army of 612,000 men in June, 1812. A fortnight cost him 135,000 men, lost through desertion, sickness, and failure of supply. Only 100,000 soldiers got to Moscow. The story of the subsequent retreat needs no retelling.

On the other hand, Arthur Wellesley, later Duke of Wellington, had a sound grasp of the problems of logistics and an immense concern for the physical well-being of his men. In the Peninsular Campaign he said, "To guide a biscuit from Lisbon into a man's mouth is a matter of vital importance, for without biscuit no military operation can be carried out." It was to be Wellington's rather than Napoleon's concept of logistics that would prevail in the nineteenth century, and the impact of a blossoming science and technology would be particularly felt in this area of communications and supply.

## NAVAL WARFARE AND TECHNOLOGY

The history of the British Navy through the eighteenth century is characterized by periods of stagnation and impoverishment during peacetime and by feverish building during war or threat of invasion. The early years of the century saw the personnel neglected, the dockyards poorly maintained, and the designing of new ships carelessly done. When the War of the Austrian Succession broke out in 1739, the fleet was badly demoralized. Rehabilitated during this war, and again during the Seven Years' War, which began in 1756, the Royal Navy always managed to frustrate the French invasion plans and to maintain British supremacy on the seas.

Fearful corruption and maladministration in the navy followed the Peace of Paris of 1763. During this period the French thoroughly reorganized their own fleet and again threatened England by joining the revolting American colonies. By 1780 England was at war with France, Spain, and Holland simultaneously. The great British victory off Guadeloupe in 1782 brought the war with France to a conclusion, and the treaty of Versailles signed in 1783 brought a few years of peace. Now for the first time the fleet was maintained at a high degree of efficiency—though the British sailor himself suffered from bad food, low pay, and extremely harsh treatment—so that when the French revolutionary wars broke out in 1792 the British Navy was fully equipped and led by skilled officers—Howe, Collingwood, Hood, Jervis, Duncan, Keith, and Nelson.

The revolutionary and Napoleonic wars saw the greatest naval battles and victories in British history, among them the defeat of the Spanish fleet off Cape St. Vincent by Admiral Sir John Jervis in 1797, the destruction of the French squadron by Nelson at the Battle of the Nile in 1798, and the tremendous victory at Trafalgar in 1805. Naval tactics changed decisively under the genius of Horatio Nelson, who modified the old single-column "line ahead" tactics which had been considered the most effective for dealing broadsides. He saw the importance of concentrating his whole fleet on part of the enemy line, which he accomplished brilliantly at the Nile. At Trafalgar he assaulted the larger French-Spanish fleet with two parallel lines of ships, breaking the enemy line at the center and putting two ships on each one of the enemy's at their rear. By the time the enemy's van was able to come around in the light wind, it was its turn to be defeated.

Britain greatly expanded her naval bases, acquiring at first Malta, Ceylon, and the Cape of Good Hope, later Aden, the Falkland Islands, and Hong Kong. In general she used her sea power to promote rather than to curtail the expansion of international trade, and the whole world benefited.

One notable advance in eighteenth-century medicine might be mentioned here, for it brought about a marked improvement in the health of the world's sailors by banishing the threat of scurvy. Though citrus fruits had been used intermittently for several hundred years as a cure for scurvy, the disease was still a deadly commonplace of seafaring. An observant Scottish doctor, James Lind, serving as surgeon on the British man-of-war *Salisbury*, decided to submit the citrus fruit cure to a clinical test. He chose twelve ailing sailors with similar symptoms and divided them into six groups of two each. Five teams he privately designated as controls and gave them innocuous remedies; the sixth received oranges and lemons. All received the same food, drink, and nursing care. The two men in the sixth group were almost well at the end of a week; the remainder were desperately ill. Lind's experiments, which he described in two papers published in 1754 and 1757, resulted in the Royal Navy's passing in 1795 a regulation which added a "citrus supplement" to the sailor rations, and the British sobriquet "Limey" was born. The Scottish doctor's method of testing drugs was accepted as a model for over 150 years.

The eighteenth century saw very little change in the technology and armament of the world's navies. The ship's cannon were still smoothbore muzzleloaders made of cast iron or bronze. The 32-pounder, a three-ton gun of about six-inch caliber, was the biggest a line-of-battle ship could handle in its broadside. It required a fourteen- to sixteen-man crew. Naval guns were still extremely inaccurate, having an effective range of less than 300 yards, though an extreme range easily ten times that. Good gunnery meant speed and therefore volume, not accuracy.

The rifled cannon predicted by Benjamin Robins had to wait upon new metallurgical developments; rifling would mean elongated and therefore heavier projectiles, and thus greater pressures within the gun for the desired muzzle velocities.

Gun carriages were still primitive, heavy timber frames riding on four small wheels. The gun was trundled up to the porthole and fired; it rolled back on its own recoil till stopped by heavy breeching ropes. The guns had to be swabbed out after each firing, and when they got too hot there was some danger of a premature firing.

The ship itself was an immense wooden machine driven by wind and muscle, bigger but not essentially different from that of the seventeenth century. Its construction of wood had caused it to reach a limit of size—about 3,000 tons in weight and 200 feet in length, with an armament of up to 100 guns, occasionally even more, but more often between 50 and 80. It required constant repair, and might disintegrate in two or three years from dry rot. On the other hand, if built of seasoned timber and kept in good condition, it might be a good ship after fifty years. Nelson's flagship at Trafalgar, the *Victory,* was forty years old, but

Fig. 28. Nelson's **Victory**

equal in fighting capacity to the majority of the ships engaged (Fig. 28). After the mid-century most ships had their bottoms covered with thin sheets of copper so that the exfoliation might drop off barnacles. Ships were hard to sink in battle; obsolescence was slow and important new inventions almost unknown.

The most valuable naval invention of the century was probably the marine chronometer, a special timepiece for shipboard use which made possible the accurate measurement of longitude from the sun or stars. Gemma Frisius of Antwerp had pointed out in 1530 the possibility of determining longitude by the use of an accurate timekeeper. The celebrated Dutch scientist Christian Huygens had tried in the 1660's to put Frisius' suggestion into practice with a pendulum clock, but it would not work because of the effects of temperature and especially of the ship's motion. And so the matter remained until the eighteenth century. Latitude could be computed fairly accurately by the old cross staff, and after 1731, when the sextant was invented by John Hadley in England, the computation could be made quite exact. But the problem of longitude remained. In 1714 the British Government offered a prize of £20,000 for any means of determining a ship's longitude within thirty nautical miles at the end of a six-week voyage. A timekeeper fulfilling this requirement would have to be true within three seconds per day, a standard not attained by the best pendulum clocks of the time.

It was not a scientist but a self-taught Yorkshire carpenter, John Harrison, who finally solved the problem after forty years of experimentation. The last of the four instruments he presented was tested on a voyage to Jamaica in 1761, and it enabled the longitude to be determined to within two minutes of a degree. Harrison had some difficulty proving his right to the prize, however. It took the personal intervention of George III to secure him the final half, by which time Harrison was seventy-nine. Harrison's instrument—still preserved, in going order, at Greenwich Observatory—was, unfortunately, too delicate and costly to provide a model for the subsequent evolution of the chronometer. That function was served by a marine timekeeper invented in 1765 by Pierre Le Roy of Paris, which was essentially the prototype of the modern chronometer. In our own times the chronometer has been superseded by the radio time signal as a means of determining longitude.

The first decisive change in the nature of naval projectiles came at the end of the eighteenth century, with the use of Mercier's shell gun during the siege of Gibraltar, 1779-1783. The new projectile was a 5.5-inch explosive shell with a short fuse fired from a 24-pounder mortar. An efficient exploding projectile had been invented by Renaud Ville in 1602, but its development had remained at a standstill. Henry Shrapnel in 1784 designed the special kind of shell which was to bear his name. But all these shells, because of their real or presumed sensitivity, had to be tossed with small propelling charges at high angles. Otherwise they might explode within the bore. The first successful low-trajectory shell gun was not built till the nineteenth century. This was the Paixhans shell gun, designed about 1822, which was destined to make the wooden battleship obsolete. Its destructive power was demonstrated in the Greek War of Independence in 1827, and still more decisively in the

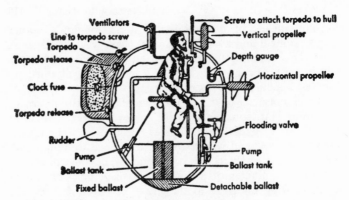

Fig. 29. Cutaway Drawing of Bushnell's **Turtle**

Battle of Sinope in 1854, which started the Crimean War.

The submarine appeared in the last quarter of the eighteenth century; though still very primitive, it was greatly improved over the amusing device of Cornelius Drebbel. It was an undergraduate at Yale College, David Bushnell, who constructed the first truly successful submarine in 1773-74, using the theory of the propelling screw, which had been advanced in 1752 by the mathematician Daniel Bernouilli. He called his craft *The Turtle* (Fig. 29). During the American Revolution, in which he was made a captain, his submarines were tried out against British frigates anchored off New York. They were designed for a single operator who maneuvered by means of a rudder and two hand-driven screws, one for horizontal and the other for vertical movement. Immersion was secured by the intake of water ballast, and the downward thrust provided by the vertical screw.

A torpedo containing 150 pounds of powder and weighted to zero buoyancy was attached to the outside of the submarine. Bushnell taught his operators to maneuver under the hull of the British ships and attach the torpedo, which would be set off by a timing device. All of the several attempts failed, but this was due as much to mischance as to the crudity of the instruments. Actually his vessels and torpedoes were theoretically sound, and with better luck he might have succeeded.

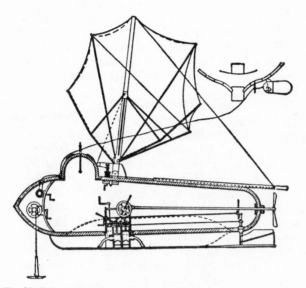

Fig. 30. Fulton's **Nautilus,** with Collapsible Sail

Bushnell's ideas were later enthusiastically embraced by
Robert Fulton, whose subsequent fame as inventor of
steamships is well known. Fulton temporarily won the interest of Napoleon and under his patronage constructed a
four-man submarine which made several trips under water
in the harbor of Brest in July, 1801 (Fig. 30). He also devised several types of torpedo carrying from 80 to 100
pounds of gunpowder to be discharged by gunlock on contact. With these he blew up several old hulks in French
waters. But Napoleon, with remarkable lack of foresight,
refused to aid him in constructing the larger vessels he
thought necessary for success against the British ships.

Fulton thereupon took his invention to the British, who
were happy enough to disengage him from the French but
not too interested in his experiments. He did persuade William Pitt to let him try out his torpedoes against the French
flotilla blockade at Boulogne, however. Fulton had his
eighteen-foot, two-ton torpedoes floated into the harbor on

the night of October 2, 1805, each attended by an operator on a small, pontoon-like raft. The operators lashed the torpedo to the enemy anchor cable, started a clockwork detonating mechanism and then paddled back to safety. The tide was expected to press the torpedo against the vessel, whereupon it would explode.

The French managed to cut all of them adrift but one, which exploded and destroyed a pinnace with its crew of twenty-one, but the British were unaware of even this success and counted the whole experiment a failure. A few weeks later they tried Fulton's device again at Boulogne but without success. Meanwhile on October 21 the Battle of Trafalgar was won, and thereafter the British took no notice of Fulton, nor of his remarkable prophecies that hundreds of bombs or mines could be strewn in the Thames Channel or along the coast and the whole British Navy could do nothing to prevent it. No one believed him when he said that the Channel could be mined from Dover to Calais against enemy submarines.

Few Englishmen had the imagination to see what torpedo warfare might mean to England. Admiral Jervis, who had become Earl St. Vincent and First Lord of the Admiralty, remarked that "Pitt was the greatest fool that ever existed, to encourage a mode of war which they who commanded the seas did not want, and which if successful would deprive them of it." Most naval officers, French and British alike, felt that torpedo attack was ungallant, immoral, and in total contravention of the accepted laws of war.

Actually the immense consequences of the invention of the submarine and torpedo boat had to wait upon more than a hundred years of slow technological evolution. They would not be of paramount importance till the First World War.

## EIGHTEENTH-CENTURY SCIENCE

Though the eighteenth century saw few significant changes in the technology of war, the same period saw a burgeoning of science and an industrial revolution of immense consequence for the wars of the nineteenth century. It saw the evolution of the steam engine, the development of iron metallurgy, the shift in fuel from wood to coal, the rise of industrial chemistry, the establishment of a machine industry—that is, machines to make machines—and the first stirrings of the science of electricity. Of all these, none had as spectacular consequences as the invention of the steam engine, which resulted, it has been said, in the first major transformation of human life since the Neolithic agriculture. Having tamed wind and water, man now succeeded in utilizing fire for his engines of production.

As we have seen, clumsy prototypes of the steam engine appeared in England late in the seventeenth century. In France, Denis Papin, working with Christian Huygens at the Académie des Sciences, constructed a vertical cylinder with a piston. Thomas Newcomen, an ironmonger at Dartmouth, invented a similar machine independently and succeeded in putting his machine to use commercially. By 1715 his engines were in use in seven English counties for pumping water out of mines. There was no great improvement on the Newcomen engine for fifty years.

Then an imaginative young scientist and instrument maker at Glasgow College, James Watt (1736-1819), became interested in the problem when he was asked to repair a disabled model of a Newcomen engine used in demonstrations before students. Watt's invention was not merely an improvement on the Newcomen engine but a wholly new creation based on his knowledge of the theory of latent heat, which he had learned from the Scottish scientist Joseph Black. Instead of theorizing only after the invention, Watt went from theory to invention. As J. G. Crowther aptly put it, "technical invention passed from the realm of perception into that of conception."

Watt's improvements on the old engine were basically two: first, where Newcomen's engine had depended on the injection of cold water to condense the steam which had already done its expansive work in the cylinder, Watt's engine kept the cylinder housing the piston as hot as possible at all times. By avoiding the alternate heating and cooling it made for far greater efficiency of performance; second, it applied steam and vacuum alternately to both sides of the piston instead of one side only as in all previous engines. By means of this double action the piston pulled as well as pushed the beam, and the steam was exhausted from the cylinder for condensation elsewhere. The first patent of Watt's steam engine was granted him in 1782.

Iron production in Britain was at this time smaller than that of France, but by 1801 it had trebled, giving Britain a commanding lead during the last phase of the Napoleonic Wars. The engine brought spectacular changes in every field of industry, and these changes in turn stimulated every branch of science. As the late Professor L. J. Henderson has pointed out, "before 1850 the steam engine did more for science than science did for the steam engine."

The eighteenth century saw several great inventions in the iron industry, which brought the transition to the modern era in the metallurgy of iron and steel. Craftsmen had been making an imperfect steel from wrought iron for a long time but it was not until this era that man began to understand what really happened in the blast furnace. The first scientist to study it seriously was René A. Remaur, who published in 1722 his *Art of Converting Wrought Iron Into Steel*. His theories, which were ingenious and sound, were not proved till many decades later.

The first great practical improvement came with Abraham Darby's development of a successful coke to be used instead of charcoal in the reduction of ores. This came around 1750. The Swedish inventor Christoph Polhem (1661-1751) transformed the roller into a practical piece of machinery for metallurgical purposes, and the British iron manufacturers went on to develop the complicated rolling process for making steel plates and the puddling process for converting pig iron into wrought iron by the use of coke.

Pig iron, an alloy of iron, carbon, and other elements, had been produced in furnaces since the fourteenth century. The use of coke instead of charcoal for converting it into wrought iron and steel was of immense importance for England, which had been forced to rely upon Swedish and American forests for much of her charcoal. Since her own coal mines were among the best in Europe, she now became the supplier for most of the world. The use of coke also marked the beginning of the great development of the Ruhr Valley. The output of iron now rose spectacularly. In 1740 the annual output in Britain was 17,000 tons; by 1800 it was 150,000. In 1840 it would be 1,400,000 tons.

The science of industrial chemistry which blossomed in England during the eighteenth century was largely stimulated by a group of industrial leaders, radical in politics and nonconformist in religion, who drew very little from the universities, and least of all from the older established universities like Oxford and Cambridge.

Basic research in pure science was beginning to be taken seriously, however, in some of the major universities of Europe, and the astonishing new industrial progress inspired the young chemists in the schools. Gradually chemists came to believe that all tangible things could be weighed and measured. The last half of the century saw the emergence of a small galaxy of truly great chemists. James Watt, who was not only a gifted engineer but also a notable chemist, did extensive work on the physics and chemistry of steam. Joseph Black (1728-1799), professor at the University of Edinburgh, was especially skillful at developing accurate measuring instruments for use in his studies of heat. He first defined the concepts of specific and latent heat and he also made the discovery that carbon dioxide is a chemically distinct gas in air.

Joseph Priestley (1733-1804), the discoverer of oxygen, greatly extended the knowledge of gases, though he refused to accept some of the consequences for chemical theory of his own discoveries. It took the work of Antoine Lavoisier (1743-1794) in France, who brought to the study of gases a ruthless logic, to clear away the phlogiston theory, to which Priestley and many other distinguished chemists had clung tenaciously. Lavoisier invented the nomenclature still used to describe classes of chemical substances, and it can be said that modern chemistry truly began with the publication of his *Traité Elémentaire de Chimie*. After him chemistry was based on the study of mass, which became the most fundamental property of the elements and their compounds.

Henry Cavendish (1731-1810) went on to make the first genuinely systematic study of gases and gave a consistent interpretation to experiments in combustion, oxidation, and reduction. Jacques A. C. Charles (1746-1823) worked out the exact relationship between the temperature and the volume of gases in 1787. The three extraordinary Bernouilli brothers, primarily mathematicians, left an impact on every phase of science they explored. Daniel Bernouilli (1700-1782) shared in ten prizes awarded by the Académie des Sciences. One of his theories dealing with the propulsion of vessels by water ejected from the stern led to the invention of the propelling screw, which in the nineteenth century made possible an efficient steam warship.

The eighteenth century saw the first elementary experimentation with electricity. Benjamin Franklin, renowned as an international scientist as well as a statesman, explained the similarity between electricity and lightning. His work had great psychological value, for it brought lightning, which had been feared for centuries as supernatural in origin, under a measure of human control. Luigi Galvani (1737-1798), professor of medicine at Bologna, first observed "animal electricity" in frogs, and his experiments led to the discovery that electricity could result from chemical action. Alessandro Volta (1745-1827) discovered the phenomenon of the electric current, and aroused enormous interest among the scientists of Europe with the publication of his findings in 1800 and with his demonstration of the electric battery. His battery differed from the electrostatic generator already known in that it was the first source of continuous current.

The science of analytical chemistry, born in the latter half of the eighteenth century, led to the discovery of many new metals. L. N. Vaquelin found chromium in Siberian minerals in 1797; J. G. Gahn found manganese in 1774;

P. J. Hjelm isolated molybdenum from molybdenite in 1782. Martin H. Klaproth, the leading German chemist of his time, discovered uranium, zirconium and cerium, and re-discovered titanium in 1794. (It had been isolated earlier by William Gregor.) The list would lengthen prodigiously in the nineteenth century. Scientists from every country felt the excitement of the new discoveries.

Medicine made a spectacular advance with the publica-tion of Edward Jenner's *An Inquiry into the Causes and Effects of the Variolae Vaccinae* in 1798. Though this great doctor was unable to explain the success of his smallpox vaccine, the concept and use of vaccination were a major milestone in medical science.

Despite the numerous wars during the century, com-munication among the scientists of the western world re-mained free. The scientist was esteemed as a man of imag-ination, like an artist or a poet, and for the most part he remained divorced from the technology of war. Even as late as the French Revolution and Napoleonic wars, political and military events did not prevent their easy fraternization. As Liddell Hart has noted, "at the height of that bitter struggle, British scientists were allowed to travel freely on the Continent and were hospitably received by French scientists."

Lavoisier, it should be pointed out, was guillotined in the Reign of Terror in 1794—though, like many others who suffered the same fate, he was not hostile to the basic revo-lutionary aims. To the extent that learned men did lend their services directly or indirectly to the art of destruction, their fellows were appalled by it. The Comte de Saint-Simon, addressing some questions to a group of French mathema-ticians in 1813, said bitterly: "All Europe is cutting its throat; what are you doing to stop this butchery? Nothing. What am I saying? It is you who perfect the means of destruction; you who direct their use in all the armies."

# 6. The Nineteenth Century

## SCIENCE, INDEPENDENT OF WAR, TRANSFORMS WAR

The early part of the nineteenth century, from 1815 to 1848, saw a long period of peace in Europe with prodigious industrial expansion. America too—excepting the war with England, 1812-15, and with Mexico, 1846-48—saw political tranquillity and phenomenal national growth up to the outbreak of the Civil War. Armaments were generally neglected, for many fondly imagined peace would be permanent. By mid-century tensions were increasing, and an intense rivalry developed again between England and France, partly as a result of the revolutionary change from sail to steam in their navies. On land the development of the railroad brought another revolutionary change; its consequences for the game of war could only be guessed at, at first.

The latter half of the century—torn with strife—saw the following major struggles: the Crimean War, the American Civil War, the Austro-Prussian War, the Franco-Prussian War, the Russo-Turkish War, the Boer War, and the Spanish-American War; after the turn of the century came the war between Russia and Japan. There was abundant opportunity for experimentation with and testing of new weapons, and for a realization of the dizzying impact of science and the industrial revolution upon tactics and strategy. Communications and logistics were completely transformed by the steamship, the railroad and the telegraph. Armies were much bigger than before and more mobile; firepower was vastly more effective, thanks to the adoption of rifles and breechloading weapons of all kinds; and war became more destructive than ever in the past. The American Civil War cost 600,000 dead out of a population of 31,000,000, and the Franco-Prussian War was equally deadly while it lasted.

Thanks to the industrial revolution the civilian was now responsible for providing the industrial means of war, and the workshop became as vital a part of the struggle as the battlefield. The soldier and civilian were now fundamentally dependent upon one another. The importance of the role of the scientist-inventor became increasingly recognized. Napoleon III, who was keenly interested in technological developments in war material, offered a reward for a cheap process of making a better armor for French ships. He had been disturbed by the success of the Paixhans shell gun, with which the Russians had annihilated the Turkish fleet at the beginning of the Crimean War. Though this gun had been developed in France—by Henry Joseph Paixhans (1783-1854)—as a means of overcoming the superiority of the British Navy, Napoleon realized that it might be turned against the French fleet.

Henry Bessemer, a young English engineer then working under Napoleon III's patronage, won the prize. His experimentation, as later developed in England, led to the famous "Bessemer process." It consisted of blowing air into a crucible containing molten pig iron. The air caused the pig iron to burn, thus removing most of the carbon. The result was a substantial increase in the output of iron and steel in both countries, and a considerable lessening of the cost.

During the Civil War, Senator Henry Wilson of Massachusetts urged the passage of a bill creating a National Academy of Science, begging for a "society of scientists" to help the nation through its "dark and troubled night." Lincoln signed the bill March 3, 1863. The academy established a new weights and measures system, drew up more accurate wind and current charts, started studies of magnetic deviation in iron ships, worked on methods to protect the bottoms of iron vessels from fouling, and sought improved methods for handling the expansion of steam. By and large, however, the scientific improvements of the century sprang up independent of any special war-stimulated research.

Chemistry made tremendous strides during the century, though there was a lag before most of the new discoveries affected military technology in any way. Particularly important was the isolation and identification of chemical elements and compounds. Sir Humphry Davy (1778-1829), the British pioneer in electro-chemistry, isolated potassium and sodium early in the century and demonstrated that chlorine was an element. John Dalton (1766-1844), the English chemist and physicist, believing with Democritus that matter was composed of atoms and that atoms were ultimate particles incapable of subdivision, made the first table of atomic weights. One discovery stimulated another till, by 1860, the table numbered sixty elements.

René Remaur in France, H. C. Sorby and Michael Faraday in England, and Adolf Martens in Germany, all contributed to the new science of metallography, the study of the structure of metals. With the discovery of X-rays in 1895 by Wilhelm Conrad Roentgen (1845-1923) there came, among many notable results in other fields, the science of crystallography, which meant still further refinements in man's knowledge of metals.

Most of the common modern military explosives—TNT, tetryl, picric acid, PETN, and cyclonite—were discovered in the nineteenth century, though their explosive behavior was utilized only later, when the technique of detonating high explosives came to be better understood. This understanding resulted largely from the researches of the Swedish inventor and explosives manufacturer Alfred B. Nobel (1833-1896). The first extensive use of picric acid and nitrocellulose would not be made till the Russo-Japanese War of 1904-05, and TNT did not become a standard explosive till World War I.

There was usually a considerable time lag between the discovery of a new explosive and its adaptation by the military engineers and gunmakers. But in at least one instance the military had expectations for a new weapon which the chemists and physicists of the day were simply not equipped to perfect. This was the rocket, which has had a fascinating and uneven history. Though abandoned completely in Europe in favor of the gun toward the end of the fourteenth century, it had seen spasmodic use in the Far East, particularly in India. A British colonel, Sir William Congreve, became interested in the weapon after seeing it fired by Tipu Sultan at the siege of Seringapatam in 1799. He improved on the Indian weapon and tested his product in the siege of Boulogne in 1806. When he had succeeded in setting the whole town afire he wrote enthusiastically, "The Rocket is, in truth, an arm by which the whole system of military tactics is destined to be changed."

For a time the British Army ordnance experts shared his enthusiasm. They produced an iron-headed rocket that would carry an explosive powder charge more than two miles, the rocket being exploded on landing by means of a time-fuse. This rocket was used against the Americans in the War of 1812 with indifferent success. The "rockets' red glare" immortalized in *The Star-Spangled Banner* came from the rockets employed in the bombardment of Fort McHenry in Baltimore Harbor; they were not sufficient to bring about its surrender. The United States Army used some rockets in the Mexican War but found them unstable and dangerous, and afterward abandoned their use altogether. The British gave them up officially in 1885.

Throughout the nineteenth century, improvements in iron and steel manufacturing were steady and cumulative. The open-hearth blast furnace came in 1824, the Bessemer process in 1856. Both improved the quality and decreased the cost of wrought iron and steel. Toward the end of the century the industry finally felt the overwhelming impact of the new chemistry. Tungsten was successfully added to steel by R. F. Mushet in 1871; chromium steel came in 1878. Robert Hadfield developed manganese steel in 1882 and silicon steel in 1889. Nickel was incorporated into steel in 1883; vanadium and chromium-vanadium steels came at the turn of the century. All of this meant improved guns and armor plate. When Andrew Carnegie was asked about the value of scientists in manufacturing steel, he said, "If faced with the loss of buildings and plants, or the services of scientists, I would prefer to lose the former. Plants would be less difficult to replace."

Thermodynamics, which deals with the relations between heat and mechanical energy, grew into a respected science with an impressive body of theory and experimentation. A not surprising result was that steam engine development accelerated, culminating in the high-pressure steam engines of the 1880's which helped to transform the world's warships. The names of most of the great men in thermodynamics are well known to students of chemistry. Many were Frenchmen. There was Nicolas Carnot (1796-1832), the young military engineer turned physicist who died before his work could be published; Joseph L. Gay-Lussac (1778-1850), who studied magnetism and the expansion of gases, making some of his observations in balloon ascents; and Pierre Louis DeLong (1785-1838), who studied the elasticity of steam at high temperatures. Henri Victor Regnault (1810-1878) did classical research on the thermal properties of steam and attracted many scientists to his laboratory.

The ferment among chemists in France early in the century was in such marked contrast to the situation in England that the brilliant young Scotch chemist William Thomson (1824-1907), later Lord Kelvin, went to France to study with Regnault. He later came back to the University of Glasgow, where he had an extraordinary catalytic effect upon the young scientists of his own nation. His researches, together with those of James Prescott Joule (1818-1889), a British brewery owner who devoted his life to scientific research, provided thermodynamics with basic theories that commanded universal acceptance.

Lord Kelvin's extraordinary talents extended through the fields of physics and electricity as well as chemistry and included a remarkable flair for invention. Extremely enthusiastic about underwater telegraphy, he helped improve the quality and manufacture of the cables which were being laid across the Atlantic. He reconstructed the mariner's compass, invented an apparatus for taking soundings in shallow and deep water, invented a tide gauge and a tidal harmonic analyzer and tide predictor, and he simplified tables for determining the position of a ship at sea. His influence on science in Britain was similar to that of Robert W. Bunsen (1811-1899) in Germany. This great chemist, professor at the University of Heidelberg, was not only a distinguished theoretician and teacher but also the inventor of many useful devices—the carbon-zinc electric cell, the filter pump, the ice-calorimeter, and the vapor-calorimeter.

The same kind of role was filled in America by Joseph Henry (1797-1878), professor at Princeton and first secretary of the Smithsonian Institution. Henry, like the others, ranged freely over the known sciences, made noteworthy inventions, and stimulated many students. He invented the first practical electromagnetic telegraph in 1830-31, devised and constructed the first electromagnetic motor—the forerunner of all electric motors—discovered self-induction and electromagnetic induction (also discovered by Faraday), invented a method for determining the velocity of projectiles, and made a serviceable system of fog signals. At the Smithsonian Institution he founded the science of meteorology by organizing a corps of volunteer weather observers who transmitted their reports by telegraph. He helped organize the American Association for the Advancement of Science and saw to it that the Smithsonian provided free publication and distribution of scientific papers throughout the world.

The effect of these and other talented men on the science of the time was inestimable. Though none of them was directly concerned with the application of science to war, inevitably many practical applications of their initial theories or experiments were put to use by the military. The science of meteorology was obviously to have wartime as well as peacetime utility; so also specific inventions like the telegraph and the telephone.

The pattern of development in electrical communications usually followed three steps: theory, experiment, and invention. The telegraph began with the theory of Faraday, continued with the experiments of Joseph Henry in America and of Sir Charles Wheatstone (1802-1875) at King's College, London, and culminated in the invention of Samuel F. B. Morse. Though his invention was complete in 1836, it took eight years of futile bargaining at home and abroad before Morse was successful in persuading his own government to appropriate money to set up a telegraph line. When it was finally completed between Washington, D.C., and Baltimore on May 24, 1844, Morse transmitted the memorable question, "What hath God wrought?" (Thirty-two years later, when Alexander Graham Bell [1847-1922] transmitted the first complete sentence over the telephone, he showed by comparison a rather melancholy deficiency in rhetoric. He said simply, "Mr. Watson, come here; I want you.")

Wheatstone guided the growth of scientific telegraphy on land wires, devised the automatic transmitter and many forms of electrical recording apparatus. As early as 1840 he was experimenting with the submarine cable, foreseeing its practical use in communication. The value of the telegraph in war did not long lack propaganda to advertise it. Though the telegraph was not used tactically during the American Civil War—battle messages were carried by mounted officers, or sent by flag or balloon signals—it was of great strategic value, for it practically obliterated the factor of time in long-distance communications. Both sides used it and it would be difficult to say whether it benefited one side much more than the other.

The interplay of science, technology, and of men in war becomes increasingly difficult to describe as science becomes more complex. Every simplification is likely to be a distortion. Divisions into land armament, naval armament, hand guns, big guns, and communications become misleading, for the new sciences affected them all irregularly and in the old world differently from in the new. The needle gun, the chassepot, the breechloading cannon—all seemed new and important to the military men of the time, but they were of little consequence when measured against the more pervasive changes wrought by the railroad or the iron-hulled warship.

Let us look now at the resulting transformation of land warfare and of sea warfare. In discussing land warfare we shall consider first the improved weapons—hand guns, artillery, and repeaters, then improved communications, especially the railroad, and finally the problem of fortifications. With sea warfare we shall look at the change from sail to steam, the innovation of the screw propeller, the introduction of iron armor and the iron ship, and finally the evolution of the big gun and of the armor plating used as a defense against it. Last in the chapter, we shall look briefly at the late developments in nineteenth-century science that would not affect war until the twentieth century.

## TRANSFORMATION OF LAND WARFARE
### Improved Infantry Weapons

There were two significant inventions in small arms during the first half of the nineteenth century, the percussion cap and the cylindro-conoidal bullet. The first had to wait upon the discovery of an explosive that detonated on concussion; this was made possible by L. G. Brougnatelli, who produced silver fulminate in 1798, and by Edward Charles Howard, who discovered the cheaper fulminate of mercury in 1799. Other explosives followed. There was no great lag in the military use of mercuric fulminate, though its speedy adaptation to firearms was made not by a scientist nor by a military engineer but by a sports-loving Scottish clergyman, the Reverend Alexander Forsyth, who had been trying to develop a percussion system of ignition since 1793. In 1807 he finally perfected one.

Forsyth employed a detonating powder which when struck a smart hammer blow flashed through the touchhole of the gun and ignited the powder in the barrel. This superseded the old flints and solved the chronic problem of misfire and hangfire due to wind and damp. The next logical development was the percussion cap, which was invented by

Joshua Shaw of Philadelphia in 1814. At first his caps were iron, then pewter, and finally copper. Since it was easy to convert the flintlocks, the percussion cap began to come into general use about 1820, though the British ordnance officers, conservative as usual, were suspicious of it and did not order its adoption till 1836. Many unconverted American military flintlocks saw service through the Mexican War of 1846-48.

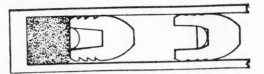

Fig. 31. The Minié Bullet

The cylindro-conoidal bullet, which exploited the rifling that made it possible, was invented in 1823 by a Captain Norton of the British 34th regiment. It had a hollow base, so that when fired it would automatically expand and seal the bore. This invention was enthusiastically taken up in France, where Captain C. E. Minié gave his name to it— though "the Minié ball" was neither Minié's invention nor a ball. The new bullet radically altered gun design and made rifling for the first time truly practicable (Fig. 31). It meant that a rifle could be loaded from the muzzle as rapidly as a musket, and therefore that the smoothbore was finally doomed. The Minié rifle with an improved bullet was employed in the Kaffir War of 1851 and in the Crimean War of 1854-56.

Improvements in the infantry hand gun now followed hard upon each other, with inventors from many nations contributing changes. American inventors produced the first successful long bullet, the "sugar-loaf," which was put in with a special ramrod. It increased the range of the American rifle to nearly 500 yards. Eli Whitney made a revolution not only in firearms but in machine manufacture generally by introducing mass production and the principle of interchangeable parts. Awarded a contract for 100,000 muskets, he had promised the American government delivery in two years, by September 1800. It actually took him ten, but his manufacturing methods set a firm precedent; henceforth the gun would no longer be the hand-tooled, specially wrought instrument of the individual gun-maker.

Eliphalet Remington II, a gun manufacturer in upper New York, greatly improved the technique of barrel-making. He learned to drill through a solid bar of cast steel, thereby banishing for good the old, laborious process of lapwelding strip iron around a core rod. His factory was among the first to develop assembly-line techniques.

Breechloading, long known to be theoretically superior, was slow in coming to the hand gun. Major Patrick Ferguson of the British Army had designed a breechloader of exceptional utility during the American Revolution, which, had it been used in quantity, might have changed the course of that war. But the British high command was unwilling to shift allegiance from their beloved Brown Bess. The chief problem with the breechloader was the leakage of gas and flame from the seams of the breech, which blew flame back into the face of the firer.

In 1811, Captain John Hall of Maine invented a breechloader which was adopted by the American Army after extensive tests and later mass-produced at Harpers Ferry. The Hall carbine was a .52-caliber flintlock with a 33-inch barrel. Its hinged breechblock, containing the lock and chamber, gave the soldiers much trouble, for the seam between the chamber and barrel was not sufficiently tight and was inclined to spurt flame from the joint. It was never popular, therefore, though used for many years.

The first really satisfactory American breechloader was developed at Harpers Ferry by Christian Sharps, whose superior gun helped make the word sharpshooter a common American noun. John Brown's abolitionist raiders carried Sharps carbines and troops used them in the outbreaks in Kansas. The perfected 1859 model became the most popular single-shot breechloader in the Civil War.

The American Civil War was a colossal proving ground for improved weapons of all kinds. For the first time the achievements of the industrial and scientific revolution were used on a large scale in war. There were rifled cannon and breechloaders for the artillery, breechloading rifles and repeaters for the infantry, and land mines, armored trains, flame projectors, submarines, surface torpedo boats, marine mines and both free-floating and spar torpedoes for the navy. This was the first war to see mass movement of troops by railroad; it saw the first duel between two ironclad ships. Steam supplied power for the warships; the telegraph directed general troop movements everywhere except in battle. It was the first war to be adequately photographed. Balloons were used for reconnaissance and for signaling messages by means of mirrors, though mostly during the first two years, when the fronts were relatively stable. One European observer watched balloon exercises from the White House lawn with special fascination; it was Count Ferdinand von Zeppelin, then a young Prussian lieutenant.

Despite the variety of new weapons, the Civil War was nevertheless a rifle war. In the beginning the Union forces entered battle with an appallingly inadequate array of weapons. The arsenals were stocked with great quantities of old-fashioned smoothbore muskets, some of them flintlocks. Many of the new rifled muskets had been captured by the Confederacy. The basic weapon came to be the 56-inch, .58-caliber rifled handarm, with an 18-inch socket bayonet. About two million of these were made and used during the war.

Lincoln, who had a keen interest in weapons, had the misfortune to inherit as Chief of Ordnance James W. Ripley, a stubborn, unimaginative officer who was implacably opposed to breechloaders and repeaters. When Col. Hiram Berdan organized a specially recruited regiment of expert marksmen and begged Ripley for Sharps breechloading rifles, the Chief of Ordnance gave them only the standard Springfield muzzleloaders. It took a threatened mutiny and great pressure from Lincoln before Ripley would give way. This regiment, finally equipped as Berdan wished, proved the worth of the new weapon in the Battle of Gettysburg.

Ripley, who at times even refused to obey explicit orders from Lincoln, was finally dismissed in 1863.

Lincoln personally tested Christopher Spencer's fine repeater, a seven-shot rifle firing rim-fire cartridges, and ordered the Army to adopt it. It increased the soldier's rate of fire to sixteen shots a minute and, had it been manufactured in quantity early enough in the war, might have shortened its duration. The Henry repeater was also used in small quantities by the Union forces. The Confederates called it "that damn Yankee gun that can be loaded Sunday and fired all week."

The Confederates suffered from a serious shortage of weapons and ammunition as the war progressed and the blockade tightened. They conducted the war with an assortment of smoothbore flintlocks, percussion conversions, and various kinds of rifled muskets. At one time the Confederate government was so fearful its troops would run out of guns and ammunition that it ordered the manufacture of thousands of pikes.

The first battles of the Civil War demonstrated dramatically that the old Napoleonic tactics of mass frontal assault were dead. After the Seven Days' Battle General Robert E. Lee saw this at once and thereafter encouraged his infantrymen to become skirmishers, spreading out and seeking cover. General D. H. Hill later wrote of the Confederate soldier: "Of the shoulder-to-shoulder courage, bred of drill and discipline, he knew nothing and cared less. Hence, on the battlefield, he was more of a free lance than a machine. Who ever saw a Confederate line advancing that was not crooked as a ram's horn? Each ragged rebel yelling on his hook and aligning on himself."

Both sides speedily learned that a few log-faced earthworks gave them an immense advantage, and the axe and shovel became almost as important a part of the soldier's equipment as his rifle. When General William T. Sherman's men were marching to the sea, they lightened their packs by throwing away their bayonets, but kept their shovels. The new entrenchments, however primitive, gave the defensive an immense advantage, and both sides learned that the attacking force had to have a majority of about three to one. By the end of the war, particularly in the lines around Petersburg, defensive entrenchments became extremely complex and their tenure prolonged. One could see a system of warfare which would be duplicated and enlarged in 1914-18—wire entanglements, trenches, dugouts, listening posts, and bombproof shelters.

Both Confederate and Union generals sometimes reverted to the Napoleonic frontal attacks, throwing waves of troops at the enemy, as Lee did at Gettysburg and Ulysses S. Grant did later at Cold Harbor. Most such attacks never carried beyond the first line of breastworks and were enormously costly. The number of battles fought during the Civil War exceeded those of Napoleon, and the battles themselves were usually far more desperate and bloody. By 1864 the superiority of the guns and ammunition of the Federal troops began to be decisively felt. By the end of the year there were a hundred thousand new breechloaders in their hands. Confederate General Alexander later stated that "had the Federal infantry been armed from the first with even the breechloaders available in 1861, the war would have been terminated within a year." The Spencer repeater, though used in small quantities, was extremely valuable in the critical battles near Atlanta and Franklin.

The rifle had made long-range fire more deadly; it had greatly strengthened the defensive, and it almost entirely abolished the cavalry as the army's "shock arm." Cavalry continued to be effective in long-range raids against communications and supplies, and was a useful morale-destroyer on both sides throughout the war. It was often used to seize road junctions and hold them till the infantry arrived. But the horse-plus-rider was extremely vulnerable to accurate rifle fire, and the cavalrymen on both sides learned early to dismount at critical moments and fight on foot. The footsoldier could move, fight, and dig in the forests or the swamps, and it was he who carried the brunt of the battle.

In, Europe, changes in the hand gun were slow at the beginning of the century and then moved forward at a constantly accelerating pace. In the early years the British armed some of their men with the Baker rifle, a 30-inch, .625-caliber gun with seven grooves. It was inferior to the American rifles of the same period. Finally the British switched to the Minié rifle, then after the Crimean War to the Enfield, and after that to the Snider, an American model. With each new gun came extraordinary improvements in range and accuracy. Queen Victoria opened a rifle match in 1860 by firing a new Whitworth. She made a hit that for accuracy was the most remarkable shot fired up to that time in the history of target competition, and it was generally recognized that the gun deserved the credit. Toward the end of the century the obsolescence of the British rifles was ever more rapid, as the army shifted from the Martini-Henry to the Lee-Metford, and then to the Lee-Enfield.

Meanwhile similar developments were occurring at an uneven pace on the continent. Prussia in 1841 developed the Dreyse needle gun, the first practical breechloading rifle of European warfare. It was provided with a long needle carried in a slender rod which was actuated by a surrounding spring. When the trigger was pulled, the rod flew forward and the needle struck a disk of detonating material, igniting the charge. Though the gun was imperfect—the needle often broke—its adoption gave the Prussians an obvious advantage over their less enterprising rivals, especially the Austrians, who clung to muzzleloaders for two more decades.

The needle gun proved decisive in the Seven Weeks' War, which broke out in 1866. Though the Austrians managed to mass as many men as the Prussians—over 200,000 on each side in the Battle of Sadowa—and sought to overcome their weapon inferiority by coming to close quarters with the bayonet, the needle gun shattered their forces. In seven weeks Prussia gained five million inhabitants and 25,000 square miles of territory in Germany. As Winston Churchill put it, "A premonitory shudder went through France."

Although the Prussian victory was due also to the brilliant generalship and meticulous advance preparation of Count Helmuth von Moltke, and to the ineptness of the Austrian Ludwig Benedek, the needle gun got the credit. Shortly afterward every army in Europe adopted some form of breechloading rifle. Sweden adopted the Hagstrom, Prussia the Carte, and Italy the Carcano, all using paper cartridges containing their own means of ignition. The French developed their celebrated chassepot. This had a longer range and faster fire than the needle gun. The caliber was reduced from .66 to .43 so that the French soldier could carry ninety rounds of ammunition, whereas the German could carry only seventy-five.

During the Franco-Prussian War the chassepot proved to have double the effective range of the needle gun, but superiority in this single weapon was not enough to make up for the appalling inferiority of the French generalship and the weakness in French artillery. In six weeks the Germans had surrounded one French field army at Metz, had destroyed another at Sedan, and were free to march on Paris. The old Vauban-type fortresses were too hopelessly out of date to withstand the bombardment they got from positions beyond the range of their own guns. When the war was over, the Germans had lost 28,000 dead and 101,000 wounded; the French had lost 156,000 dead and 143,000 wounded.

It took the Battle of Plevna in the Russo-Turkish War of 1877-78 to demonstrate to Europeans what the Americans had learned at such cost in their Civil War, namely that massed attacks were futile against infantrymen armed with the breechloader if they were protected by even the most primitive and hastily constructed breastworks. The Turks under Osman Pasha were armed with an excellent American rifle, the Peabody-Martini, a drop-block-action breechloader. The Russians, who greatly outnumbered the entrenched Turks, attacked three times, and each time were forced to retire. In the second battle the Russians lost 7,300, the Turks 2,000; in the third Russian casualties were

18,000 against 5,000 for the Turks. When Plevna finally fell, it was due to lack of supplies.

By the end of the century every government in the western world had come to take a keen interest in the rapidly evolving hand gun. They conducted elaborate tests of new weapons, subsidized research in their own armories, and made fortunes for the lucky inventors whose weapons were adopted for general use.

### Artillery Changes

Although the nineteenth century saw improvements in artillery quite as striking as in the hand gun, there was more reliance on the latter in battle. Napoleon had used concentrated artillery with telling effect, but later nineteenth-century commanders counted the rifle the decisive instrument, despite notable artillery successes, particularly in the Franco-Prussian War. There were four main improvements in the artillery of the period: first, the adoption of rifling; second, the change to breechloading; third, improvements in interior ballistics; and fourth, the development of a better recoil mechanism.

The change to breechloading became universal after the invention of the interrupted-screw breechblock. The first successful rifled cannon were made by Cavelli in Italy in 1846. His guns had two spiral grooves and used a cylindrical shot. Joseph Whitworth of England built a gun with a twisting hexagonal bore. This 3-pounder when elevated to 20 degrees threw a shot 7,000 yards—a range previously unheard of for a field gun—with an accuracy that astounded the observers. With a 35-degree elevation the gun had a 9,500 yard range. Both the Cavelli and Whitworth cannon were breechloaders.

Smoothbores continued to be built, however, since the elongated projectiles of the new cannon could not at first deliver as powerful a blow at short ranges as spherical shot of equal caliber. The latter, being lighter, had greater velocity and therefore much greater impact energy $(E = MV^2)$ in the early portion of their trajectories, though they lost their velocity faster than the heavier and sharper-pointed elongated shells. John Dahlgren, an American, invented his "soda-bottle" gun in 1850, a smoothbore muzzleloader which had the merit that the thickness of metal along the bore corresponded to the changes in internal pressure rather than being determined mostly by convention. It was considered so superior to the rifled cannon in use against ironclad ships that it was maintained as standard armament in the American Navy for twenty years after the Civil War —though this says less for the continuing merit of the gun than for neglect by the United States of its armaments. It was certainly badly out-of-date by 1880.

Napoleon III, who had a keen interest in artillery, and who had in fact written two treatises on the subject while still a pretender to the throne of France, ordered secret experiments in Algeria. The result was the adoption by the French Army of a rifled, breechloading fieldpiece which proved its worth later, in the battles of Magenta and Solferino against the Austrians in 1859. The French guns had double the range of those used by the Austrians. So rapid was the evolution in guns, however, that by 1870 the Prussians were manufacturing still better cannon. When war broke out, the French fieldpieces proved to be hopelessly outdated; the Prussian guns were better and there were far more of them.

The science of interior ballistics, which uses a combination of chemistry, mathematics and physics to study the various strains and reactions within the gun itself when fired, led to remarkable improvements in artillery. Gunmakers shifted first from cast iron to wrought iron, but though the wrought-iron guns of the forties were clearly the most powerful the world had seen up to that time, artillerists distrusted them because of several disastrous burstings. The worst was the explosion in 1844 of the "Peacemaker," Captain Robert F. Stockton's great 12-inch, wrought-iron smoothbore, aboard the *Princeton*. It killed several prominent members of the U.S. government, including the secretaries of State and Navy.

The great German inventor and gun-maker Friedrich

Krupp (1787-1826) had succeeded in manufacturing cast steel; his son Alfred Krupp (1812-1887), who was to be called the Cannon King, manufactured a 3-pounder muzzle-loader of cast steel which attracted much attention in the Great Exhibition of 1851 in England. The gun was a marvel of lightness, and had a tensile strength about four times that of cast iron and twice that of wrought iron. Several unfortunate fractures of the Krupp guns made artillerists fear their brittleness, so the adoption of these steel guns in the armament of nations was considerably delayed. However, the decided Prussian artillery superiority over the French in 1870 was in good part the result of Prussian adoption and French rejection of these guns.

In the United States Robert Parrott designed a cast-iron rifled gun which had wrought-iron bands around the breech for extra strength. These were used extensively as field and naval guns in the Civil War; they ranged in size from 10- to 300-pounders. Captain J. T. Rodman, whose *Reports of Experiments on Metals for Cannon* (Washington, D.C., 1861) is a useful document on the research of the time, designed a smoothbore gun cast with a hollow bore, but the interior metal was chilled first, so that the exterior shrank upon a hardened interior. The result was a compression of the exterior metal upon the interior, which meant that when the gun was fired the interior received support at the very instant of explosion rather than only after expansion from the pressure. Rodman's gun foreshadowed the built-up gun. His improvements were combined with those of Admiral Dahlgren to produce the powerful naval gun of the American Civil War—the 11-inch gun mounted on the famous *Monitor,* for example (Fig. 32).

The most notable improvement in interior ballistics came with the invention of the hooped or built-up gun. As early as 1829, A. Thiéry, Chief of Squadron in the French Army, had started experiments with hooped guns by shrinking a wrought iron envelope over a cast-iron barrel. Professor Daniel Treadwell of Harvard University built a small number of hooped guns for the United States government in 1843. Sir William Armstrong in England utilized the built-up principle with tubes constructed by coiling wrought-iron bars. This system of construction, which bore Armstrong's name, made for much stronger guns than the solid forgings of wrought iron. The Armstrong gun was both rifled and breechloading, and the projectiles were coated

Fig. 32. Dahlgren Guns on the **Monitor**

with soft metal to cut into the lands of the rifling. The Armstrong "system" was applied to the British 110-pounder naval gun in 1859. This was the forerunner of the huge 300-pounder and 600-pounder naval guns of the 1860's.

Captain A. T. Blakely, another inventor of the hooped gun, was the first to demonstrate mathematically, and to reduce to a working system, the reinforcement of guns with hoops placed under initial tension. He was the first to propose guns formed of concentric tubes having different degrees of elasticity, the inner tube being the most elastic because of the greater demands made upon it. A. Noble's crusher gauge, invented in 1860, made possible the measurement of pressure inside a gun.

By 1863 almost every major principle embodied in the gun of the present day had been incorporated in the ordnance of the time. Recoil mechanisms, however, were still primitive. Though ammunition and cartridges had improved, the use of slow-burning powders had scarcely been tried, and good fire-control instruments were as yet unknown. The use of high explosive in the shell would not come until after 1870.

Late in the century an improved gun carriage and recoil mechanism evolved from proposals put forward by General Wille in Germany, and Colonel Langlois in France in 1891. These allowed the gun to recoil in a slide or trough without moving the carriage that supported it, the recoil force compressing springs which thereupon ran the gun back to its original position. The new guns could fire at a rate of twenty shots to the minute. The carriage permitted the construction of a bullet-proof shield to protect the gun crew, thus reintroducing armor to the field of combat.

The first satisfactory smokeless powder was made by Vieille, a French chemist, in 1884. Alfred Nobel in 1890 produced ballistite, one of the earliest of the nitroglycerin smokeless powders. Cordite, a mixture of nitroglycerine, guncotton and acetone, was in use in England after 1890. These new smokeless powders neither gave away the gun's position nor obscured the field with clouds of smoke. They were thus essential to the development of the machine gun. Another great advantage of smokeless powder, not evident in the name, was its slower, more controllable burning. With its adoption the large gun lost its beer-bottle shape and began to take on the long, slender lines that we know today. Slower burning in a longer bore meant more over-all thrust with smaller maximum pressures in the gun. The result was greater range or a greater weight of shell fired, or a combination of both. Larger guns could be built, not only because it made sense to use more weight in added length, but also because the thickness of metal at the breech did not have to be so great, relative to bore diameter, as formerly. This advantage was naturally reflected in larger bore diameters.

By the end of the century mathematicians like H. Resal and E. Sarrau had worked out ballistic equations which were substantially modern in form. All the technical and mathematical improvements of the last quarter of the century were reflected in the famous French "75," adopted in 1897. This gun, named for the 75mm. diameter of the bore (2.95 inches), had the particular advantage of a superb hydro-pneumatic recoil mechanism which permitted the gun to be fired rapidly and accurately with a minimum of re-aiming between shots. Most American field artillery units in World War I used 75mm. guns bought from the French.

### The Coming of the Machine Gun

Inventors had struggled with repeater guns during the renaissance, producing some complicated mechanisms that came very close to being practical guns. The nineteenth century saw a return to this kind of experimentation, now with decisive results. Revolving cylinders were an old story to gun inventors, but the cylinder had usually contained complete gun barrels. An American inventor, Samuel Colt of Hartford, Connecticut, finally devised a method of revolving a short cylinder containing cartridges and of locking it into alignment with a fixed barrel—both by the same action that drew back the hammer as the gun was cocked. Colt, who seems to have been inspired by an ancient weapon in the Tower of London, took out his first patent in 1836. Some of his repeaters were used during the Mexican War, but were not satisfactory because of the inferior ammunition.

By 1851 repeating rifles and pistols were appearing in considerable numbers. As we have seen, Christopher Spencer's fine repeater was used to some extent by Union troops in the Civil War. Military men held that one man operating a Spencer repeater from cover was the equal of eight men in the open armed with regulation muskets. Confederate generals mistrusted repeaters, fearing wastage of their ammunition, which was always scarce.

The first practical machine gun used as a fieldpiece was

the French mitrailleuse, developed by Faschamp and Montigny between 1851 and 1869 under the patronage of Napoleon III (Fig. 33). This was a 37-barreled one-ton gun mounted on a carriage and pulled by four horses. It could

Fig. 33. The Montigny Mitrailleuse, 1851-1869

deliver the contents of ten magazines, about 370 shots, in one minute, and was extremely effective at close range. The French, who had great hopes for it in battle, kept news of it so secret that their own men were insufficiently trained in its use, but not so secret that the Prussians did not know about it. The result was that when it first appeared in battle in 1870 the Prussians concentrated all the fire of their new Krupp breechloading artillery upon it. The mitrailleuse was hopelessly outranged and quickly destroyed. When, by an accident, it was used against infantry at close range, it did admirably, but the French generals missed the significance and persisted in thinking of it as an artillery piece. As a result the deadliness of the machine gun would not be convincingly demonstrated till World War I.

In America a successful machine gun was designed by

Dr. Richard Gatling in 1862. It can be considered the first real machine gun, since charges were fed into the chambers, fired, and extracted all by the operation of machinery. Gatling made it first with four, then six, then ten barrels.

Fig. 34. The Gatling Gun

Though Gatling tried to get it adopted during the American Civil War, it was not officially adopted till the war was over. It was used in the Spanish-American War. (The Gatling principle, and name, were revived in a very high-speed 20mm. machine gun designed for fighter aircraft after World War II.)

The chief objection to the Gatling gun was that it had to be operated by a hand crank (Fig. 34). The British inventor Sir Hiram Stevens Maxim (1853-1927) ended the crank-turning in 1885 when he devised a gun which used its own recoil energy to load itself, fire, and eject its own empty shells. This was the first truly automatic machine gun, for the gunner had only to squeeze and hold the trigger. Maxim used a mechanically-fed canvas belt with 250 rounds conveniently packaged in it. The British Army adopted it in

1889. A large Maxim was used in the Boer War. As big as a fieldpiece, it was fed by 25-shot belts containing 37mm. shells called "pom-poms," and was an ancestor of the automatic guns of comparable caliber which performed so well as antiaircraft guns in World War II.

The Colt-Browning machine gun, invented in 1895 by the American John M. Browning, used gas pressure rather than recoil for its operating power. An air-cooled gun mounted on a tripod, it could fire 400 rounds a minute. This gun saw service in the Spanish-American War. Both the recoil and the gas pressure forms of activation continue today to be used in the most modern types of automatic and semi-automatic guns and hand arms.

Quick-firing cannon were used by Menelek of Abyssinia in his victory over the Italians at Adowa in March, 1896. This battle marked the end of a long period where the white man had a monopoly of scientifically devised weapons. Throughout the nineteenth century it had been easy for the white man, armed with the rifle, to colonize most of Africa and a good part of Asia. Now it was clear that the non-white races could, and would, use the new armament of war.

In the Boer War at the end of the century one can see the transitional tactics between the Civil War and World War I. This was the first war where both sides were armed with new smokeless repeating rifles. The Boers had the Mauser, the British the Lee-Metford. Heavy artillery, now brought directly into the field of battle, once more assumed the supreme tactical importance it had lost after the Napoleonic Wars. The deadly power of the rifles and heavy artillery meant the ever-increasing use of entrenchment on the battlefield, new difficulties in reconnaissance, the increasing importance of camouflage, and the decreasing importance of high ground. All the troops were dressed in khaki; conspicuous marks of rank were abolished, buttons and buckles were dulled. Officers no longer wore the sword in action. The "apparent emptiness" of the battlefield became the new phenomenon of war. Beyond 600 yards the artillery fire was dangerous; within 600 yards the rifle fire was deadly. The big problem in land fighting was how to cross the last 400 yards.

## The Coming of the Railroad

The coming of the railroad and the application of steam to the warship were the two most important strategic developments of the nineteenth century. The railroad revolutionized strategic geography, increased the pace and power of strategical maneuver, made armies more massive and more mobile, and stimulated a whole new science of logistics. The debilitating long marches of the past, which had wasted an army's strength before it even crossed a frontier, largely disappeared. Speedy mobilization and great concentrations of manpower along frontiers even in advance of war were now possible. For a time it almost seemed that a war could be won by advance planning, or decided by the first few battles. Nations with the greatest industrial resources, particularly in railroads, seemed to have a great advantage over their neighbors. These attitudes developed late in the century, however, for it took time for generals to learn how to use railroads effectively in war.

Richard Trevithick put a steam locomotive to work on a Welsh coal road as early as 1804; this was the first time a steam engine operated on rails. Hosts of designs for locomotives were drawn up between 1804 and 1820, but the first truly practical one was designed by George Stephenson, who not only built the locomotive but also the railroad line upon which to operate it. This line, running between Stockton and Darlington, was begun in 1822 and opened in 1825. It caught the attention of the world.

The first railroad in America was built in 1828, and continental nations quickly followed suit. By the time the Crimean War broke out, western nations had seen a quarter of a century of railroad building. Yet the allied governments made no attempt to use the railroad in that war. In the terrible winter of 1854-55, the French and British had between them 56,000 troops. Nearly 14,000 ended up in the hospital, where many died because of the appalling lack of care. Florence Nightingale, by instituting some primitive nursing techniques, was able to reduce the death rate at Scutari from 42 per hundred to 22 per thousand. "Amid storms and blizzards the British Army lay," wrote Winston Churchill in his *History of the English Speaking Peoples,* "without tents, huts, food, warm clothes, or the most elementary medical care. Cholera, dysentery, and malarial fever took their dreadful toll. Raglan's men had neither transport nor ambulances, and thousands were lost through cold and starvation because it did not occur to the Government of the greatest engineering country in the world to ease the movement of supplies from the Port of Balaclava to the camp by laying down five miles of light railway."

In the beginning it was believed that the railroad would give the advantage to the nation on the defensive, but this notion was shattered in 1859 when large French armies fighting the Austrians in the Italian War were carried with heretofore unheard-of speed to the chosen front of attack in northern Italy. In the American Civil War the role of the railroad was all-important, though in the beginning neither side was in a position to mobilize an army from trained reserves. Since the land frontiers of the Confederacy in 1861 were 2,700 miles long, railway and steamship transportation were absolutely essential. There resulted a war of movement on a scale absolutely unprecedented.

Large bodies of troops were moved speedily over tremendous distances. With only slight warning and preparation, twenty-three thousand men were sent by rail from the Army of the Potomac to Nashville, Tennessee—a journey of 1,192 miles—in seven days. General W. T. Sherman's celebrated march to Atlanta in the summer of 1864 would have been impossible without his use of rail and water transportation. He used his wagon trains as moving storehouses to carry supplies from the railheads to his 100,000 men and 35,000 animals. Later he estimated that had he not had the railroad it would have required 36,800 six-mule wagons to have duplicated this successful logistics operation.

There was, of course, always the danger that the railroad could make troops less rather than more mobile if they became too dependent upon it for supplies. And for a time in the Civil War it did seem that the railroad was making strategy "run on straight-forward lines." Sherman demonstrated, however, that the railroad did not necessarily hamper an army's flexibility and mobility in this fashion. In his march to the sea he had to cut loose from his own railroad communications, but he had made his own troops mobile by cutting down drastically on their equipment and by developing the art of foraging off the country. His "flying columns" were almost completely self-sustaining. Once he reached the sea, he reopened communications by ship. He incidentally took pains to destroy Confederate railroads, as well as their foundries, arsenals, and machine shops.

During the nineteenth century no European nation utilized the railroad as effectively in war as Prussia, who had laid out her railroad system with an eye to its use in future wars. Though her attempts to mobilize by railroad in the crisis with Austria in 1850 were a fiasco, her general staff, led by the great Count Helmuth von Moltke, took the lesson to heart, and in the wars of German Unification the Prussians demonstrated that they had learned much. The Austro-Prussian War of 1866 was largely shaped by the railroad systems of the two countries. By 1870 Prussian railroad strategy had become a highly complicated art. Where French mobilization was inept in the use of railroads, Prussian mobilization, like everything else Prussian, was thoroughly planned in advance and worked with marvelous precision. Sixteen days after mobilization began 400,000 Prussian soldiers were deployed along a 125-mile front. On the twentieth day the first action was fought at Weissenburg. This record was not to be bettered even in World War I, for then the general advance began seventeen days after the beginning of mobilization, and the opening battles again came on the twentieth day, though of course the armies of 1914 were four times as large.

The necessity of destroying the enemy's railroad system, which today would seem so obvious as not to require comment, was not always taken for granted. In the Russo-Japanese War of 1904-05, the Japanese took no real advantage of the fact that the Russians were entirely dependent upon the single line of the Trans-Siberian Railway. As Liddell Hart put it in his *Strategy, the Indirect Approach,* "Never in all history has an army drawn breath through so long and narrow a windpipe, and the very size of its body made its breathing more difficult. But all that Japan's strategists contemplated was a direct blow at, and into, the teeth of the Russian Army. And they held their own forces more closely grouped than those of Moltke in 1870. . . . there was an abundance of indecisive bloodshed."

## The Fundamental Problem of Fortification

The Crimean War saw the first serious tactical challenge to the Vauban fort when the Russian general Count Franz Todleben, responsible for the defense of Sevastopol, extended light earthen rifle pits out beyond the fortified lines. Though not bombproof, they were extremely effective, and cost the allies tremendous casualties. Thereafter in Europe the trend was toward small, bombproof infantry redoubts with artillery placements outside the regular forts. The old idea of the "enceinte" or enclosure was abandoned for flat, small, strategically placed trenches and casements.

The Franco-Prussian War decisively ended Vauban's reign over French military doctrine. French engineers now built a new system of ring forts on spurs of land as far as 15,000 to 18,000 yards from the stronghold. The redoubts were armored with two to three meters of concrete and three centimeters of steel, a combination which successfully withstood tests of shells containing melinite, a new explosive made with picric acid.

A Belgian military engineer, Henri Alexis Brialmont, seeing the construction of the new French forts, concluded reasonably that the next German invasion would be down the Meuse Valley through Belgium, and advocated the fortification of a few strategic places controlling communications. He made Antwerp especially a great entrenched camp ringed by forts and linked with trenches. Similar though lesser forts were built elsewhere in Belgium. The new forts were white concrete mushrooms, sometimes sod-covered, built to withstand the nine-inch howitzer shell, the largest known at the time. Guns were placed in revolving turrets which would rise up out of the pit for firing. A vast labyrinth of trenches and tunnels surrounded the gun emplacements, with magazines of powder and ammunition and barracks for the armies and squads of mechanics.

If we may anticipate at this point some events of the twentieth century, we see that by the time these fortresses came up for testing, in 1914, the Germans had designed and built two kinds of giant howitzers specifically for dealing with them, the larger one being of 420mm. (16.5-inch) caliber. The guns succeeded very well in doing what they were supposed to do, thereby underlining the fundamental weakness of fortresses, which is not that they can be destroyed by big guns, or even that they are immobile, but rather that the enemy who intends to attack them usually has a long period of time and plenty of accurate information for deciding how to go about it. What is static is not so much the emplacement but the conception. In a word, the defense in such instances has no surprises; it is the attacker who is invited to produce them, and he usually does.

That is not to say, however, that the wall of steel or concrete, which can always be defeated by the appropriate weapons, is always useless. It all depends on the context. What else does the attacker have to do? What else is the defender doing? An analogy can be seen in the battleship, which may now be considered to have terminated its career after about three and a half centuries of existence. What characterized the battleship was always its armor, whether of oak or iron. Yet it was never, or almost never, invulnerable to the weapons of its own time. Its characteristic was not that it could take any punishment, but that it could take more punishment than any other type of ship and at the same time be handing out powerful blows of its own. In test after critical test during more than three centuries of war, the armor paid its way.

The collapse of the Belgian fortresses in 1914 caused the French as well as others to conclude that fortresses were useless. They therefore hastily removed the guns from most of their own, including Verdun, so that they could use them elsewhere. But the war turned out to be one long siege of fortress warfare, except that the forts took the form of trenches. And in the main the defense had the upper hand. The most terrible and grueling test of that most terrible of wars was probably Verdun, and in the course of that test the French brought back the guns they had removed, plus hundreds of others. And Verdun held.

After that war the French built the Maginot Line, named after André Maginot, who had been both a deputy and a soldier in World War I, and was Minister of War when the construction of the line was undertaken. The Maginot Line was by far the most extensive and elaborate system of fortifications ever built. It is now generally referred to as a folly—and worse, as *the* folly that betrayed France in 1940. Insofar as there is a measure of truth in this extravagant judgment, it is that the French put too much into the line, not merely of resources but of themselves; their soldiers became too involved and too preoccupied with it. But that is not to say that a line or zone of fortifications was necessarily a bad thing.

And in a matter very pertinent to the present, a phrase like "Maginot Line complex" should not be used, as it often is, to deride any and all suggestions for armoring or "hardening" such things as missile-launching sites. Catch phrases are usually poor substitutes for analysis anyway, and that particular one could be dangerous.

### SEA POWER IS REVOLUTIONIZED
#### The Coming of the Steamship

The adoption of steam on the warship during the nineteenth century changed the whole geography of maritime strategy. There had been no revolution of such consequence since the displacement of the galley by the sailing ship. Ships crossing the ocean could now go in direct line instead of in sweeping deviations determined by the winds. Tactics, which had previously been dominated by the direction and velocity of the wind, now had to be completely revised. Thus, both naval tactics and naval strategy were profoundly affected. The new reliance upon machinery was naturally to the advantage of Great Britain vis-à-vis her continental rivals, since she had the most highly organized machine industry and the best supplies of anthracite coal.

On the other hand, though machine propulsion gave new vigor and speed to maneuvers on the seas, the necessity of keeping the fleet supplied with fuel acted as a tether upon it. The battle fleet became more dependent upon its base, and its range of action narrowed. This change favored the defensive strength of powers that were separated from their rivals by wide oceans, and thereby favored the contemporary aspirations of the United States and Japan. England finally solved the problem of range by establishing coaling bases all over the world; these bases were possible only as a result of her enormous nineteenth-century colonial expansion, which they in turn stimulated.

The coming of steam made contact between enemy fleets in narrow seas more probable, since the inferior fleet would be much less often lost to the superior through vagaries of the wind. Inferior forces therefore chose not to cruise extensively, and there were few decisive naval actions. Steam made close blockade more difficult, because of fuel supply problems, as the Union Navy discovered in the American Civil War when the southerners managed to run $200,-000,000 worth of goods through the northern blockade. However, the Union Navy finally succeeded in plugging the leaks by increasing its forces and by capturing the basic ports. Thus northern sea power was decisive in the end, for it choked off the basic supplies needed by the South.

The fact that blockading ships had to report back to base for fuel resulted, incidentally, in much better rations for the seamen, who in the protracted blockades of the past had often had to subsist on the vilest of victuals. The days were gone forever when a midshipman could write home as one did in the blockade of Brest in 1802: "We live on beef which makes your throat cold in eating it owing to the maggots, which are very cold when you eat them. . . . We drink water the color of the bark of a pear tree with plenty of little maggots and weevils in it, and wine, which is exactly like bullock's blood and sawdust mixed together."

The introduction of steam propulsion on the fighting ships was for a long time strongly resisted, for reasons good and bad. The first successful steamboat, William Symington's *Charlotte Dundas,* was built in 1802, and in 1807 Robert Fulton sent his paddle-wheel steamer, the *Clermont,* 150 miles up the Hudson River in thirty-two hours. Merchant marines began to move eagerly toward acceptance of steam. But the British Admiralty, full of suspicion, issued a statement in 1816 saying that they felt it their bounden duty to discourage the use of steam vessels; they felt that the introduction of steam would strike a fatal blow at the naval supremacy of the empire.

The early paddle-wheel steamers were, of course, extremely vulnerable to gunfire, especially since their engines had to be above the water line. This dilemma was incidentally avoided in the first steam warship, built by Robert Fulton in 1814 and called the *Demologos* (Voice of the People). Intended for defense of the Port of New York against the British in the War of 1812 (which lasted almost three years), it was completed too late to see action. It was a formidable warship with five-foot-thick walls and thirty long 32-pounder guns. Its single paddle wheel was in a channel-way down the middle, and its engines were below the water line. But it was built for defense only, and had no seagoing qualities. Still, it was to be several decades before another ship of comparably bold conception would be built.

British naval officers were contemptuous of the first "tea kettles" in their service. Even by 1840 there were only 29 steamers out of 239 ships in commission in the British Navy, and none of them were genuine fighting ships. Many believed that the ships-of-line would never give way to steamers. By this time, however, another invention had appeared which made possible the design of a much more efficient and less vulnerable steamship. This was the propelling screw, which not only permitted the exposed paddle wheels to be dispensed with but also enabled designers to put the engines below the water line.

Although the principle of the driven screw (as in the windmill) was as old as Archimedes, the principle of the propelling screw was not advanced until 1752, when it was formulated by the mathematician Daniel Bernouilli. There was some experimentation with propelling screws in the latter part of the eighteenth century, noteworthy especially in the primitive submarines built by David Bushnell and Robert Fulton, but the first screw-driven vessel of substantial size was not built till 1839. This was appropriately called the *Archimedes,* a ship of 240 tons.

In a field where all knowledge was empirical, early designs were bound to be inept, but trial and error—and even accident—brought improvements. In one case a mishap to the screw, in which a large portion was broken off, caused the ship using it to pick up speed! John Ericsson, who as early as 1836 had demonstrated a screw-driven boat on the Thames to members of the British Admiralty—a technical success that failed to convince—was persuaded to come to America, where together with Captain Robert F. Stockton he designed and built the first screw warship. This was the *Princeton,* completed in 1843, a ship of remarkable efficiency and performance. The French followed two years later with their first screw-propelled man-of-war, the *Pomone.* From this time onward no new warship could reasonably be built without steam.

The shift from sail to steam stimulated among the British a series of invasion panics. Their fear was expressed in the words of Lord Palmerston that the Channel was now nothing but "a river passable by a steam bridge," permitting the French to invade their island at will. Actually it permitted nothing of the sort. As Winston Churchill was to put it in the House of Commons on June 4, 1940, when a *real* threat of invasion hung over the country, "In the days of Napoleon . . . the same wind which would have carried his transports across the Channel might have driven away the blockading [English] fleet. There was always the chance, and it is that chance which has excited and befooled the imaginations of many Continental tyrants."

The introduction of steam meant that much less depended upon chance, upon the vagaries of the wind, and upon expert seamanship. Now the factor of simple superiority in numbers was likely to be far more decisive. And the British saw to it that their fleet was always larger than that of the French—larger in fact, than those of all their continental rivals put together.

When in 1850 the French constructed the *Napoléon,* their first true line-of-battle ship equipped with a screw propeller, the British finally realized that they could not be content with a steam force only one-fourth the size of the fleet, but must convert the whole British Navy. The financial burden, though trivial by today's standards, looked appalling at the time. Marine engines were undergoing a rapid evolution; steamer design was still a matter more of guesswork than of engineering, and the conversions of old sailships to steam sometimes had ludicrous results. One ship, cut in two, lengthened, and fitted out with engines, sank so low in the water she could scarcely float when loaded with fuel; she was promptly dubbed "the Porpoise of the Navy."

The Crimean War saw very little naval action, though a great deal of naval transportation. There was enough action, however, to demonstrate that sail warships were worse than useless when fighting with steamships. Of the British fleet sent into the Black Sea only two of the ten line-of-battle ships were steam-propelled, though the proportion among those sent to the Baltic was thirteen out of nineteen. In the Black Sea it was the small steamers that performed brilliantly, towing the larger ships into line and playing the chief role in the attack. The British took the lesson to heart; by 1857 the line-of-battle sailing ship had disappeared from the British fleet. Sails were kept, but only as auxiliary power to save fuel. The first British warship to abandon sails altogether, the *Devastation*—the first modern battleship—would not be built till 1873.

The shift to steam, and especially the success of the

*Merrimack* (or *Virginia*) against the *Cumberland* in Hampton Roads, rekindled a remarkable enthusiasm for the ancient tactic of ramming in war. For some fifty years thereafter, ships were designed with huge cumbersome rams which impaired their seaworthiness. The tactic was certainly anachronistic, better suited to galleys than to steamships, as improvements in guns and the development of the torpedo were to prove.

## Warships of Iron

Another technological revolution, second only in importance to the change to steam, was the widescale adoption of iron in the world's navies, first in armor plating, and even more important in the basic construction of the hull. The new hot-blast furnace, invented by Neilson in 1834 and operating on greatly reduced amounts of coal made it possible for iron to compete economically with wood in shipbuilding. The advantages of iron over wood were many. It made possible ships that were larger, stronger and lighter for their dimensions than wooden ones; it also made possible greater variety in design, less vulnerability in storms, and more immunity to fire and lightning. Iron permitted cellular construction or compartmentation, which was to prove an important safety factor in battle. The iron ship was not subject to dry rot, which could sometimes destroy a wooden vessel in two years. It provided a more solid gun platform, and because it permitted greater size it also permitted the carriage of larger guns and heavier armor against gunfire and ramming.

The French in 1859 built the first iron-armored ship, *La Gloire*, a wooden frigate with an iron belt 4½ inches thick on its sides. The British followed with the *Warrior*, which carried the same thickness of armor but on a hull built of iron. The *Warrior* thus sets a landmark as the first armored warship of battleship size to be built of iron, although the first iron ships to engage in battle, the *Phlegethon* and *Nemesis*, had been built in 1839 and had fought in the Chinese War of 1842. They had demonstrated the superior capacity of iron vessels to bear the concussion and recoil of heavy guns firing from their decks. However, they were armed merchant ships. The first iron warships designed for naval use had been ordered, oddly enough, by the Mexican Government and had been built in London in 1842. The British themselves had been fearful of the tendency of iron plates to splinter under shot, but by the time of the *Warrior* the brittleness of iron had been largely corrected through metallurgical advances.

There remained, however, the serious problem that iron hulls fouled badly in sea water and had to be cleaned frequently, by putting them either in drydock or in fresh water for a time. The wooden ships had carried copper sheathing on their bottoms, which kept marine life from accumulating. Iron ships, however, could not carry such copper sheets because of the galvanic action set up. Various devices for solving this problem were to be tried during the nineteenth century, including that of shielding the copper from the iron with an intervening layer of wood, but the problem was not to be fully solved until effective anti-fouling paints were perfected during World War II.

The doom of the unarmored wooden ship had been demonstrated in the Battle of Sinope, which started the Crimean War. There the Russians had annihilated the Turkish fleet at little cost to themselves by using the Paixhans shell gun, which had been developed in France some three decades earlier. Paixhans, who had hoped that his gun would give the French the means of neutralizing the superior British fleet, was now himself one of those to suggest the use of iron armor to make the ship less vulnerable. But armored ships, and especially iron-built armored ships, returned the advantage to the British, because they were industrially in a far better position to build them.

The famous *Merrimack-Monitor* battle of 1861 in America, which was not only the first real duel between two ironclads but also one of the first between two steamships, had great dramatic impact in Europe. It confirmed the wisdom of the step the British and French had already taken. As Sir John Hay put it: "Henceforward the man who goes into action in a wooden ship is a fool, and the man who sends him there is a scoundrel." Sir John no doubt meant "unarmored" rather than "wooden" ships, since the *Merrimack* herself, though iron-plated, was a wooden ship.

Actually, it was in iron construction rather than in iron armor that the shift away from wood was decisive. As guns were to grow more and more powerful, armor had to become thicker and thicker (as well as more resistant in quality) until it became necessary to restrict it to the larger warships and to restrict its coverage even on them. The lighter vessels were to become mostly or totally unarmored (like the destroyers of today) and to seek security in speed and the compartmentation of their hulls.

In 1862 the Siemens-Martin open-hearth process for making steel was developed. The regenerative furnace, which was controllable at all times, made possible careful testing, a more uniform product, and much larger charges of ore. For the first time cheap steel plates became available. Napoleon III, as we have seen, had earlier encouraged the development of the Bessemer process for making steel, and when steel plates finally became cheap enough to compete with iron in shipbuilding, the French were the first to use them. On the other hand, Napoleon III, mindful of the fate of his uncle, was careful not to appear to be challenging the British lead, and the British were the first to construct warships entirely of steel.

Another signal improvement in warship building came later with the invention of the reaction steam turbine, which abandoned the energy-wasting reciprocating piston and produced power by playing high pressure steam jets on the vanes of a rotating shaft. This was perfected in the 1880's by Sir Charles Parsons. His compound turbine gradually displaced the reciprocating engine in new construction of steamships, especially in naval vessels.

The Race Between Guns and Armor

The tremendous evolutionary development of the warship that took place in the last half of the nineteenth century was unlike anything in the preceding three centuries. It affected basic construction, machinery, and ordnance—the latter being a term which covers both guns and armor. The same metallurgical advances that made possible the forging of thicker and more resistant armor plates, and the plates and framing of the iron hulls, also made possible the construction of stronger guns. The naval guns in use till 1860 were not much different from those used three centuries earlier. The metal was better cast, the powder superior, and the bores more precisely cut. The larger naval guns were 32-pounders (about 6 inches in caliber), or 8-inch shell guns. The British had introduced the 68-pounder in 1840, but as a pivot gun only, of which no more than one appeared on any ship. The guns were all smoothbore cast-iron tubes, markedly limited in power. The gun carriages were still extremely primitive, most of them being made of wood.

When Alfred Krupp built the first steel gun in 1847, it was clear that naval guns could expand considerably in power. And expand they did. Several things were responsible, including the adoption of rifling, though this advance was not fully exploited till after 1880 with the introduction of slow-burning powders which permitted a more gradual thrust for the elongated and therefore heavier projectiles. After 1881 all new naval guns were built-up weapons made of steel. Breechloading, abandoned long before, came back into use with a significant increase in ease of loading.

A. Thiéry, Joseph Whitworth, T. A. Blakely, and William Armstrong all contributed to the development of the big naval gun, as they had to that of the big field gun. From 1860 to 1885 the changes in naval guns were fantastic. The maximum weight of the British naval gun rose from the 4¾ tons of the 68-pounder smoothbore to the 111 tons of the British 16.25-inch rifled gun, with a much more than proportionate increase in power. The 16.25-inch gun of 1884 could hurl a 1,800-pound projectile which would penetrate 34 inches of wrought iron at 1,000 yards. After 1870, shell was substituted for shot in the naval projectiles. After 1873, the guns were increasingly housed in revolving turrets, and the recoil mechanisms were vastly improved. However, firing accuracy at any considerable distance was poor, because the fire control instruments of the twentieth century remained to be developed.

Every advance in the gun stimulated a corresponding ad-

Fig. 35. British Destroyer of 1893

vance in the strength and thickness of the ship's armor. The rate of obsolescence of warships during this period was wholly unprecedented. In the two decades from 1860 to 1880 armor increased from 4½ inches to 24 inches at the water line, a thickness never since surpassed. Wrought-iron armor gave way to composite armor, and in 1893 to nickel-steel armor face-hardened by the Harvey process. Then in 1895 Krupp invented at his ordnance works in Essen an armor with twenty to thirty per cent more resistance to armor-piercing projectiles. This "new process" armor was adopted in most navies by 1898.

The rapidity of development in armor and guns helped speed changes in existing power relationships. Because of the rapid obsolescence of ships, four nations which had never before been influential maritime powers reached positions of naval eminence by essentially moderate efforts. The United States, which after the Civil War and in fact up to 1883 had not a single warship worthy of representing a great nation, attained considerable maritime stature before the end of the century. From the Spanish-American War of 1898 she emerged as a recognized naval power of the first rank.

Japan's successful war with China in 1894-95 brought her to the fore as a naval power to be reckoned with, though she fought with ships that had been built elsewhere. It was still mostly with British-built ships that she defeated overwhelmingly in 1904-05 the supposedly superior but inefficient and ineptly handled Russian Navy, and emerged as the great power of the Far East. The tremendous industrial growth of Germany after the Franco-Prussian War would make it possible for her to challenge seriously the naval supremacy of Great Britain with only a few years of concentrated building before World War I. Italy was welcomed to the international arena in 1861 by Lord Clarence

Fig. 36. Cruiser of 1900

Paget, who expressed the "hope and trust that that glorious people will speedily rank among the first maritime nations of the world." Though she lacked the essential raw materials, she purchased so many ships abroad and constructed so many of her own with imported materials that Great Britain soon felt compelled to build "replies" to specific Italian models.

Along with the prodigious improvement in naval armor and guns there was a continuous search for means of underwater attack. The second half of the nineteenth century saw the further development of the mine, the introduction of the automotive torpedo, and the evolution of the submarine from primitive prototypes into deadly weapons of warfare.

Fig. 37. The Confederate Submarine **Hunley**

In the first war between Prussia and Denmark over Schleswig-Holstein, 1848-51, a Professor Himmly of the University of Kiel devised a mine intended to protect the harbor from the Danish fleet. Explosions were controlled by electricity from the shore. In the same war a submarine boat, the *Brandtaucher,* designed by Wilhelm S. V. Bauer (1822-1876) was put into service, but it sank in the port of Kiel in 1851 with the loss of all its crew. The Russians used contact and electrically discharged mines for the defense of the Black Sea and Baltic coasts in the Crimean War, but those of the latter type were failures.

During the American Civil War, a Confederate submersible boat named the *Hunley* (Fig. 37), after its builder, did succeed (while operating awash) in sinking the Federal corvette *Housatonic* with a spar torpedo, a large bomb rigged to the end of a pole. But the explosion also finished the *Hunley* with the loss of her whole crew, while the crew of the *Housatonic* was saved. One Federal boat sank the Confederate *Albemarle,* also with a spar torpedo. Floating torpedoes—which we would now call mines—were sent down the rivers, and it was these that Admiral David Farragut damned at Mobile Bay. Considering the state of the electricity and chemistry of the time, the success of the Confederate torpedoes was remarkable. They sank seven monitors and gunboats and eleven wooden ships, and damaged others.

After this, all wars saw the use of mines and torpedoes. The first truly automatic torpedo was designed by a Scotchman, Robert Whitehead, in Fiume, Austria. His weapon was purchased by Austria, and by 1873 all other navies had adopted it. It was a prototype of the modern weapon, with depth control achieved through a hydrostatic valve and pendulum balance, and with propulsion provided by a small reciprocating engine working by compressed air. Later a gyroscope was introduced to control the rudder, which greatly increased directional accuracy.

The first truly practical submarine ever constructed was designed by two Frenchmen, Bourgeous and Brun, in 1863. France was keenly interested in the submarine, as well she might be, and she preceded all other nations in its development. The first submarine built to order for the French Navy, *Le Gymnote,* was fitted with two torpedo tubes. Several were in service by 1899. Their motive power was entirely electricity provided by storage batteries, which meant a limited range, rarely over 150 miles. Meanwhile an all-electric British submarine was built in 1884 by two Englishmen, Campbell and Ash. It was propelled by two 50-horsepower electric motors and had a 100-cell storage battery. Its effective range was 80 miles.

In 1897 Simon Lake built a submarine powered for its surface cruising by a gasoline engine. John P. Holland was the first submarine inventor to use submergence by water ballast and horizontal rudders, or elevators. His *Plunger* (Fig. 38), the first submarine contracted for by the United

Fig. 38. Holland's **The Plunger**, 1893

States Navy, was propelled by a steam engine for surface cruising and by storage batteries for submerged cruising. It was completed in 1900. The periscope, which had been invented by Thomas H. Doughty during the Civil War, was now adapted to the submarine, for which it was a well-nigh indispensable aid.

The later nineteenth-century naval developments, particularly the growth of firepower and the perfection of the torpedo, tended to put an end to close-action naval combat. Fleets would fight at longer ranges, which tended to make decisive actions rarer. Automotive or "fish" torpedoes saw their first use in the Russo-Turkish War of 1877. The Russians launched five and, though all failed, the strategic consequences were considerable. The Turks, despite an overwhelming naval superiority in the Black Sea, now kept at a respectful distance from Odessa. There was, in fact, only one action between large ships during this war; all others were between ships and torpedo boats.

The availability of the automotive torpedo near the end of the century encouraged the development of the torpedo boat. Naval men feared again for the security of their battleships, as they had when the Paixhan shell gun was developed. The answer to the torpedo boat was the torpedo-boat destroyer, carrying quick-fire guns, which soon drove the simple torpedo boat out of existence and then itself usurped the functions of the boat it had been created to destroy. The modern destroyer is its direct descendant.

In the Spanish-American War there were no instances of successful torpedo tactics. Admiral Dewey expected to find the channel in Manila Bay mined, but he did not let this alter his movements. No mines exploded. In the Russo-Japanese War of 1904-05, the Japanese initiated hostilities by a successful torpedo-boat attack on the Russian Port Arthur Squadron. Two Russian cruisers and one battleship were disabled as a result, though the most elementary precautions would probably have saved both ships. On the other hand, had the Japanese been more efficient in their torpedo attacks they might have destroyed the entire Russian squadron. Both sides suffered extensively from anchored mines, and in the decisive Battle of Tsushima the Russian flagship *Suvaroff* was sunk by a torpedo, as were three other ships. Nevertheless, the major engagements of the war were essentially gunnery duels, and the opinion prevailing among naval experts afterward was that the torpedo successes were not great enough to encourage increased reliance upon the torpedo, or certainly not at the expense of the gun.

Though the torpedo's engine had been much improved, close approach was still necessary. Accurate aim was difficult, and in daylight the wake of the torpedo was clearly visible to the intended victim. Since the torpedo moved at little more speed than the target ship, it was often possible to maneuver clear of the approaching weapon. It is not surprising that the massive destructive potential of the torpedo would not be felt until World War I, for it could not be utilized with maximum efficiency until both it and the submarine had been improved. The latter improvement could not come about until the perfection of the internal combustion engine, and of the electric generator, both of which had been slowly evolving for many years.

## LATE DEVELOPMENTS IN NINETEENTH-CENTURY SCIENCE

The full impact of electricity upon war would not be felt until the twentieth century, though as we have seen it was put to some use in mine and submarine warfare before

1900. The theory was well advanced, the invention tardy. Part of the difficulty was the slow development of the electric generator. Faraday's simple copper disk rotating edgewise between the poles of a horseshoe magnet, demonstrated in 1832, was the first electric generator. The next forty years saw successive improvements, but it was not until Thomas A. Edison (1847-1931) set his mind to the problem that a generator was properly designed.

Edison's invention of the incandescent lamp in 1879 and his system of 1882 for central power production gave great commercial impetus to electric-generator and power development. Production now speedily followed invention. The first practical electrical locomotive was designed by Sir William Siemens (1823-1883) in 1879; Edison demonstrated his own electric car in 1880; and only three years later the first all-electric track was opened at Portrush, Ireland.

Charles F. Brush invented a compound generator in 1881; thereafter larger and larger multi-polar generators, run by reciprocating steam engines, came into use. The invention of the first alternating-current system of power generation and distribution came with L. Gaulard and John D. Gibbs, in Europe, and with William Stanley in the United States in 1885.

The end of the century brought the invention of the wireless telegraph. James Clerk Maxwell (1831-1879) had formulated the underlying physical theory in 1873; Hermann von Helmholtz (1821-1894) added his studies of electric oscillations in 1870-75; Heinrich Rudolph Hertz (1857-1894) proved experimentally the existence of electromagnetic waves and paved the way for Guglielmo Marconi (1874-1937), who put the conception to practical use. Marconi made a device which could detect these waves and in 1897 transmitted a wireless message a distance of nine miles. By 1901 his wireless telegraph spanned 3,000 miles. Communications in wartime, already speeded by the telegraph and the submarine cable, were now made much more flexible, since sender and receiver were no longer tied to systems of cables and wires. Although throughout the latter part of the nineteenth century wire systems were to be found on land wherever railroads ran, the wireless was especially important strategically to naval operations, since ships were otherwise devoid of any but visual communication while at sea.

The internal combustion engine, destined to revolutionize first transport in war and then the implements of war themselves—like the tank and the airplane—showed the same leisurely development through the nineteenth century as the electric generator, with tremendous acceleration in the final decade. As early as 1794, R. Street in England had made drawings of a proposed engine driven by a flame-ignited explosive mixture of vaporized spirits of turpentine and air. The first commercially useful gas engine was Samuel Brown's primitive "gas-vacuum" creation, invented in 1832. William Barnett made important improvements in 1837. A free-piston engine was invented in Italy in 1859, and the essential theoretical requirements for a really efficient gas engine were laid down in Paris by Beau de Rochas in 1862. But it was not until 1874, with the invention of Dr. N. A. Otto of Germany that a satisfactory gas engine was finally built.

One difficulty of the engines of the time, including Otto's, was that they were extremely heavy. It took Gottlieb Daimler (1834-1900) of Germany to devise in 1882 the first successful light-weight gasoline engine, and to him belongs the principal credit for the development of the automobile. Fifteen years after the first Daimler patents the world's first auto race was held. Cars journeyed from Paris to Bordeaux and back at an average speed of fifteen miles an hour.

The slowness in the development of the gasoline engine was partly due to the difficulty in finding and producing a satisfactory fuel. The transformation of crude petroleum to gasoline is a true test-tube miracle, requiring the resources and ingenuity of many kinds of scientists and complicated industrial facilities. The Diesel engine, invented in 1895 and using low-grade fuel oil, was a significant achievement in bypassing this problem. It was also a tremendous boon to the submarine, which needed an internal combustion engine that did not give off dangerous explosive fumes.

The first commercial production of petroleum began in Rumania in 1857 and in the United States in 1859. By 1900 the world consumption was already 150 million barrels annually, though the motor car had barely arrived on the roads. But the refining industry, which would be several times transformed by scientific research in the twentieth century, was still primitive in 1900.

The development of rubber was also indispensable for the efficiency of motor transport. Though rubber was known in Europe and America very early in the nineteenth century —and was in fact given its name by Joseph Priestley, the eighteenth-century discoverer of oxygen—it was little more than a toy until 1839, when Charles Goodyear discovered the process of vulcanization. By the outbreak of the Civil War in 1860 rubber was being used for footwear, rubberized clothing, and odd items like bumpers for railroad cars. But a uniform rubber product could not be made before 1906, when George Oenslager of Akron, Ohio, discovered how to use organic accelerators to speed up the process of vulcanization.

Nineteenth-century medical discovery—the germ theory of Pasteur, the discovery of antisepsis by Joseph Lister, the bacteriological research of Robert Koch and others, the development of the science of nursing—had enormous consequences for armies and navies, which in battle suffered casualties and between battles subjected their men to crowding, exposure, poor food, and fatigue. During the Napoleonic Wars far the greatest number of deaths among the troops resulted from illness. In the Crimean War 19 per cent of the British brought to Crimea and 27 per cent of the French died of disease. Few escaped serious illness. The twentieth century would see phenomenal progress in medicine, but since the emphasis here is on weapons technology, this story must be told elsewhere.

One is tempted to say now that no scientific advance in the nineteenth century matched in significance the beginnings of the science of radioactivity. In 1895 Wilhelm Conrad Roentgen (1845-1923), while experimenting with vacuum tubes on the conduction of electricity through gases, observed the fluorescence of a barium platinocyanide screen. Further investigation showed that this radiation could pass through substances opaque to ordinary light and still affect a photographic plate. He called the force X-rays.

The following year Henri Becquerel (1852-1908) accidentally locked some sensitive photographic plates in the same cabinet with some uranium salts. The exposure of the plates led him to the discovery that uranium at ordinary temperatures emits invisible rays which can affect a photographic plate even after passing through thin plates of metal. His rays resembled Roentgen's X-rays in this. Becquerel's discovery inspired Pierre and Marie Curie in their own research and labors. The story of their isolation of radium and polonium from pitchblende in 1898, one of the most dramatic in the history of science, needs no retelling here. Its importance, like that of the discovery of X-rays, was recognized almost immediately. Roentgen was awarded a Nobel prize in 1902, and the Curies shared a Nobel prize with Becquerel in 1903.

Sir Joseph John Thomson (1856-1940), the British physicist, demonstrated in a highly original study that cathode rays—now known as the electron beam—were particles of high velocity which could be deflected by an electromagnet. His student Ernest Rutherford (1871-1937) was one of the first to ask, "Why does an unsplittable atom give off rays?" Scientists leaped at the new problem with imagination and talent. The quantum theory of the great German physicist Max Planck (1858-1947) was first designed only to meet the facts of radiation. Formulated in 1900, it proposed that the energy of radiation varies in multiples of a minimum indivisible quantity called a quantum; it proved to be a valuable tool for investigating the fundamental nature of matter and energy. In 1903 Ernest Rutherford and Frederick Soddy proposed the hypothesis of atomic disintegration. This bold reappraisal of the theory of matter led to portentous consequences which will be the subject of chapter 10 of this volume.

# 7. World War One, The Use and Non-Use of Science

With the twentieth century we enter into a period when science becomes so intertwined with the technology of war that within the remaining chapters we can do little more than suggest the complexity of the tapestry. During World War I the scientist in military work became so ubiquitous that he began to be anonymous. Most of his achievements were accomplished in teams working under pressure to solve specific weapons problems. But, as we shall see, the full resources of science did not begin to be utilized. The hideous slaughter in the stalemate on the western front went on year after year without anyone's calling on the scientists to make a serious and concerted effort to find means to break it—except in the use of poison gas, which demonstrated fairly early its inutility for decisive victory. In sea warfare, however, the use of scientists on both sides was considerable, and the ingenuity of the allied group may well have been responsible for saving England from defeat.

The First World War demonstrated that the twentieth century had put into the hands of each great nation a war machine of far greater power than any known before. This change was accompanied, however, by a near-collapse of the forces previously serving to limit war, including that of common prudence. All rational concern with the proper political aims of war seems to have been suppressed. World War I was the purposeless war which no one seemed to know how to prevent, and which, once begun, no one seemed to know how to stop. Politically, the world it brought in its wake was in many respects a worse place than before.

The technology of World War I is immeasurably more complicated than that of any previous war. Much of it is a story simply of the improvement and perfection of previous weapons. Metallurgists and ballistics experts, for example, made machine guns and artillery weapons ever more accurate and powerful. Railroads were more efficient; communications, which now included the telephone and wireless, were swifter; and logistics became ever more voluminous, and therefore complicated, as transport was gradually motorized. We shall concentrate chiefly, therefore, on the great innovations—the airplane, the tank, poison gas, and particularly the submarine. All but the submarine were new in war, and in effectiveness the submarine too was new. It was the most nearly decisive instrument, and the airplane was potentially the most revolutionary.

## THE COMING OF THE AIRPLANE

Considering that the dream of flying is as old as man, and that the example of the birds has been with him constantly, it seems astonishing that the development of aerodynamics came so late in scientific history. Robert Bacon had written of flying machines and Leonardo da Vinci had designed a helicopter with an aerial screw 96 feet in diameter. Newton had been interested in the flight of birds, and so had Daniel Bernouilli. The philosophical papers of Newton, Jean and Daniel Bernouilli, Jean Le Rond d'Alembert (1717-1783), Leonhard Euler (1707-1783), Osborne Reynolds (1842-1912) and others, had advanced fundamental laws of fluid resistance basic to modern aerodynamic theories. John W. S. Rayleigh (1842-1919) had written a provocative paper on the mechanical principles of flight in 1899. But no organized scientific attack had been made on the questions raised by flight before the turn of the century.

Inventors of course had directed immense ingenuity in this direction. A wind tunnel had been designed by Francis H. Wenham in England as early as 1871. The successful flying machine had to wait upon the development of a lightweight motor, but even the motorless glider was not invented till the last quarter of the nineteenth century. It was a German inventor and aeronaut, Otto Lilienthal (1848-1896) who first established gliding as a science. He made over 2,000 flights before being killed in a glider, and

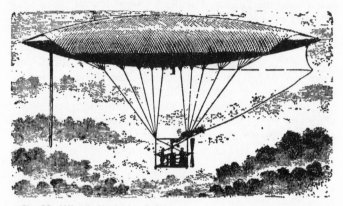

Fig. 39. Giffard's Navigable Balloon

he left a valuable book on gliders which pointed out the superiority of arched over flat wing surfaces, and the necessity of studying air currents and airfoils.

A 3-horsepower steam engine had been adapted to a balloon as early as 1851 by Henri Giffard, who piloted his airship from Paris to Trappes (Fig. 39). After the development in Germany by Count Ferdinand von Zeppelin of rigid-frame airships called "dirigibles," we had the beginning of useful and maneuverable flying ships. But balloons —rigid or non-rigid—were fundamentally different objects from airplanes, and the development of the one contributed little to that of the other—except in engines and air screws.

The first scientist who tried seriously to combine aerodynamic theory with practical invention was Samuel Pierpont Langley (1834-1906), U.S. astronomer and physicist, and secretary of the Smithsonian Institution. In the late 1880's he made quantitative experiments on the lift and drag of a plane moving through the air at measured speeds, using a recording dynamometer carried on the arm of a whirling table. He established the fact that a plane could be driven through the air by then-existing engines at speeds which would make it support more than its own weight. He also explained scientifically for the first time how birds

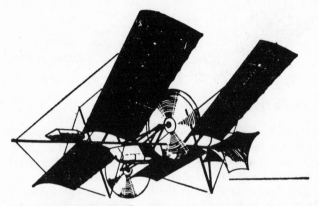

Fig. 40. Langley's **Number 5**

could soar without appreciable motion in their wings. His influential book *The Internal Work of the Wind* was published in 1893.

In 1896 Langley made a steam-driven model plane which flew 4,200 feet over the Potomac River, but it had no pilot and no proper means for taking off and landing (Fig. 40). Later he built at great expense a plane to be flown by a pilot, but the launching from a houseboat failed and the plane fell into the Potomac River (Fig. 41). Other experiments in powered flight by Clément Adler, Sir Hiram Stevens Maxim, and others, were also failures.

The builders of the first successful airplane were not scientists but two remarkable inventors, Wilbur Wright (1867-1912) and his brother Orville Wright (1871-1948), bicycle builders in Dayton, Ohio. They had read about the experiments of Lilienthal in Germany and became immediate captives of the age-old dream. They studied the known theories of flight, experimented with kites and gliders, and corresponded with Langley in Washington. Wilbur Wright in 1905 acknowledged his debt to the American scientist: "The knowledge that the head of the most prominent scientific institute of America believed in the possibility of human flight was one of the influences that led us to under-

Fig. 41. Langley's Piloted Model

take the preliminary investigations that preceded our active work. He recommended to us the books which enabled us to form some ideas at the outset. It was a helping hand at a critical time, and we shall always be grateful."

Concluding finally that the literature on the subject was inadequate, they devised a small wind tunnel where they made their own measurements of lift and drag, and devised two important techniques—aileron control and the horizontal rudder, or elevator. The first airplane they actually constructed weighed 750 pounds with the pilot, and had a four-cylinder gas engine. On December 17, 1903, at Kitty Hawk, North Carolina, the brothers achieved the first powered flight. It lasted twelve seconds. On October 5, 1904, Wilbur Wright flew for 38 minutes.

Five years later, on July 25, 1909, Louis Bleriot spanned the English Channel in thirty-one minutes. Though it was generally unrecognized at the time, the flight of his fragile craft, with potentialities as yet undreamed-of, marked the end of the long period of British invulnerability to attack from abroad.

Airplane design and production thereafter made phenomenal advances, much of the rapidity of which was due to the swift development of aerodynamic theory. In 1904 Ludwig Prandtl in Germany introduced the idea of the boundary layer—a thin layer of retarded air in contact with the surface of the plane—and went on to make mathematical formulations on the nature of the flow in the vicinity of the wingtip, one of the most useful contributions ever made in the field of aeronautics. A. F. Zahm measured air velocity, pressure, and friction on various forms of surface. M. W. Kutta in Germany, Nikolai Joukowski and D. Riabouchinski in Russia, and Frederick W. Lanchester in England worked on the problems of airfoil and lift.

Meanwhile governments became interested. The National Physical Laboratory in England had an advisory committee for aeronautics as early as 1909; and the United States established in 1915 the National Advisory Committee for Aeronautics for the supervision and direction of the scientific study of flight. It was quickly discovered that more empirical data was needed to solve the immensely complicated problems, and by 1915 all the leading western countries had wind tunnels.

Airplanes were first used in war in the Italian Tripoli campaign of 1911-12, where the aviators succeeded in discovering and warning the Italian generals of gatherings of Arabs and Turks. They also tried dropping bombs, which produced local panics but no military advantage. In the Balkan War of 1912-13 the Bulgarian army hired foreign aviators for reconnaissance purposes. The Germans seem to have been more impressed with the military possibilities of the airplane than any other nation; when the First World War broke out they had 200 first-line planes, which was twice as many as the French or English.

The British Air Battalion was but three years old, and the Naval Wing of the Royal Flying Corps was even younger. Nevertheless, it should be pointed out that the British planes, though few in number, were being used with much imagination and daring. By 1914 they had already been used experimentally for most of the functions they were to assume in the war. British naval aviators experimented with the use of aircraft for torpedo attack as early as 1911; they tried hunting submarines with planes in 1912; in 1913 they experimented with bomb dropping, wireless telegraphy, machine gunnery, and fighting. In 1911 a plane took off from the deck of a cruiser at anchor. A parallel record was established in the same year by officers of the United States Navy.

The high commands on either side, however, seemed at first to have little comprehension of the versatility of the airplane in war. They considered it primarily a reconnaissance tool, designed to be the eyes of the ground forces, as balloons had been in earlier wars. But planes were so successful in reconnaissance that it became important for each side to destroy those used by the other. Planes were made with greater speed, and armed with machine guns; thus the fighter aircraft was born.

In the beginning, military leaders left the creation of such instruments as bombsights and aerial machine guns to individual inventors, to be developed on their own initiative and without military encouragement. Once an invention came to the military and successfully passed their often cautious scrutiny, it might be put to use. In 1915 the Germans accepted the invention of a Dutch airplane designer, Anthony H. G. Fokker, of a synchronizing gear which allowed a fixed machine gun to be fired through a revolving propeller without striking it. It gave them an enormous advantage, until the Allies discovered the device on a captured German plane and were able to duplicate it.

The British attempted sending aircraft massed in considerable numbers; finally their De Havilland II and the French Nieuport, each with 110-horsepower engines, proved more than a match for the Fokker. The Germans then replied with the Albatross and Halberstadt. So the race began in earnest, each country seeking desperately for superiority in speed, firepower, and maneuverability. In 1917 as many as 100 planes were taking part in single air battles.

The Germans used Zeppelins for bombing England, and the early raids over London were fairly destructive. It took some time before the British learned how vulnerable the hydrogen-filled Zeppelin was to attack by aircraft armed with explosive bullets. Churchill rightly predicted that the "gaseous monsters" would fall before the airplane, and the

Zeppelin raids dropped from 22 in 1916 to 4 in 1918. Of the 61 Zeppelin airships attached to the German fleet only ten were left at the armistice.

The plane, however, did not share this hopeless vulnerability. The Germans organized systematic strategic bombing forays over England, using bombs up to 660 pounds. By 1918, however, British antiaircraft defenses were so improved that in the last German raid on London, May 19-20, 1918, six out of thirteen Gothas and Giants reaching the city were destroyed. The Germans then abandoned London and took Paris as their target. During the war the Germans sent 435 aircraft over England and 208 airships; the results were 1,300 killed, 3,000 injured, and considerable material damage.

The British developed their own Handley-Page bomber, which was capable of carrying a 1,650-pound bomb, the largest dropped in the war. They concentrated on railroad stations and airfields, and tried to destroy the Zeppelin factories. Most of the airplanes on both sides, however, were used not for strategic bombing but as an adjunct to the ground forces. General William A. Mitchell in 1918 developed the idea of creating an airborne parachute division and even obtained General Pershing's approval, but too late to implement the idea before the war was over.

In the spring of 1918 the Germans managed to concentrate 900 aircraft for their great offensive, but they could not wrest control of the air from the Allies. In their own offensive of August, 1918, the Allies used 2,000 planes, as against 365 for the Germans. They managed to concentrate 1,500 planes in September to help in the offensive to flatten the German salient at St. Mihiel. Though the numbers seem large, actually the planes were so small and the bombs so ineffective compared with those of World War II that one cannot in any sense accord the airplane the importance in the First World War that it proved to have in the second.

The airplane was not the factor at sea that it was on land —except for its success in hunting submarines. The seaplane remained deficient in reliability, range, speed, and weight-carrying capacity. At the Dardanelles in 1915 the British sent seaplanes carrying torpedoes slung along the fuselage to attack German and Turkish supply ships, but it was never dreamed on either side that the airplane could threaten the existence of the battlefleet. The plane in sea warfare was used mostly to improve the accuracy of the gunfire of the surface warships, and it was a great aid in reconnaissance.

Although ships called "aircraft carriers" made their appearance during World War I, none had a flight deck running the entire length of the ship and thus large enough to permit planes to land as well as to take off. Planes which took off from their decks usually alighted on the water, where they floated upon air bags until hoisted onto the mother vessel. There were also seaplane carriers which functioned as tenders, using derricks to lower the planes into the water and hoist them up at the end of the flight. The first vessel constructed with a clear deck which could be used both for taking off and landing was the British *Argus,* completed September 1918, too late to be of use in World War I, though it served well in World War II.

The role of the airplane in the naval war was deceptive in that it gave no promise whatever of being the colossal threat to the warship it proved to be in World War II. Certainly the airplane would have revolutionized naval war even if the submarine had not done so, but its full impact, as in land warfare, came a generation later.

### THE SUBMARINE STORY

In the first few years of the twentieth century France led all the other powers in submarine building, but Great Britain and the United States had substantial flotillas, and the smaller powers were buying submarines singly or in pairs. Oddly enough in view of later history, the Germans lagged far behind the other great powers. Admiral Von Tirpitz for a time stubbornly opposed the submarine altogether for the German navy, insisting that it was a purely defensive weapon. But after 1905, when the Krupps proved with the

*Karp* class that a diving boat with real fighting value had been developed, the German navy began cautiously to build them. The gyroscopic compass had by now been perfected, and the Germans saw to it that this device, indispensable for submerged navigation, was adopted on all their underwater boats.

A basic defect in all early submarines was their dependence upon the gasoline engine for surface cruising; it restricted their range, gave off clouds of smoke, and was extremely dangerous. The Germans began experimenting with Diesel engines in their U-boats (for *Unterseeboote*) in 1905, but did not succeed in building a satisfactory Diesel-powered U-boat till 1913. By 1914 they had ten of these built, seventeen more in the building, and eighteen pre-Diesel boats. By contrast, the British had fifty-five boats and the French seventy-seven, most of them very small, and the Americans had thirty-eight. Few of these could match the German boats in performance and military value.

The British knew the range of the German U 18, and thought their own boats appreciably superior. They had no idea that the U 19 had a range of 5,000 sea miles, four times that of the U 18. Neither side expected a war on commerce, perhaps because the American naval writer, Rear-Admiral A. T. Mahan, whose prestige was enormous, had sharply discounted the importance of commerce-raiding.

Torpedoes had been perfected on both sides. The British in 1914 had a 21-inch torpedo, the largest then in use, with a range of 7,000 yards at 41 knots. On August 8, 1914, the U 15 fired a torpedo at the British battleship *Monarch* without success. This was the first time an automotive torpedo had been fired against an enemy from a submarine. Though it was unsuccessful, the attack caused great uneasiness in the British fleet, for it threw into doubt the security of the Grand Fleet's anchorage at Scapa Flow. Shortly afterward the Admiralty ordered the fleet to Loch Ewe, and, after further submarine scares, to Loch Swilly in North Ireland, meanwhile ordering submarine defenses to be built at Loch Ewe and Scapa Flow. Even Loch Swilly was found to be insecure, for one of the newest super-dreadnoughts, the *Audacious,* sank there after hitting a mine laid by the surface raider *Berlin;* at the time it was not clear whether she had struck a mine or been hit by a torpedo.

Fortunately, the Germans had no idea that a few submarines had forced the most powerful battle fleet in history to retreat from its main base to a second base, and then to a third, each more remote from the main theater of the war —the North Sea. Had they known, they could have roamed that sea with impunity, destroying all the shipping they encountered. Neither did they learn, for a considerable period, of the sinking of the *Audacious.*

The submarine war on commerce began October 20, 1914, when a U-boat commanded the scuttling of a small steamer, the *Glitra.* The U-boat commander returned to port expecting censure, but instead was formally applauded. The German High Command determined now to declare the area around the British Isles a war zone, dangerous to neutral and enemy alike. Realizing that it was more efficient to sink smaller ships with shellfire than with the costly and bulky torpedoes, of which only a few could be carried by each submarine, they secretly fitted out their larger submarines with guns. The Kaiser on February 4, 1915, gave the formal order, and the sinking of commercial vessels began in earnest.

American protests became so vehement that the Germans promised to curtail the war on commerce despite the startling success of the U-boats. Had the United States not demanded the curtailment of the U-boat attacks, the submarines would perhaps have succeeded in doing what they failed to do in 1917—bring Great Britain to her knees by causing the collapse of her shipping. German naval officers considered it intolerable for the United States to demand that Germany withhold so powerful and perhaps decisive a weapon so that a handful of American citizens could blithely traverse the war zones without danger of loss of life. Finally the Kaiser consented to the resumption of unrestricted submarine warfare beginning August 1, 1916.

Meanwhile deliveries had begun to the German fleet of two larger and superior types of submarines, the UB 18-29, and UB 30-47.

In the face of renewed American protests the Kaiser retreated again, and the number of orders for new submarines under construction was actually lowered. The result was that when the unrestricted campaign finally opened in earnest February 1, 1917, there were fewer U-boats available than might have been. Even when submarine warfare was conducted in accordance with cruiser prize rules (which required that the submarine surface and see to it that all hands on the doomed ship were safely in lifeboats before sinking her), the toll of merchant shipping was enormous. And when the Germans decided to defy American demands and return to unrestricted submarine warfare, the result was that of every 100 ships leaving the British Isles 25 never returned. Such losses, had they continued, would have meant certain defeat for Britain.

But the delay in the all-out submarine warfare caused by American protests was just sufficient to give Britain the time to marshal her resources for the antisubmarine fight. In 1914 she was completely unprepared to handle the menace. Even in mid-1917 all the scientific ingenuity and technological resources of the nation gathered together during the preceding eighteen months had not been enough to stem the appalling sinkings. Churchill wrote of this period later: "I watched with a fear that I never felt at any other moment of that struggle the deadly upward movement of the curve of sinkings over the arrival of new construction. . . . That was, in my opinion, the gravest peril that we faced in all the ups and downs of that war."

In the five months prior to February 1, 1917, the average monthly toll of British ships had been about 37; March saw 103 ships sunk by submarines and mines and 24 by surface raiders. The following month, when the United States entered the war, a total of 169 British ships were sunk. The British gross tonnage sunk in that terrible month of April reached 545,000.

Nevertheless there had been time to set into motion a

great variety of antisubmarine measures, the most important single one of which was organizing the ships into escorted convoys. These measures slowly began to take their toll of the U-boat and to afford protection to Allied shipping. After this same month of April the number of Allied sinkings went down and the toll of U-boats went up. British physicists, chemists, and mathematicians, responding with immense dedication, had perfected two technical devices of great value, the hydrophone and the depth bomb. On April 23, 1916, the hydrophone was first used successfully to detect the UC 3, caught in a mine net. The underseas craft was quickly destroyed. On July 6, 1916, the motor boat *Salmon* used hydrophones to hunt down the submarine-minelayer UC 7 and dropped a depth charge that detonated her mines. U-boat commanders whose job it was to lay mines in British waters came to fear this combination of disasters more than any other, and there was a noticeable deterioration in their morale.

British scientists also developed a special type of shell for use against submarines. The U-boat with its low freeboard and minimum buoyancy was always relatively vulnerable (nineteen were destroyed by ramming during the war), and a hit from a small gun in a vulnerable spot could cause it damage that might prevent its diving. At first the British used decoy vessels—their famous Q-ships—armed vessels disguised as innocent merchantmen. Later, as gun production increased, they were able to arm merchantmen in great numbers. This meant that the submarines had to abandon the use of their surface guns and stay submerged in order to survive, thus using up their limited stock of torpedoes.

It was not until the spring of 1917 that British scientists perfected an antisubmarine mine, the Mark H. Delivery began in July and minelaying started over a large area in the Heligoland Bight, in the Straits of Dover, and elsewhere. Unlike World War II, in which the Germans were to control the whole French coast and submarines could set forth from any port in France or the Low Countries, the Germans in World War I could venture forth only from a narrow coastal area, and had to pass through either the North

Sea, or the English Channel. England in effect blockaded the Germans by her geographical position. It was this fact that made large-scale minelaying feasible and useful.

In the last quarter of 1917 the British laid 12,450 mines. In the following year they decided to lay a mine barrage across the North Sea, an audacious undertaking requiring the invention of a special deep-sea mine, its manufacture in a quantity over 150,000, and the employment of hundreds of minelayers to lay them. Altogether the Allies laid 172,000 mines. Only the manufacturing resources of the United States made it at all possible to produce this number in so short a time, and yet the line was not complete till well into 1918. The Straits of Dover were at this time floodlighted from one side to the other, so that patrol craft could force the U-boats passing at night to dive into the mine barriers.

The airplane was also used for submarine detection. Unlike the surface ship, it could see a submarine as a shadow beneath the water, and could then signal its position to destroyers or drop depth charges itself. A special type of aerial bomb was devised for exclusive use against the undersea boat. The plane greatly discouraged minelaying activity by submarines and kept the U-boats submerged, which vastly reduced cruising range and efficiency.

Allied submarines were also employed against the U-boats; they developed a wholly unexpected usefulness in stalking them. The British built a special type for this purpose, the "R" class, which had a greater speed on its electric motors while submerged—about 14 knots—than on its combustion engines while afloat.

By and large, however, the greatest offensive threat to the U-boat came from the increasing number of destroyers and smaller naval craft armed with depth charges, which hunted the submarine in patrols. In 1914 the supply of British destroyers was hopelessly inadequate, but by the end of the war the United States, using her tremendous facilities for mass production and prefabrication, was building destroyers in six weeks. When the war was over there were 400 to 500 available, and a vast number of smaller craft. In the early months of the war there were so few depth bombs in production that destroyers were limited to four each; by the beginning of 1918 every destroyer carried from thirty to forty.

The usual submarine had several critical weaknesses: lack of speed, especially when submerged, low cruising radius when submerged, vulnerability to underwater attack, and poor vision. Moreover the submarine required water of a sufficient depth for safe submerged cruising, and this had to be considerable when she was diving to escape bombs. This requirement was not easily met in the shallow waters around the British Isles. Even when the U-boat was totally submerged and sitting on the sea floor with engines off, the sensitive hydrophone could sometimes detect the sound made by the motor of her gyroscopic compass.

Her torpedoes, which were propelled by the expansion of compressed air, left a broad white wake, which meant that a destroyer could rush to the end of the wake and drop a pattern of depth charges. After October, 1917, the number of submarines destroyed began to exceed the number of those being built. It is clear now that even at that date the submarine campaign had failed, and worse than failed, for it had brought the United States into the war. But during the war this was by no means clear, and the submarine threat seemed monumental. Sinkings continued despite the antisubmarine offensive measures, and also despite vast defensive precautions, including convoy, the arming of merchant ships, and the sweeping up of mines laid by the submarines. The focal areas in the western approaches to the British Isles and the several bottlenecks of the Mediterranean became the graveyards of 11,000,000 tons of Allied and neutral shipping.

Convoy was of enormous aid in helping reduce submarine sinkings, for it was a rare U-boat that would attack a convoy adequately protected by destroyers. But convoy presented problems; it drastically reduced the fruitfulness of the available shipping, since all ships were held down to the speed of the slowest, and the assembling of the convoy required much time. Minesweeping was imperative, though it required the services of some 600 small boats, for the Germans managed to lay 43,600 mines in four years, 11,000 in British home waters.

Late in 1917 the Germans developed a delayed-action type of mine that gave the Allies great trouble. It was designed to rise from the bottom of the sea to its effective position at periods varying from one to four days after being laid. Thus after fields were swept and reported clear, mines would reappear in them even though no new laying activity had taken place.

For defense against all types of anchored mines the "otter gear" was developed, a system of paravanes designed to be fitted to the prows of ships, both of war and of commerce. These pushed out to the side and cut the moorings of whatever mines they reached. The mines would then float to the surface, where they could be spotted and destroyed.

It will be seen that the mine, like the submarine, was used both offensively and defensively. It helped bar the Allies from the Dardanelles and the Germans from Riga. The use of mines in the Baltic enabled the Germans to check the naval arm of Russia with an inferior force and concentrate their battle fleet in the North Sea. The British used mines to help close the Dover defile with a force inferior to the German battle fleet, making possible concentration of the Grand Fleet at the Orkneys for offensive purposes.

It would have been impossible to predict in advance the effects of science on naval strategy during World War I. No one foresaw that the submarine would be the colossal threat it proved to be, and at the height of the U-boat successes few were confident that the forces of science and industry, and the dogged courage of the British in the face of disaster, would combine to bring about its final failure.

On the other hand, the German high command expected great successes from their surface commerce raiders, the most famous of which were the *Emden, Wolf, Möwe,* and *Seeadler.* While these successes were not inconsiderable, especially in 1916-17 when Britain was already reeling under the great submarine attack, they were surprisingly short-lived. The cruising radius of the raider was curtailed by her dependence upon the fuel supply at her base. But more important, the coming of the wireless meant that merchant ships could be warned away from the areas where her presence had been felt, or, they could aid their own cruisers in hunting her down. The famous light cruiser *Emden,* whose exploits eclipsed those of all the other German raiders, had a career of only two brief months before the wireless betrayed her to the larger guns of the *Sydney.* Other raiders became more cautious, and the sum total of their successes was not militarily impressive. In World War II, with the airplane to hunt her down, the surface raider would become little more than a fugitive, though the careers of a few of them were spectacular enough.

Insofar as the two great battle fleets of World War I were concerned, the war gave very little opportunity for either side to test the technological developments that had taken place in ordnance since the turn of the century—except in the Battle of Jutland. Both fleets had capital ships of the dreadnought and super-dreadnought types. (The name comes from the *Dreadnought,* built by the British in 1906 and incorporating a single type of primary armament —ten 12-inch guns—instead of the mixed armament—four 12-inch and four 8-inch guns—of pre-dreadnought types. This innovation made fire control much easier.) Their guns ranged from about 11-inch to 15-inch caliber, the latter being on ships of the great *Queen Elizabeth* class. All guns were of tremendous power. Both fleets had adopted the "director" system of fire, where all the big guns were placed in nearly parallel alignment and aimed and fired together through electrical control by a gunnery officer, who followed the target with a "director" which automatically tied into computers that adjusted for the speed and direction of both firing ship and target. The shot could thus be controlled till it "straddled" the target.

These developments had produced a phenomenal increase in accuracy. Gunnery practice before had been considered largely a waste of ammunition, but hits now could be scored at 20,000 yards. Sea battles could take place at far greater ranges and ships could be sunk miles away from their attackers. Fleets with a decided fire superiority could entirely destroy an enemy without suffering serious damage, as the British battle cruisers under Admiral Sturdee demonstrated at the Falkland Islands in December, 1914, when they annihilated the smaller squadron of Admiral von Spee (who in turn had destroyed the weaker squadron of Admiral Cradock). This was a decisive change in naval war.

The Battle of Jutland saw the use of every new technological naval device and also involved the use of airplanes and dirigibles. The threat of submarines in the vicinity affected the maneuvering of both fleets. The battle demonstrated among other things that not only gun power but also ability to withstand hits is the test of battle strength. The four heavily protected *Queen Elizabeths* received many hits at long range from the German 11-inch and 12-inch guns, but none of them penetrated the armor. On the other hand, the British ships that were lightly armored, especially the battle cruisers—which had the size and gun caliber of battleships but had fewer guns and carried lighter armor to allow them more speed—suffered heavily from the German guns. The British lost three battle cruisers, three armored cruisers, and eight torpedo craft as against the loss of one old battleship, one battle cruiser, four light cruisers and five torpedo craft for the Germans. The British lost over 6,000 men, the Germans about 2,500.

Though the battle was indecisive in the sense that the German High Seas Fleet remained undestroyed, nevertheless the fight ended with the German commander, Admiral Spee, prudently refusing to renew the battle. He fled back to port, leaving the British in a command which was in all essential respects undisputed for the rest of the war.

## THE STALEMATE ON LAND

In striking contrast to the stories of the airplane and submarine, where imagination and audacity in science and in strategic and tactical thinking became commonplace on both sides, the land fighting is largely a story of stupid rigidity and waste. The first blunder was the complete underestimation of the power of the machine gun by both sides, but particularly by the French general staff. General Ferdinand Foch and his school, obsessed with the idea of *l'offensive brutale et à outrance,* helped guarantee that the French would enter the war with an allotment of two machine guns per battalion as compared with the Germans' six. Foch's protégé, Colonel de Grandmaison, chief of the operations branch of the general staff, stated the French strategy succinctly: "In the offensive, imprudence is the best safeguard. The least caution destroys all its efficacy."

As it turned out, imprudence against the machine gun was outrageous folly. When the French armies in 1914 went charging off to the east while the Germans wheeled down on their flank and rear, they met a scourge of fire in the opening battles of the frontiers that sent them reeling backward with appalling losses. They were barely able to regroup for the Battle of the Marne, which stopped the German advance. The battles of the Marne and the frontiers cost each side 500,000 casualties, a larger figure than that which represented the whole manpower of the Prussian army in the Austro-Prussian War of 1866.

By late 1914 the armies were already stalemated. The firepower of the machine gun was so devastating that armies could no longer live upon the surface of the battlefield. As General J. F. C. Fuller put it, "there was no choice but to go under the surface; consequently trenches five hundred miles long were dug, and armies went to earth like foxes— each side turned itself into an immense spider and spun hundreds of thousands of miles of steel web around its entrenchments." Soon the trench barrier extended from Switzerland to the North Sea. The fronts became flankless, and penetration became the tactical problem.

Meanwhile the high commands on both sides continued to mount offensive after useless offensive in the teeth of the same terrible and confounding weapon, which was by then being produced in immense quantities and constantly improved. This became the longest and bloodiest war of attrition in all of history.

The rifle was now hopelessly outclassed, with its bayonet a useless encumbrance. The machine gun, relatively immobile, could not be used effectively to destroy other machine guns, though this was tried. The only answer to the machine gun that either side could think of for a long period was artillery bombardment. Field artillery on the Allied side included the most-fired cannon of the war, the French 75mm., as well as the 105mm. howitzer, both operating from positions close behind the front-line trenches. Medium artillery included the 155mm. howitzer, which was pulled by a five-ton tractor and could hurl a shell over twelve thousand yards twice a minute. Heavy artillery consisted of 155mm. rifles (with longer barrels for given caliber than howitzers), and the 8-inch and 240mm. howitzers, which could be moved with tractors at about eight miles an hour. There were also railway guns, usually converted naval guns of 14-inch caliber, which could shoot twenty miles but had to remain on their tracks.

German artillery advances were impressive. A secret weapon at the outset of the war was their heavy 420mm. (16.5 inch) howitzer, popularly known as the "Big Bertha," which was designed for reducing the Belgian forts—something it succeeded in doing without difficulty. The most famous German gun was the "Paris gun," which held the record for long-distance shooting and managed to hurl 250-pound shells seventy-five miles into the French capital (Fig. 42). This was made by putting portions of three large naval guns end to end and binding them together with an inserted tube which reduced the bore to about eight inches, though the length was about 100 feet. It was largely a terror weapon, and its several models succeeded over several months in killing only 256 Parisians.

The artillery on both sides hurled mostly high-explosive shells which on bursting scattered lethal fragments. The shrapnel shell, on the other hand, actually a kind of shotgun in itself, was filled with iron balls which were shot forward just as the shell arrived over the target by a pre-set time fuse. The setting of the time fuse was a matter of fixing the length of a variable powder train.

The great artillery bombardments of the war solved nothing. The time taken for massing the artillery gave warning

Fig. 42. The Paris Gun

of the coming attack, and the preliminary bombardment warned the enemy of the point of attack. The bombardment itself shattered the ground, turning it into such a monstrous upheaval of mud and shell holes that the advance was crippled before it started. Surprise was impossible. The nineteen-day bombardment by the British at the Third Battle of Ypres, or Passchendaele, in 1917, used 321 trainloads of shells, a year's production for 55,000 war workers. Because of the rain, the result was a chaos of mud and swamp. The British took forty-five square miles in five months at a cost of 370,000 men. "Each square mile," wrote General Fuller, "cost us 8,222 casualties."

Despite repeated failures and mass slaughter of proportions that had been inconceivable before, the Allied high command believed for two and one-half years that prolonged bombardment was the only key to success, that "the quantity of the shells was the key to victory." Before the war was over, France, with a population of only forty million, would lose 1,400,000 men dead and 4,500,000 wounded.

During the stalemate scientists and inventors worked hard to improve the weapons which produced it. Colonel I. N. Lewis, an American, perfected a light, air-cooled machine gun; the Americans mass-produced the new French recuperator mechanism for countering the recoil of the howitzer; Major F. R. Moulton, previously a professor of astronomy at the University of Chicago, designed a streamlined shell which would more consistently follow its designed trajectory. Physicists invented the geophone for detecting the location of enemy mining operations, and, by triangulation, the sites of large enemy cannon. Precision optical instruments took the guesswork out of gunfire—rangefinders, the aiming circle, elevation quadrants, deflection boards, wind indicators, and panoramic sighting instruments. Communications devices for use within the trench network improved, including telephone and radio. None of these did anything to the tactical or strategic picture except to increase the efficiency of the slaughter. Tactics had become completely ossified.

The Germans were the first to turn to science in earnest for a device to break the stalemate. Chemists very early in the war had pointed out to the German high command the possibilities inherent in chemical warfare, but the generals had been reluctant to adopt the proposals. As the stalemate lengthened, they turned to Fritz Haber, the greatest authority of his time on the relations between chemistry and industry and professor at the Kaiser Wilhelm Physical Institute in Berlin. Haber held the post of head of the raw materials department in the war ministry. He had already solved the serious crisis resulting from the low supply of nitrates by synthesizing ammonia from nitrogen in the atmosphere. The increased supplies of ammonia—which jumped tenfold—could be converted to nitric acid, an essential for high explosives.

Within six months, Haber and Walther Nernst, professor of chemistry at the University of Berlin, had prepared the materials for a chlorine-gas attack and had devised a satisfactory gas mask. Haber was made chief of the chemical warfare service in 1916 and directed the research, supply, and personnel training thereafter. His department introduced mustard gas in 1917 and experimented with hundreds of other substances.

The Germans were not the first to consider gas as a

Fig. 43. French and British Gas Masks of World War I

weapon of war. Charles XII of Sweden had used smoke successfully during a river crossing in 1701. During the siege of Sevastopol in 1855 Admiral Lord Dundonald submitted a plan for the use of gas for the reduction of the Russian forts—400 tons of sulphur and 2,000 tons of coke —but the English government had refused to sanction it. During the American Civil War, John W. Doughty had tried unsuccessfully to persuade Secretary of War Stanton to use chlorine gas, and he had devised a practical scheme for dispersing it.

The British had advance warning that a gas attack was forthcoming but simply refused to believe it. The first gas attack was launched north of Ypres on April 22, 1915; it broke the strength of two Allied divisions. The Germans lacked the reserves to exploit their success, which was much greater than they had anticipated. At first the Allied soldiers used pads of cotton dipped in water—chlorine being highly soluble—and tied over the nose and mouth; then a crude respirator was distributed. The gas mask saw continual improvement through the war (Fig. 43).

Five months after the first German gas attack, the British launched a gas attack at Loos, and it continued to be used on both sides till the end of the war. Diphosgene, a poison gas with a marked tear-producing effect, was used, and so were phosgene, chloropicrin, hydrocyanic acid, which attacked the central nervous system, and mustard gas, which caused slow-healing burns on the skin and respiratory tract. Although gas was deplored as inhuman and barbaric, and feared by the soldiers themselves more than the artillery shells, it was actually less lethal than other weapons. About one-fourth of the 258,000 American casualties in the war were caused by gas, but of this fourth only two per cent died, while among casualties from other weapons 25 per cent died. Three-fourths of the American gas casualties were caused by mustard gas.

The German use of gas stimulated the Allied governments to draw more heavily upon the resources of their own chemists. (President Wilson did not set up a special chemical warfare service until the spring of 1918.) Not only did they prepare new gases to attack the Germans but they also developed incendiary bombs, smoke funnels, smoke screens, smoke grenades, colored rockets, and flame throwers. They improved high explosives and did work on such varied projects as sanitation, soldiers' rations, optical glass, nitrates, and metallurgical problems. They discovered methods for preventing meat spoilage, and worked on many different raw materials. They cracked petroleum for the purpose of producing toluene, useful in the production of TNT.

None of these improvements or special devices was successful, however, in bringing to an end the stalemate of the western front with all its useless slaughter. Churchill, minister of munitions, stated to the War Cabinet early in March, 1918, that the British were "merely exchanging lives upon a scale at once more frightful than anything that had been witnessed before in the world, and too modest to produce a decision." Neither the German nor the Allied generals seemed capable of thinking of anything but their increasing demands for manpower. Their narrow strategic doctrine knew no horizons beyond the immediate needs of the battle.

The British, despite their history, ignored the sea as an avenue for turning the enemy's flanks and refused to make use of their immense amphibious power. As Harvey De-Weerd has written, "Sir Henry Wilson held that the British fleet did not have the value of 500 bayonets; Joffre and Castelnau did not value it at one bayonet."

The instrument that finally broke the sand-bag and barbed-wire blockade and restored the offensive to what it had been before the invention of the machine gun was the invention not of a scientist but of a colonel in the British Army. As early as October, 1914, Colonel Ernest Swinton, after watching some American Holt caterpillar tractors tow heavy artillery behind the lines, conceived of the idea of armoring the tractor, mounting it with guns, and using it as an answer to the machine gun.

Swinton developed his idea in detail and won the enthusiasm of Winston Churchill. But the war office, incredibly, abandoned the Swinton proposals at the end of February, 1915. It was Churchill who rescued them and developed the tank under the auspices of the admiralty, using naval guns as armament.

The Swinton idea was not especially a marvel of originality. The notion of an armored car was at least as old as Leonardo. The idea of making a machine gun mobile had been developed in 1898 by F. R. Simms, who successfully mounted a Maxim gun on a motorcycle. The jointed track, so necessary for maneuvering on soft ground, had been invented by Thomas German back in 1801. Turreted armored cars built by the firm of Charron, Giradot and Voight in France had been sold to the Russians as early as 1904. Americans had been using caterpillar tractors in agriculture for a considerable period with great success, and the technology of their construction was already highly perfected.

The success of the caterpillar tractor in hauling heavy artillery might well have suggested the idea of the tank to scores of influential men; it simply didn't. But even the widespread use of the caterpillar was not demanded by the military, who were content to see most of the work of transport done by the horse. All through the war, horses

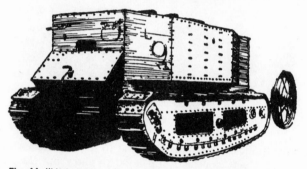

Fig. 44. "Little Willie," the First Experimental Tank

and men, rather than tractors, moved artillery into position, the tractors being reserved for the heaviest pieces. The British actually shipped more tonnage of oats and hay—5,500,-000 tons—to the western front than of ammunition.

The first British tank was a thirty-one-ton machine mounting two 6-pounders and four machine guns; next came a thirty-ton tank with six machine guns. The tanks were powered with 105-horsepower Daimler water-cooled engines and had a maximum speed of 3.7 miles per hour. The early French tanks were armed only with machine guns.

The first serious use of the tank came in the Battle of Cambrai on November 20, 1917, when the British sent forward 381 fighting tanks employing 1,000 guns. Huge bundles of brushwood were carried on the nose of each tank and released on reaching the Hindenburg trenches. The tanks worked in successions of three so as to cross three trench barriers. The preparations were made with great skill and the attack was launched without preliminary bombardment, so that it came as a complete tactical surprise. The tanks overran the enemy's main defense system and made a four-mile penetration; only a half-finished line and open country lay beyond. But, by then, 179 tanks were out of action, and the tank crews and original divisions were exhausted. Thanks to lack of faith in the new weapon, there

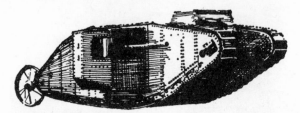

Fig. 45. "Big Willie," the First Rhomboidal Tank

were not sufficient reserves on hand to exploit the victory. The cavalry was hopelessly unsuited to carry out this role in the face of the machine-gun fire, though Allied officers continued to depend on it. Field Marshal Douglas Haig, the British commander-in-chief, had after all been a cavalry officer, and he continued to believe in it to the end.

Though the Battle of Cambrai had clearly pointed the way to decisive victory, the Allied high command did not accept the lesson. Thereafter they used tanks only fitfully and in small groups. Individual tank crews did astounding feats, sometimes fighting and maneuvering for forty hours at a stretch. But a group of fifty tanks could never do what required hundreds, even when fighting at forty-hour stretches. The proper tactic was to bring up hundreds of them by surprise, feed them with ammunition and fuel by tank carriers, and back them with plentiful reserves.

Most surprising, the Germans never woke up at all to the tremendous potentiality of the tank, though it was they who had exploited the machine gun sooner and better than the Allies, who had gauged more correctly the potentialities of the heavy howitzer, who were faster to awake to the scale of ammunition needed. When they did begin to build tanks, it was on a scale much smaller than that of the Allies; first priority was not given to their construction until the summer of 1918, and only 45 German tanks ever saw action. The British alone built 3,000.

On August 8, 1918, the British Fourth Army led a surprise attack with 450 tanks in front of Amiens and made an eight-mile breakthrough, killing or capturing 28,000 men and capturing 400 guns. The success was all too convincing to the Germans, who now finally abandoned all hope of victory. General Erich Ludendorff declared it "the black day of the German army in the history of the war." An invention relatively simple in conception, relying upon no new scientific ideas and no radically new technology but simply upon the proper assembling of technical devices already long in use—this was the weapon that finally revolutionized land warfare and brought an end to the stalemate. The fact that it was so long in coming and had to overcome such apathy and want of imagination before it could be used at all only serves to point up further the senselessness and futility that seems so much to characterize the first great world war.

# 8. World War Two

In World War II the scientist in the laboratory touched almost every aspect of the war operations and
profoundly influenced tactics and strategy. The Germans
believed that no new weapon could be introduced, or in
fact needed to be introduced, in a short war; Hitler was
confident of winning, with the weapons he had already developed and massed, weapons which were largely those of
World War I, though enormously improved technically.
What he relied upon chiefly was a novel tactical use of these
weapons, particularly the airplane and the tank.

"Who says I'm going to start a war like those fools in
1914?" he said. "Are not all our efforts bent towards preventing this? Most people have no imagination. . . . They
are blind to the new, the surprising things. Even the generals are sterile. They are imprisoned in the coils of their
technical knowledge." And on another occasion he said, "If
I were going to attack an opponent . . . I should suddenly,
like a flash of lightning in the night, hurl myself upon the
enemy."

His contempt for the expert and his reliance upon his
own "creative genius" were in the end to prove fatal for
Hitler and for his kind of Germany. For though his contempt for the military tactics of 1914-1918 was well justified, and though the new tactics which he favored proved
amazingly successful—the fluid war of movement that con-

centrated on creating confusion in the enemy, on causing annihilation rather than exhaustion, and the remarkable integration of tank, airplane, and infantry—there were very basic flaws in his capacity as a general. To the great failures of his strategy—his underestimations of British doggedness, of Russian fighting prowess, and of American productive capacity—one must also add his failure to mobilize the scientific talent of his own people until it was too late.

So confident was he of quick victory, and so contemptuous of the need for weapons other than those he had already developed and massed, that he put most of his young scientists in uniform and left the older academic scientists to their peacetime pursuits until late in 1942. Incomprehensibly, he ordered basic research on radar stopped in 1940; it was not renewed till 1942, when it was clear that the war could not be won quickly. Even before the war started he had driven out of Germany the group of Jewish scientists and mathematicians who were uniquely equipped to develop the A-bomb, and he gave no encouragement to the nuclear physicists remaining.

When the scientists were finally seriously mobilized, they made tremendous advances, particularly in ordnance, aerodynamics, and rocketry, but it was then too late. Professor William Osenberg, assigned in 1943 to the *Reichsforschungsrat,* an agency like the Office of Scientific Research and Development in the United States, complained just before the German surrender that "Germany lost the war because of incomplete mobilization and utilization of scientific brains." It is frightening to contemplate what might have happened had Hitler pushed scientific achievement with fanatic zeal and with all the resources of the German state. As it was, without marshaling the scientific talent at his disposal he almost won the war.

It is the opinion of James Phinney Baxter III, whose *Scientists Against Time* has been of great value to us in thinking through this chapter, that the British utilized the talents of their scientists with greater efficiency than did other nations, including ourselves. Like the Germans, the Americans in the beginning drafted into the military services

an immense pool of scientific talent, and were obliged belatedly to pull out one man after another and place him in
the spot where his training could best be used. The Japanese
organization of science, on the other hand, was far less
effective than the British and American. Japanese scientists
were even mistrusted by the military for their political
views, especially if they had been educated in Britain or
America.

After the fall of France, President Roosevelt acted
quickly to put the resources of American science at the disposal of the desperately imperiled United Kingdom. He
permitted the full interchange of scientific information between Britain, Canada, and the United States, and appointed
Dr. Vannevar Bush to head a National Defense Committee
for the purpose of co-ordinating the efforts of American
science. The British sent Sir Henry Tizard, Rector of the
Imperial College of Science and Technology, to head the
first scientific mission to the United States.

These moves marked the beginning of what was to grow
into a gigantic co-ordinated effort, in which hundreds of
academic scientists, all the leading British, American, and
Canadian universities, and an immense number of industries, as well as the research departments of all the armed
services in all the Allied countries, worked at top speed to
perfect old weapons, to invent new ones, and to invent
countermeasures which could lessen the deadliness of
enemy weapons. It is hard even now to imagine what was
left undone that might have been done. The dedication was
universal, the sense of urgency constant, and the results
phenomenal.

The stupendous achievement of the A-bomb will be considered in a separate chapter. The story of the fascinating
developments in military medicine, which directly affected
the life of almost every soldier, must be told elsewhere. One
can only survey briefly the new scientific achievements
which directly affected the battles, and suggest something
of their impact on the strategy and tactics of the war.

It is unfortunately impossible within a single chapter to
give proper credit to all the scientists and institutions in-

volved. One can note that rocket development was largely the work of the California Institute of Technology, that Harvard, Columbia, and the Woods Hole Oceanographic Institute operated laboratories to study underwater sound and underwater explosives, that Princeton specialized in ballistics, Pennsylvania State in hydraulic fluids, Michigan in explosives, and the University of Chicago in nuclear fission. But this is only a fragmentary listing.

A detailed account simply of the names of the industrial laboratories involved would take several pages. And it is impossible here to make clear exactly what was done under the authority of the Office of Scientific Research and Development, headed by Dr. Bush, or under the Naval Research Laboratory, the Signal Corps Laboratory, the Aircraft Radio Laboratory, the National Advisory Committee on Aeronautics, the Chemical Warfare Service, the National Inventors Council, or any of numerous other agencies. In England research was chiefly centralized in three agencies, the Telecommunications Research Establishment of the Ministry of Aircraft Production, the Air Defense Research and Development Establishment of the Ministry of Supply, both at Great Malvern, and the Admiralty Signal Establishment at Farnborough.

Except for the A-bomb, the most important of the new scientific developments of World War II concerned radar, the proximity fuse, electronic fire control equipment, anti-submarine devices, incendiaries, and rockets; and most of this chapter will be given over to describing their development and use. But it should be kept in mind always that an immense amount of scientific and engineering talent went into the perfection of World War I weapons—guns, airplanes, tanks, torpedoes, mines, submarines, and surface ships—and it was these that dominated the fighting.

## THE SUPREMACY OF THE AIRPLANE

In World War II the full potentialities of the airplane were finally realized. Winston Churchill had predicted gloomily in Commons in January, 1937, that while the day would come "when the raiding airplane will almost certainly be clawed down from the sky in flaming ruin . . . I fear that perhaps ten years, ten critical and fateful years, will pass before any such security will come, and . . . in the interval only minor palliatives will be at our disposal." The "minor palliatives" were enough to save Britain from defeat, but they were available, and before the war was over science had succeeded in making the airplane far more vulnerable, though it was a long way from being "clawed down from the sky in flaming ruin." (Actually Churchill's prediction was on its way to being realized in the late fifties and the sixties, but by then the ballistic missile had come along to supplement and partially replace the airplane.)

The Germans put considerable faith in the airplane as a tactical instrument, and went into the war with an impressive superiority in number and training over any of their opponents. Long before the war began they were mass-producing Heinkels, Dorniers, Messerschmitts, and Stukas. The Stuka, a two-seater, low-wing cantilever monoplane, was armed with two fixed machine guns, one in each wing, and a movable one in the after cockpit. Though a relatively slow plane with fixed landing gear, its vulnerability could not be an issue in a sky almost free of enemy planes. The Messerschmitt single-seater fighter, armed with a 23mm. fully automatic machine gun firing explosive shells and four 7.7mm. machine guns, was nearly 100 miles an hour faster than the standard British fighter of 1937. The French went to war with 520 war planes—100 bombers and 420 fighters; the Germans had more than 4,000.

German dive bombers destroyed communications, prevented counter-attacks, aided tank assaults, and paralyzed morale everywhere. In Belgium and Holland the Germans attacked the airdromes, first with bombers to drive the enemy antiaircraft gunners to shelter, then with dive bombers to keep them there, then with transport planes and gliders carrying troops armed with tommy guns to take and hold the fields. Parachute troops were decisive in the occupation of Belgium and of the Meuse bridges, the Albert Canal, and the strongest forts in the Liège area.

German tanks were bigger, faster, and better armored than French and British counterparts, and they were accustomed to working in large concentrations. German airplane pilots were trained to assist efficiently in the tank advance. Against the quick thrusts of the highly mobile Germans, the French infantry, relying on outmoded tactics in which tanks were used in scattered units as a support to the infantry rather than as a spearhead, was systematically divided, surrounded, demoralized, or annihilated.

Göring was confident that the 2,750 planes available to the *Luftwaffe* after the fall of France could destroy the RAF and also the British fleet. Neither Göring nor Hitler had believed an actual invasion of Britain would be necessary to victory, but after the surprising refusal of the British to accept defeat Hitler ordered the preparation of Operation Sealion. The first step was destruction of the RAF. Two things, besides courage and skill, made it possible for the British to win the Battle of Britain. One was the new British fighters just coming into production, which were superior to the German planes; the other was radar. The Germans knew the British were developing radar, as they were themselves, but they underestimated the quality and operational status of British radar.

During the years when the Germans were mass-producing planes and making few changes the British had been building few but making many changes. The result was that the new Hurricanes, and especially the faster Spitfires, had marked advantages. Both types had eight .30-caliber machine guns mounted in the wings, almost twice as much firepower as the Messerschmitts. The Spitfire could climb faster, and the Hurricane was more maneuverable. The only difficulty was that there weren't nearly enough of them. The British had only 700 fighters, 620 of them new, as against a thousand fighters and many more bombers for the Germans.

What saved the RAF was the fact that it had the greatest air surprise of the war at its disposal—radio location, or radar. This made it possible to tell when the Germans were crossing the channel, in what strength, and from what direction. Thus the RAF planes could wait on the ground, without using up their fuel, until an attack began, and could then be sent where needed. The effect was as though they were multiplied in numbers. Losses of Nazi aircraft soared. The last large daylight raid was made on September 30, 1940, after which the Nazis abandoned the battle to destroy the RAF and turned to night bombing. Shortly afterward the projected invasion, Operation Sealion, was abandoned.

And so began the attempt at the systematic destruction of British docks, factories, and cities, which was expected to destroy both Britain's productive capacity and the will of her people to resist. In both respects the Germans failed, partly because their equipment for strategic bombing was simply not equal to the task. Neither were the Germans able seriously to damage the British fleet.

When the Japanese entered the war, however, they taught the world that the airplane was capable of shifting the balance of naval power in the Pacific in a single week. On December 7, 1941, they sank or competely disabled five of the eight United States battleships at Pearl Harbor and destroyed most of the U.S. planes there and in the Philippines. Three days later they sank the *Prince of Wales* and the *Repulse* off the Malayan Peninsula. These ships, a new battleship and an old battle cruiser, went down without firing a single shot from their main batteries of 14-inch and 15-inch guns.

Churchill wrote later: "In all the war I never received a more direct shock. . . . There were no British or American capital ships in the Indian Ocean or the Pacific except the American survivors of Pearl Harbor, who were hastening back to California. Over all this vast expanse of waters Japan was supreme, and we everywhere were weak and naked." Japan was free to roam the stretches of the Pacific, annexing whatever islands she chose, conquering great sections of the continent and threatening even Australia and India. At no other point in the war did the airplane rank so high, and it seemed to many that the warship, except for the aircraft carrier, had become obsolete altogether.

Actually the warship was not as vulnerable as it seemed.

Had the defenses at Pearl Harbor been alert, or even awake, the story would have been very different, and the *Prince of Wales* and *Repulse* were shockingly underarmed with anti-aircraft guns. After Pearl Harbor not a single American battleship was sunk or even seriously damaged by the action of enemy planes, and before the war's end the American fleet was cruising practically at will in Japanese waters. Science came to the aid of the fleet as it had come to the courageous little group of fighter pilots of the RAF, bringing many protective devices and enormously increasing her offensive power. Of all these the most valuable new device was again radar.

### RADAR

The word radar is derived from the initial letters in the phrase "radio detection and ranging." This "electronic watch dog," based on the principle of the echo, grew out of directional short-wave radio. The fundamental research leading to radar began when Heinrich Hertz, the discoverer of radio waves, proved in 1887 that these waves were reflected from solid objects. Then in 1925 Gregory Breit and Merle A. Tuve of the Carnegie Institution of Washington, D.C., demonstrated how to use radio pulses to measure the height of the ionosphere, the layer of ionized gas near the top of the atmosphere which because of its ionization reflects radio waves. With the electronic tube called the cathode-ray oscilloscope, comparable to the television picture-tube, it was possible by radio echo, the same principle that accounts for "ghosts" on television screens, to measure time in such infinitesimal amounts that, despite the high speed of light, the ranges of objects miles away could be read within yards.

The idea of using a radio pulse and echo technique to detect aircraft and ships occurred to scientists in several countries about the same time, though the work seems everywhere to have been kept highly secret. The Naval Research Laboratory was working on radar in 1935. In England, Sir Robert Watson-Watt, head of the radio department of the National Physical Laboratory, was the first to work out a satisfactory plan for the radio pulse-echo detection of aircraft, and his system was set up experimentally in the late spring of 1935. This radar system could detect planes at considerable distance no matter what the weather, and measure their range with extraordinary accuracy. By following the changes in the direction and range of the aircraft, it was possible to compute instantly their true speed and direction.

In December, 1935, five radar stations on the east coast of England comprised the first operational radar system in the world. Fifteen additional stations were authorized in August, 1937, and from then to the end of the war there was an uninterrupted radar watch. It was these stations— built largely as a result of the extraordinary foresight of Sir Henry Tizard—that gave the RAF such a desperately needed advantage in the Battle of Britain. In effect it provided England with a curtain through which only very low-flying aircraft could pass undetected; the others were located before they were halfway across the North Sea, or just as they left their French and Belgian coastal bases. Radar proved especially valuable for maritime use, whether on ships or on coastal stations, because of the absence of terrain obstructions over the water.

The United States, France, Germany, and Japan all developed radar independently. Scientists at the Naval Research Laboratory built a set early in 1939 which was tested at sea during battle maneuvers on the *U.S.S. York*. The Coast Artillery Board of the United States Army tested radar position-finding equipment designed for control of antiaircraft guns in November, 1938, and Army long-range aircraft detection radar was successfully demonstrated in November, 1939.

By 1940 the British physicists had developed the multicavity magnetron, which made possible a remarkable improvement in radar performance. This instrument permitted a shift in wave length from a meter and a half to ten centimeters, which is in the region of the microwaves. This made possible many new refinements, especially a clearer picture on the scopes and greater accuracy in the readings.

The British turned over the whole of their radar research findings to the Americans in 1940, and the resources of the American electronics industry were virtually put at their disposal for the manufacture of radar equipment. Much of the new research in America was done at the Massachusetts Institute of Technology's Radiation Laboratory, which was opened in November, 1940; it was headed by Lee A. Du-Bridge and staffed by physicists from universities all over the country. The personnel rose from 40 to 4,000. The Naval Research Laboratory increased its radar section to 600; the Signal Corps Laboratories and Aircraft Radio Laboratory also did basic radar research.

Radar was adapted to ships, airplanes, antiaircraft guns, and submarines. It was used for aircraft warning, aircraft identification, control of aircraft interception, antiaircraft position finding, surface search, and fire control. Even where visibility permitted the use of optical instruments for range-finding, the radar was much more accurate. Later radar was used also for beacon bombing systems. Airborne navigation radar was used for navigation and bombing.

The refinements in radar research and production can be described only as fabulous, and the maintenance of secrecy on the subject, considering the thousands of men who were involved in production, was extraordinary. Just as 10cm. radar was going into production in 1942, the Radiation Laboratory completed the invention of 3cm. radar, which had wonderful clarity and was excellent for detecting night fighters. Before the war was over, this laboratory alone produced 150 different radar systems.

The best high-power warning radar was called the MEW, or Microwave Early Warning; it was conceived early in 1942 but not put into service till 1944. This was the "Big Bertha" of radar. The most powerful set built was set up on the Devon coast; it had a range of 200 miles, and its performance exceeded every expectation. During the Allied invasion of Normandy it guided fighter and bomber sweeps around the area and was in large measure responsible for the high ratio of kills to losses achieved by fighter aircraft.

The superior SCR-584, which has been described as the first Allied ground radar to surpass the German Würzburg, excelled not only in the control of antiaircraft fire but also in the direction of tactical air forces. It was used with excellent results in conjunction with MEW for the navigational control of fighter bombers. The Oboe member of the radar beacon or "racon" family was an exceptionally accurate navigational and blind-bombing aid. As Baxter puts it, Oboe "enabled two men sitting in trucks on British soil to know within a few yards each way the position of a British or American airplane over the Ruhr, and to know it much better than did the crew of the plane." By that time planes were equipped with IFF (Identification, Friend or Foe) transmitters which enabled them to be identified as friendly by Allied radar.

An airborne radar system for navigation and bombing was first developed as the $H_2S$, but was not very accurate. Then the $H_2X$ was developed, out of a 3cm. version of the $H_2S$. This became famous as the Mickey, a radar bombsight of considerable accuracy. The Mickey made it possible for bombers to take off for Germany from England and bomb their targets through a solid overcast. Until its adoption in the autumn of 1943, the Eighth Air Force had been often grounded by bad weather, operating at times no more than twice a month during the winter. Improvements on the Mickey followed, one of the most outstanding being called Gee.

Loran—Long Range Aid to Navigation—was a system that used two stations to provide intersecting arcs indicating one's position. It had the big advantage that it did not advertise to the enemy the position of the plane or ship using it. Eventually Loran stations spread around the world.

Countermeasures designed to neutralize German radar, and the "counter-countermeasures" required as the Germans retaliated with countermeasures of their own, called for continuing scientific imagination and audacity. They seem never to have been lacking. Even in the Battle of Britain scientists had used radio countermeasures to deflect the blind-bombing beams the *Luftwaffe* was using. By 1942 the Germans were using five major types of radar at frequencies from 100 to 600 megacycles for early warning, coast watching, aircraft interception, fighter control, and flak control.

Radar was basically easier to jam than radio and could be jammed by either electronic or mechanical means. The Germans were using jamming devices early in 1942. When their battleships *Scharnhorst* and *Gneisenau,* which had been operating successfully as commerce raiders, returned to Brest, they were repeatedly but unsuccessfully attacked by scores of planes. Finally the battleships were ordered to find a safer port, and under cover of fog and snow made their way up the English Channel. The American and British public, appalled at their escape, did not know that the success was due in large part to the fact that the Germans had jammed the British radar.

A simple but remarkably effective means used by aircraft to confuse enemy radar was to drop metallic strips cut to a special length so that they were resonant to the frequency of the radio waves sent out by radar. These strips, which were called by the Allies "window" or "chaff," returned echoes similar to that of planes. The Germans had experimented with such devices themselves, but realizing that they had more to lose than to gain if the Allies adopted them, they kept the whole investigation secret. When the RAF first used window in a raid on Hamburg, July 1943, the German radio operators were dumfounded. Window cluttered the scopes of the German radars and made them, in Baxter's words, as "impotent as a long-distance movie camera in a blizzard." By the end of the war the Eighth Air Force alone had dropped ten million pounds of aluminum foil over Europe.

Once the Allies began using window the Germans also adopted it. Then the Radio Research Laboratory developed an airborne electric jammer known as "carpet," designed to cripple the small Würzburg radars which were controlling the German flak and inflicting such deadly losses on Allied bombers. Carpet-jammers were tuned to send down into the ground radar signals having the same frequencies as those on which the radar sets operated. Carpet would fill a whole Würzburg scope with "grass," whereas chaff and window had affected only a portion of the screen. The first Eighth Air Force raiders using carpet suffered only half the losses of those without it.

Had it not been for these countermeasures, bombing over Germany might well have had to be suspended in 1943, so heavy were the losses to the radar-controlled German flak. When carpet and window were used together, Allied bombers could ride above the German flak "as if they were on a magic carpet." The desperate German scientists found too late that their countermeasures to chaff helped carpet, and the countermeasures to carpet helped chaff. When they finally turned to microwave radar, they were too late to get it into effective use.

The effectiveness of countermeasures was often quick and dramatic. In the Pacific the Japanese used radar as an aid to their torpedo bombers in the Battle of Leyte Gulf. When it was discovered that the frequency of the Japanese radar sets was below the lowest frequency of the high-power magnetron jammers then used to screen the American fleet, a call for aid went back to the scientists at the laboratory at General Electric. After a week of furious experimentation and activity, the laboratory delivered fifty new tubes. When jamming was again turned on, the Jap bombers on the radar scopes could be seen to waver, turn away, and finally turn back.

The Radiation Laboratory solved the problem of warning a pilot that a plane was approaching from behind. This system used a radar set standardized as the AN/APS-13, which rang a bell and lighted a light in the cockpit.

The most imaginative use of countermeasures came with the invasion of Europe. Baxter describes it as follows: "Tactical surprise saved thousands of lives, at the very least, if not the success of the whole operation. Here the radar-countermeasures experts gave full rein to their imagination and turned loose a bewildering array of jammers and deception devices. They blinded the eyes of enemy radars to conceal the true direction of the Allied attack and filled the German scopes in the Pas-de-Calais area with the fanciest

assortment of simulated echoes imaginable. A ghostly pro-
cession of non-existent battleships, cruisers, destroyers,
transports, landing craft, and air squadrons swam into the
Germans' ken, thanks to the most sophisticated faking in
the history of man. . . . We created the illusion of sweeps
around both ends, and smashed straight ashore through the
center."

Radar and radar countermeasures never gave the Allied
bombers complete immunity to German flak or fighters, nor
did radar bombsights provide the kind of accuracy in strategic and tactical bombing that was desired. Nevertheless
radar enormously aided the defense of Britain, and greatly
enhanced the offensive power of Allied planes over Europe.
In the war at sea it was particularly decisive and can be
said in truth to have saved the warship. In 1945 the U.S.
fleet could sail in the Pacific very nearly where it pleased,
something that would have been impossible in 1942. Radar
had extended the eyes of the fleet, making it possible to scan
the Pacific waters for 150 miles in any direction, regardless
of weather, night or day.

## THE PROXIMITY FUSE

It has been said that the most remarkable scientific development of the war, save for the A-bomb, was the proximity
fuse, sometimes called the variable-time (V.T.) fuse. This
was a small radar set—power plant, transmitter and receiver—which was built into an explosive shell. It activated
the detonator of the shell when it was properly located with
respect to the target. Among other things, it did away with
the necessity of computing the correct time of flight and
setting the fuse before firing the projectile.

The British were the first to experiment with proximity
fuses. They had done considerable work on both photo-
electric and radar fuses, particularly in connection with
their rocket research. American scientists built upon their
beginnings. A fuse had to be designed whose tubes and
metal envelopes would not break and whose delicate cath-
odes, grids, and plates would not be thrown out of align-

ment during firing and flight. Moreover it had to be tiny. The proximity fuse first designed for the shell of the U.S. Navy 5-inch, 38-caliber gun—the mainstay of the Navy's antiaircraft defenses—was about the size of an ice cream cone.

The first tests of this 5-inch shell took place on the cruiser *Cleveland* in Chesapeake Bay on August 10 and 11, 1942. They yielded spectacular results. The device was so successful in shooting down airplanes, however, that American military authorities feared that were it used over Europe the Germans might easily find a dud or capture an unused supply and reproduce the mechanism. This would mean that the RAF and Eighth Air Force would be largely erased from the skies. The rule held for many months thereafter that it could be fired only over water.

The proximity fuse enormously improved the safety and mobility of the American forces in the Pacific, having increased the deadliness of the naval 5-inch shell at least five-fold. It was adapted to the 6-inch dual-purpose gun and, later, it was used successfully against the kamikaze, or suicide pilots, who took off—often after less than two months' flight training—with gasoline enough for only a one-way flight, and who were likely to press home their attacks with great damage to the fleet.

When Allied intelligence in Europe brought news of the new German buzz bomb, the V-1, it was realized that this was a formidable weapon against which all the resources of science must be mobilized. It was agreed, therefore, that the VT fuse could be released for this purpose. Even before the first V-1 bombs were launched, the Allies were ready with an answer—the combination of the SCR-584 radar, the M-9 electrical predictor, and the proximity fuse.

The new fuses were released for general use on December 16, 1944, when victory in Europe was in sight and it was clear that the Germans would have neither the time nor the industrial facilities to copy them. In land warfare their merit lay in the fact that the shell could be set to burst over the target a very short distance from the ground, where its fragmentation effects could be maximized. They were used in the howitzers that stemmed the German advance toward the Meuse and ended the threat to Liège. When the Germans discovered that neither fog nor foxhole was any longer an effective cover against shell fragments, their general demoralization was accomplished. In the Pacific the fuse was used successfully in combat on Okinawa and Luzon.

## FIRE-CONTROL MECHANISMS

Along with the proximity fuse had come greatly superior fire-control mechanisms. Here mathematicians played a role in developing precision instruments that brought successes which would have seemed inconceivable a few years earlier. Fire control for antiaircraft guns posed special difficulties. The problem was to compute the proper angle to "lead" the target, which in the case of aircraft was a large angle that had to be computed swiftly. A notable development among several was that of Charles S. Draper of M.I.T., who, working with the Sperry Corporation, invented the celebrated Mark 14 sight, the gyroscopic lead-computing device used with the 20mm. Erlikon antiaircraft machine gun. Then came the M-9, a marvelously successful electronic director adapted from naval gun directors, which was widely used, and which was absolutely essential in the defense against the V-1.

Once the gunnery officer had trained the naval gun directors on the target, he could then merely follow the target. This was true especially of the 5-inch/25 and 5-inch/38 dual-purpose guns. (The second number times the caliber gives the length of the bore; "dual-purpose" refers to the fact that the guns were equally useful against surface and aerial targets.) The guns, which might be at some distance from the director on the ship, were synchronized electrically to move with it while allowance was automatically computed in the director for lead on the target, roll and pitch of the ship, and even the parallax between director and guns. The men at the guns merely loaded and reloaded, confident that the aiming and firing were being accurately handled elsewhere.

With these directors went remarkable new automatic and semi-automatic guns. The fully automatic gun was simply a machine gun which automatically reloaded and fired so long as the trigger was held. What was novel about the fully automatic gun in World War II was the dimensions which it reached, especially in the Bofors 40mm. gun, which fired a shell over an inch and a half in caliber weighing more than two pounds. Mounted in double and quadruple mounts, each mount having its own director, the Bofors handled our intermediate-range naval antiaircraft defense, the 20mm. Erlikon being reserved for the closest ranges.

The longer-range naval antiaircraft defense was with 5-inch and 6-inch dual-purpose semi-automatic guns, which had to be loaded for each shot but which after firing ejected the spent cartridge case while holding on target during the reloading. Thus, with a trained crew, the 5-inch gun could easily be fired at the rate of 20 shots per minute. This was a very different kind of antiaircraft gun and director system from that which men like Generals Billy Mitchell and Guilio Douhet had scoffed at in the 'twenties.

Near the end of the war scientists developed a single workable system of fire control for the aircraft themselves —the PUSS, Pilot's Universal Sighting System—which made it possible for a pilot to handle automatically his bombs, guns, rockets, and torpedoes, all of which could be carried on a single plane at the same time.

The electronic computers used in the director systems were the forerunners of the great wartime and postwar electronic computers, which have been and are increasingly used to solve a multitude of calculations in fantastically brief periods. U.S. military ballistic research laboratories have been using the large electronic computers since 1947, when the first ENIAC was designed and built at the University of Pennsylvania especially for integrating ballistic trajectories.

World War I seemed to have demonstrated that the submarine could be controlled, though at enormous expense and trouble, and the British were inclined to make light of the submarine threat at the beginning of World War II. In fact the early months of the war saw many U-boats sunk and the shipping losses kept at levels that seemed not too alarming. The Germans had developed a tricky magnetic mine, but the British had developed a countermeasure for this even before the mine was used. The answer was a "de-gaussing belt" consisting of cables around the ship carrying an electric current which neutralized the magnetic effect of the hull.

With the fall of France the whole strategic picture with regard to submarine warfare was transformed. The Germans now had an ocean front extending 2,500 miles; there was no bottling up the U-boat with mine barrages, and they cruised virtually unimpeded over the whole surface of the Atlantic and Mediterranean. Neither side had gone into the conflict prepared for intensive submarine warfare, for the Germans had only twenty 500-ton and ten 750-ton U-boats. But once their rapid building program got under way they were launching twenty submarines a month. Admiral Doenitz said in 1940: "I will show that the U-boat alone can win this war. Nothing is impossible to us."

Tactics changed. Whereas in World War I the submarine commanders had worked as individuals, now all their activities were controlled by an admiral on shore who was informed by reconnaissance planes of the exact positions of the convoys to be attacked. They often worked in packs, usually attacking at night on the surface as torpedo boats and keeping submerged in the daytime to avoid air attack.

The British were hopelessly inadequate in escort vessels; they went to war with 180 destroyers, though at the end of World War I they had from four to five hundred available. France had only fifty-nine destroyers, and losses during the first year of the war were high. Sinkings amounted to

515,000 tons in March, 1941, and to 589,000 in April. From then to December they averaged 360,000 tons monthly. The shipbuilding industries of Britain and the United States together could hardly replace in a year what was going down every fifteen weeks. In 1942 six and a quarter million gross tons of shipping went down, over 40 per cent of the total loss to submarines during the whole war. These were catastrophic losses, and it is frightening to think what might have happened had the Germans started the war with 300 to 450 submarines, the present size of the Soviet underwater fleet.

At the end of World War I the British had developed a sounding apparatus called Asdic (after Anti-Submarine Defense Investigation Committee) which exploited the piezo-electric effect of quartz crystals. It had long been known that plates of quartz crystal can be made to vibrate electronically at very high frequencies, thus producing trans-sonic or inaudible sound waves which, because of their high frequency, have the quality of being highly directional in both air and water. These waves, which can be sent in any direction at will, will rebound upon striking a hard surface, and the echo can be detected by an appropriately tuned apparatus. The time interval between emission and return indicates the distance of the reflecting object.

The French physicist Langevin had long before demonstrated the possibility of echo-ranging with crystals, and Lord Rutherford and his associates had developed the Langevin method further. Early tests with the Asdic, or echo-ranger, revealed that the ultrasonic waves are reflected by natural phenomena as well as the hulls of submarines, so the instrument was not wholly exact. But as an adjunct to the hydrophone it gave excellent results, and possession of the device had lulled the British into a false sense of security. They had forgotten that the invention required great quantities of destroyers and other craft to carry it and to attack those submarines whose presence it might reveal.

In the United States during the war the Asdic was developed considerably further by the Harvard Underwater

Sound Laboratory, which applied to its group of products the name "sonar," for "sound navigation and ranging."

The first airplanes assigned to hunting German submarines carried only 100-pound bombs unsuited for the task. In the first two and a half years of the war, planes destroyed very few U-boats, and it seemed to be true that, as Admiral Doenitz had said, "An aircraft can no more kill a U-boat than a crow can kill a mole." But in May, 1942, the Wellington bombers were equipped with searchlights for night attacks and had depth charges filled with a new explosive, Torpex, a mixture of RDX, TNT and aluminum which was 50 per cent more destructive than previous depth charges.

RDX, or cyclonite, had been known since 1899, but had been considered too sensitive and too expensive for use in war. The British had learned to desensitize it by mixing it with beeswax, but there were not enough domesticated bees to take care of this particular need. Scientists in Britain pressed the development of RDX upon American Army and Navy chemists. Army ordnance people, having tested it themselves, were hostile, but Rear-Admiral W. H. P. Blandy, Chief of the U.S. Navy Bureau of Ordnance, was ready to push the experimentation. The American chemists who were given the job greatly improved the method of manufacture and developed a substitute for the beeswax; the result turned out to be one of the most useful scientific contributions of the submarine war.

Meanwhile both planes and surface vessels had been fitted out with radar. To counter this the Germans put search receivers on board which made it possible for them to detect when they were being "floodlit" by radar and to dive before being detected on the Allied radar screens. The Allies replied by installing 10cm. radar sets against which the German search receivers, designed to pick up transmissions at 200 megacycles, were ineffective. Once more the Allied planes could dive on the submarines without warning. The desperate Germans believed for a time that the Allies had switched to infrared detection and wasted much scientific effort trying to counter this.

The German admiralty, meanwhile, ordered the commanders to hunt in packs in the 600-mile gap in the mid-Atlantic which was out of reach of the deadly shore-based aircraft. The results were temporary but spectacular. In the first three weeks of March, 1943, Allied losses again reached three-quarters of a million tons. The Allies now used desperate measures to close the patrol-plane gap in the mid-Atlantic. Liberators provided with extra gas tanks and microwave radar ran a shuttle service between America and Britain, making it impossible for the U-boats to refuel in mid-ocean as they had been doing, and also helping to warn the convoys and to make attacks on the packs.

An ever-increasing number of escort vessels—destroyers, destroyer-escorts, and corvettes—were equipped with centimeter radar, close-in detection gear, and superior Torpex depth charges. A "spigot" mortar called Hedgehog was developed to throw out a pattern of multiple depth charges ahead of the ship instead of behind, which had required breaking sonar contact. The twenty-four tear-shaped charges were designed to sink through the water quickly and to explode only on actual contact with the hull; thus they could be lethal in spite of being small. If the exact position of the U-boat remained undetected, planes would parachute expendable radio sonobuoys equipped with hydrophones. U-boat noises would activate radio transmitters on the sonobuoys, which would summon planes or surface ships to the spot.

By June, 1943, the U-boats had virtually retired from the North Atlantic. The same tactics were used successfully against submarines in the Mediterranean, and Magnetic Airborne Detection was used to cork the Strait of Gibraltar. Grand Admiral Doenitz, boasting no longer, wrote frankly on December 14, 1943: "For some months past the enemy has rendered the U-boat ineffective. He has achieved this object not through superior tactics or strategy but through his superiority in the field of science; this finds its expression in the modern battle weapon—detection. By this means he has torn our sole offensive weapon in the war against the Anglo-Saxons from our hands. It is essential to victory that we make good our scientific disparity and thereby restore to the U-boat its fighting qualities."

The German scientists were by no means idle. They equipped the U-boats in 1944 with radar to detect approaching planes and with Naxos search receivers designed to pick up 10cm. radar transmissions. They applied to their U-boats a Dutch invention called the *Schnorkel,* a retractable air intake and exhaust pipe which made it possible for the U-boats to run on their Diesel engines while submerged at periscope depth, and to charge their batteries while hidden from the planes. They could run without surfacing for days at a time, though the crews suffered much discomfort from the constantly varying air pressure as the *Schnorkel* valve opened and shut. The U-boats were also equipped with antiaircraft armament to shoot down attacking planes.

None of this was enough. The intensive campaign against the submarines was finally so successful that they were absolutely unable to interfere with the invasion crossing. And American shipyards were turning out a million tons of shipping a month, making up for past losses and providing an ample supply for the Pacific war.

Some of the scientific devices used against enemy submarines were also put to use in a reverse fashion to perfect the safety and increase the offensive capability of the Allied submarines. The bathythermograph, for example, perfected by the Woods Hole Oceanographic Institute, became a standard instrument for determining the acoustical character. of the water through which our own submarines had to travel, and was useful in suggesting the maneuvers best calculated to provide safety against the Japanese.

American torpedoes, particularly those intended to be dropped from planes, were much improved by American technicians. The Japanese had developed a superior torpedo; it used pure oxygen under compression instead of air for combustion of its fuel and was able to develop at full speed over 300 horsepower. Because it was run mostly on steam, which condensed in the water, it left only a trace of wake; this made it much more difficult for ships to spy an approaching "fish" in time to maneuver out of its way. In torpedoes as in few other things, Japanese technology was for a time superior to the American, but in the later months of the Pacific war the gap was closed and the situation reversed.

American torpedo bombers had proved to be extremely vulnerable in the beginning of the war because they had to come in close to the target to make successful torpedo launches. In the Battle of Midway the Japanese had shot down every plane in Torpedo Squadron Eight, and the guns of the *Scharnhorst, Gneisenau,* and *Prince Eugen* had shot down every torpedo bomber attacking them in the Channel in 1942. A torpedo was needed which could be dropped from relatively high altitudes without losing its fins or suffering other damage.

Scientists at the California Institute of Technology, using a high-speed water tunnel and a 300-foot torpedo tube erected at Morris Dam, were able to throw new light on the behavior of underwater projectiles. Eventually a new torpedo was developed. It could be dropped from a high altitude at considerable speed into either shallow or deep water, it did not splash or roll upon striking the water, and it would run a straight and true course to the target. Finally, the torpedo was given a sorely needed "influence exploder." This utilized very sensitive electrical components and some of the parts developed for the VT fuse, but it became available too late for use in the Pacific war.

The Germans developed a deadly acoustic homing torpedo, the "Gnat," or "Wren," which was designed to home on the high-pitched sound of an escort vessel's propellers. They introduced it in August, 1943, but the Allies had had advance information about this torpedo and NDRC scientists had been able to develop a countermeasure which was ready for use before that date. It was called the Foxer and was towed astern of the ship to provide a better attraction than the ship's propellers. Since the war various "homing" devices which seek out the target have been perfected for American torpedoes, and propulsion techniques have been so improved that the torpedo leaves no wake whatever.

Controversy continued throughout the war among military men and scientists concerning the relative merits of incendiaries and high-explosive aerial bombs. Many felt that incendiaries provided a much more valuable bomb load, and they were later proved to have been right by the findings of the U.S. Strategic Bombing Survey. Against targets classified as really inflammable, the M-47 incendiary, weighing 70 pounds, was twelve times as effective bomb for bomb as the 500-pound High Explosive, and one and a half times as effective against targets classified as fire resistant. The Germans had had far greater success with incendiaries in the blitz over London than they had realized, but they did not continue to exploit the weapon.

The 4-pound British magnesium bomb was an efficient incendiary weapon, but unfortunately there was a shortage of magnesium. The Americans developed as a substitute the 4-pound thermite bomb. The British had also made jellied gasoline with rubber, and it was generally recognized to be an excellent incendiary because of its easy ignition, high heat of combustion, and controlled burning rate. But when Japan's conquests cut off the rubber supply, it was essential to find a new formula. Scientists at Harvard and on the staff of Arthur D. Little, Inc., and Nuodex Products Company, investigated the potentialities of aluminum naphthenate as a thickening agent for gasoline and developed Napalm.

The M-47, a 70-pound incendiary bomb using this gasoline jelly, was developed by the Chemical Warfare Service, and Harvard scientists later improved it by adding an inner core of TNT surrounded by white phosphorus. Since a rain of incendiary bombs could mean a real hazard to formation flying, they were produced in "aimable clusters," which meant that they would fall unopened with the same trajectory as a large demolition bomb to within a few thousand feet of the target, and then burst open, scattering the small bombs in a deadly shower. By the end of the war some thirty million of these M-69 bombs had been produced.

On January 6, 1945, two hundred and seventy-nine bombers carried out an attack with the M-69 incendiaries against Tokyo. They loosed 1,900 tons. The city, as one pilot reported, "caught fire like a forest of pine trees." Later the 20th Air Force stated that "Never before or since has so much destruction resulted from any single bombardment mission regardless of the number of airplanes involved or the types of bombs employed." Fifteen square miles in the center of the city were utterly destroyed by the firestorm.

Major attacks followed on Nagoya, Osaka, and Kobe; then the supply of incendiaries at the bases in the Marianas ran short, and the sorties had to be discontinued from March 18 to May 15. After this date all the major cities of Japan save Hiroshima, Nagasaki, and Kyoto were effectively attacked by incendiaries, coupled with fragmentation and demolition bombs. The air attacks on Japanese cities caused 260,000 deaths and 412,000 injuries and burned out 40 per cent of the built-up area of sixty-six cities, which is to say over two million houses—at less than one-eighth the weight of bombs dropped on Germany.

Napalm was also adapted to flame throwers, giving them a formidable control and power they had not had in World War I. The British Petroleum Warfare Department worked intensively on the problem of flame throwers early in the war and developed the large mechanized flame throwers which were later used by the Americans. With the introduction of Napalm as a fuel, the flame thrower's range and accuracy greatly improved. The back-borne flame thrower did signal service in the Pacific against the strongly entrenched Japanese.

During World War I smoke screens had been used to protect ships against submarine attack and fire from naval artillery. It was a simple matter to cut down the air intake of the furnaces of the oil-burning vessels and produce clouds of dense black smoke. With the coming of the airplane it was no longer easy to use smoke effectively for camouflage, though far more imperative. When German planes first attacked British cities, factory owners were instructed to make as much smoke as possible whenever an air attack was imminent or under way.

When British chemists first turned, under Churchill's orders, to the problem of making better smoke screens, the resultant smokes were poisonous, corrosive, or even explosive. The Germans used chlorosulphonic acid in screening the *Gneisenau* and *Scharnhorst* at Brest. The British used a hexachloroethane smoke at Malta. Neither was satisfactory. The Admiralty Fuel Experimental Station at Haslar developed a successful oil-smoke generator which produced a brownish cloud useful under certain circumstances. The best that the Chemical Warfare Service of the U.S. Army had at the beginning of the war was a relatively primitive oil-smoke pot, not unlike the smudge pots used in citrus groves.

Irving Langmuir, a Nobel prize chemist at General Electric, and Victor LaMer, at Columbia, worked on the problem by going to the fundamentals; they studied aerosols—suspensions of particles of liquids or solids in air—and their relation to the scattering of light. They asked in advance exactly what a screening smoke ought to do, cut off all the light or simply confuse the vision. Langmuir devised a generator which used highboiling fractions of petroleum, producing small droplets and blowing them apart fast enough so they would not coalesce. Later it was discovered how to produce this type of smoke for long periods without forming coke and tar, and without danger of spontaneous ignition to the oil vapors.

Smoke generators of considerable variety were produced by the thousand and used successfully overseas. They seem to have helped save the Anzio beachhead and they assisted the Allies in maintaining regular supply routes to ports in North Africa. Generators screened the Normandy beaches, and a huge smoke screen prevented the Germans from seeing the preparations for crossing the Rhine in the late winter and spring of 1945. Smoke had to be used with care, however, for it could easily become a hindrance and confuse friendly troops and aircraft as well as those of the enemy.

THE COMING OF THE BALLISTIC MISSILE

World War II saw the reappearance in many forms of an old weapon that had been almost completely abandoned for a hundred years, the self-propelled projectile called the rocket. It saw the development, too, of missiles which are often confused with rockets, like the German "buzz bomb," the V-1, which is equally well described as either a flying bomb or an unmanned airplane designed for a single one-way mission. The word "missile," which can properly apply to a hurled stone, or a bullet, or even a bomb dropped from an aircraft, has become peculiarly narrowed in our time, and usually applies specifically to flying weapons which are both unmanned and self-propelled, and which may be of the ballistic or non-ballistic type. To confuse the semantic problem further, we have guided and unguided missiles, the former having some kind of guidance after they leave the launching device, the latter being aimed like a bullet from a gun.

The rocket is a *ballistic* missile which, after its engine has stopped functioning, either because its fuel supply is burned up or because it is shut off, continues on its path through space entirely on its own momentum, following a trajectory which, like that of any freely flying object, tends to be parabolic. The other kind of missile, like the V-1 (or the more recent Snark or Hercules) does not describe a parabola at all but uses wings, or surfaces analogous to wings, to gain lift while passing through the atmosphere. This latter type is almost always "air-breathing," that is, it sucks in air to burn its fuel, just as do almost all powered aircraft.

The ballistic missile, or rocket, carries not only its fuel but also a supply of oxygen for burning that fuel, just as gunpowder and the modern gun propellants and explosives have always contained within themselves the oxygen for their own combustion. The ballistic missile, if its range and therefore its maximum ordinate are great enough, may thus have a trajectory of which far the greater part lies outside the atmosphere. Either type of missile may be of the "guided" variety, and the guidance may be either external or internal, or a combination of both. The V-1 was internally controlled, like the old-fashioned torpedo, with gyros set before launching. With external control, the missile can be directed either by the sender (through radio or radar-beam control), or by the target, through homing devices which may depend on radar, infra-red radiation, or possibly even acoustic signals. Combinations are possible, and there is at least one kind of short-range modern rocket that is controlled electrically through wires it unrolls in its flight.

German military officials began experimenting with rockets as early as 1927; the British were at work on them in 1936 under the direction of Sir Alwyn Crow; the first to employ them successfully in war were the Russians. Though the Smithsonian Institution had experimented to some degree with rockets during World War I under the direction of Robert H. Goddard, there was no serious research effort with military rockets in America until after July, 1940. Goddard, a physicist at Clark University, was the leading figure of his country in rocket research between the wars. Some of his patents had features used later by the Germans in the V-2. He had urged in Washington the development of rockets of the V-2 type, but until 1940 he was not taken seriously.

Basically the rocket is a tube, closed at one end and open at the other, provided internally with a propellant. When the propellant is ignited, the gas formed rushes out under great pressure through the open end, its reacting force being exerted against the closed end. The simplicity of the rocket has always been alluring to inventors, but they were stopped over and again by the lack of a suitable propellant, or of suitable control over the burning process, which amounts to nearly the same thing. The fuel must burn fast enough to give sufficient thrust to lift the rocket vertically (after which the rapidly diminishing weight of the rocket as fuel is burned helps in its acceleration), but not so fast as to give an explosive and thus erratic impulse. The subsequent rate of fuel combustion must then be accurately predictable or accurately controlled. The problem of control is much more difficult than in the gun because most of the combustion and thrust takes place after the rocket leaves its launching device.

One of the rocket's chief virtues is that it exercises no backthrust or recoil upon the frame which launches it. Therefore it requires no heavy gun to discharge it, but simply a frame to hold it and perhaps to guide it during the initial phase of its flight. This means that projectiles of fairly large caliber can be discharged from light aircraft or from small naval vessels like landing ships. For example, in World War II German fighter planes used against our bombers a rocket projectile of 8-inch caliber, whereas the largest gun ever fired from an aircraft was a specially built 75mm. (2.95-inch) weapon used in some American B-25's during World War II and subsequently discarded because of its weight and recoil problem.

Early rockets were cursed with inaccuracy. Nor did they have the kinetic energy necessary for penetrating armor; but once the "shaped charge" was adopted, as in the bazooka, the projectile could blow a hole in armor by virtue of the peculiar mechanics of its own explosion against the armor face. Accuracy was improved by controlling the burning rate. World War II saw surface-to-surface rockets as well as air-to-air, air-to-surface, and surface-to-air types. Among these were both guided and unguided varieties. The Russians used surface-to-surface rockets with success as early as 1941, and their rocket barrages are said to have been decisive in the Battle of Stalingrad. Their standard rocket launchers were 16-tube 132mm. and 12-tube 300mm. weapons mounted on trucks. The Japanese developed a rocket to increase the final glide velocity of their suicide bomber planes.

British rocket research was well advanced by the time war broke out; it continued throughout the war. Twenty-two different kinds of rocket weapons were approved for British services. Co-operation with American scientists was thoroughgoing, and one of the most successful results was the 5-inch, high velocity aircraft rocket, the HVAR, which came to be called the Holy Moses. Designed for a good underwater trajectory at the end of its flight through air, it was used with success against submarines. It was also used in attacking enemy shipping, for supporting landing forces, and for knocking out pillboxes and coconut-log fortifications in the Far East. It could penetrate an inch and a half of steel armor and a substantially thicker slab of reinforced concrete. A single fighter equipped with 5-inch rockets could fire a salvo comparable to that of a destroyer.

Rockets were used for strafing during the invasion of Europe and were especially effective in supporting the breakthrough at St. Lô. The bazooka, a portable anti-tank and anti-pillbox weapon, became extremely popular. It fired a rocket with a shaped-charge warhead 2.36 inches in diameter and 21.6 inches long. It weighed only 3.4 pounds and was fired like a shotgun, simply by pulling a trigger. The Allies were deficient in anti-tank weapons, and the bazooka came as a great lift to the morale of the GI in Italy, who needed it as an answer to the ravages of the Mark VI tank. General Sherman tanks in Germany used the 60-tube "Calliope," which fired 4½-inch rockets at the rate of 120 rounds per minute. Barrage rockets, light in construction, were much used in amphibious operations, particularly in the Pacific, where they proved to be an excellent antipersonnel weapon, keeping the Japanese down after the barrage by the big guns had lifted.

The biggest Allied rocket during World War II was the Tiny Tim, weighing 1,284 pounds, with a propellant charge of 146 pounds, and designed to be launched· from planes. It was more than ten feet long and 11.75 inches in diameter. A squadron of Grumman Hellcats carrying Tiny Tims could fire the equivalent of a broadside from a division of heavy cruisers. The U.S. Navy considered the rocket the best of all airborne weapons and at the end of the war was ordering a hundred million dollars' worth a month.

The Mousetrap rocket, developed for antisubmarine use on surface craft, was fired from a simple multiple-rail launcher pointing forward. It was a good deal heavier than the British Hedgehog projectile, which in its action was comparable to a gun (though the projectile fitted outside and around a spigot rather than inside a tube). When the Mousetrap launcher was fired, six contact-type depth bombs fell about seventeen feet apart along a line 220 yards ahead of the ship and at right angles to its course.

All these weapons were controlled entirely by aiming the launcher. Few American guided missiles were used in World War II, as their development came too late to be of much importance. Douglas Aircraft developed ROC, a missile which could be slung beneath the wings of existing bombers and guided along its path, which showed up on a television screen. A heat-homing bomb called FELIX developed out of the idea that a ship could be detected at night by its own heat or infrared radiation. The NDRC developed a controlled or "guided" 1,000-pound general purpose bomb with an extended tail which carried a flare, radio receiver, gyrostabilizer and rudders for steering. This was called AZON. It was designed for alternative control by radar, infrared homing, television, or direct-sight steering. It was used for precision bombing in the Brenner Pass, on the Danube River locks, on the Seine bridges, and on bridge communications in Burma.

BAT, the first completely automatic target-seeking guided missile developed by the Americans, was a glider bomb which located its target and steered itself to it by radar. It destroyed considerable Japanese shipping after May, 1945.

The German V-1, or flying bomb, and the much more dangerous V-2, a long-range rocket, were remarkable engineering successes that dwarfed comparable feats among other nations. The V-1 was a pilotless, jet-propelled, gyrostabilized airplane or winged bomb. It was controlled in flight by an automatic pilot and various clockwork devices. It had a wing span of 16 feet and was about 25 feet long. Its warhead consisted of a ton of high explosive, and it had a maximum velocity of 350 to 400 miles per hour and a radius of 150 miles. Its fuel consisted of a liquid hydrocarbon carried in tanks, which combined with air admitted through flap valves in front of the combustion chamber. It was propelled by successive ejections of gas from this chamber. About 7,400 were launched from France and 800 from Holland. Some 2,300 got through to the London region. About 7,800 were launched against continental targets, chiefly Antwerp.

The Allies, who knew of the V-1 from intelligence reports, made feverish advance preparations to counter it, including the bombing of Peenemünde and other German rocket-research centers as well as the launching sites. Though the experimental work was unaffected, the bombing of the launching sites was of somewhat more value. The Germans had hoped to deliver 5,000 a month, but because of the bombings only 10,500 were launched against Britain in an 80-day period. The best the British could do was to try to shoot them down, either with antiaircraft guns or fighter craft. Their antiaircraft fire was surprisingly successful, thanks to the combination of the SCR-584 radar, the M-9 director, and the proximity fuse.

In the beginning the V-1 did immense damage, but the antiaircraft guns were redeployed from London to the coastal area and the gunners became ever more successful in bringing them down, as did the fighter pilots assigned to the job. Examining only the last four weeks of the 80-day period of attack, we find that 24 per cent of the V-1's fired were destroyed in the first of these weeks, 46 per cent in the second, 67 per cent in the third, and 79 per cent in the fourth and final week.

The V-2, the long-range rocket, was an immensely more portentous invention. This was a 47-foot projectile weighing 15 tons, with a warhead of 2,100 pounds of explosive. Its maximum velocity near the end of its flight was 3,500 miles an hour, and it had a maximum range of 200 miles, with a trajectory rising to 70 miles of altitude. Steered by fins working in its jet stream, it was a complicated projectile—often erratic and inaccurate, but with immense potentiality. The fuel consisted mainly of 7,600 pounds of alcohol and 11,000 pounds of saturated hydrogen peroxide to provide the oxygen.

Against this rocket with its enormous speed British defenses were absolutely helpless. None of the clever contrivances which were used with such success against the

V-1 was of any use against the V-2. Being guided only at the beginning of its flight while its engine was operating, it was immune to enemy jamming, and it was too fast for interception by antiaircraft projectiles or airplanes. The best the Allies could do was to drop 100,000 tons of bombs in the vicinity of the launching sites, which were extremely well camouflaged and hard to hit. The only real defense was the capture of those sites. Had not the invasion of Europe already been successful before the V-2 launchings began, the invasion preparations—according to some opinions, including that of General Dwight D. Eisenhower—might well have been seriously hampered.

On the other hand, its accuracy in the area of the target left much to be desired, especially considering the non-nuclear character of its warhead. It could be aimed against a city, but, especially at maximum range, hardly against anything less extensive. However, it was the prototype of a weapon which after the war was to be much more accurate, enormously longer ranged, and incomparably more dangerously armed—with a nuclear or thermonuclear warhead.

# 9. The Nuclear Revolution

"One hears a lot of talk," the mathematician David Hilbert is supposed to have said at Göttingen one day, "about the hostility between scientists and engineers. I don't believe in any such thing. In fact, I am quite certain it is untrue. There can't possibly be anything in it, because neither side has anything to do with the other." Whether true or not, the anecdote suggests why we can speak of scientists as having rather little directly to do with the progress of military technology prior to the coming of the atomic bomb. The remarkable advances in pre-atomic technology during the nineteenth and twentieth centuries were, with a few notable exceptions, the work of engineers utilizing the theories of scientists, or of scientists temporarily working as engineers or inventors under the pressure of war.

The coming of the atomic bomb changed all that. Besides being the most revolutionary military development of modern times, if not of all time, it was the first in which the very boundaries of scientific knowledge were pushed outward on a grand scale in the pursuit of a weapon. Of course an enormous amount of engineering ingenuity and effort was also necessary to the accomplishment, but one sees in this instance scientists pacing and overseeing a major development with their eyes fixed on the weapon that was to issue from it.

Where does the atom story begin? The discovery of radioactivity by H. Becquerel in 1896 led directly to the researches of Pierre and Marie Curie with radium, from which they concluded that the element that was emitting so strange a form of energy was at the same time transmuting itself into another (and somewhat lighter) element, lead. The old laws of the conservation of energy and of mass began to yield to new conceptions which postulated an equivalence between mass and energy. As early as 1905, Albert Einstein, in his great formulation of the relativity theory, provided us with the famous formula $e = mc^2$. This formula indicated for the first time how the sun and the stars might go on producing and radiating their tremendous energy for billions of years; for since the constant "c" represents the speed of light, which is a number as large as $3 \times 10^{10}$ cm./sec., and since that number is squared, we see that the transmutation of very little mass can account for the production of a vast amount of energy.

An anecdote gives us a good starting point for the development of nuclear weapons proper, and, appropriately, its time is set towards the end of World War I. The great British physicist Ernest Rutherford had been appointed to serve on a committee to find new ways of dealing with enemy submarines, and when he was chided one day for having been absent from a meeting, he is supposed to have replied: "Speak softly, please. I have been engaged in experiments which suggest that the atom can be artificially disintegrated. If this is true, it is of far greater importance than a war." The insight and the conviction were certainly right, but the statement itself is clearly wrong. His discoveries could not be more important than a war because they have made war so much more important.

The results which Rutherford achieved in his researches at the time were published in June of the following year in the *Philosophical Magazine*. They indicated that by bombarding atoms of the element nitrogen with alpha particles (which are the nuclei of helium atoms), he had caused some of the nitrogen atoms to break down into atoms of oxygen and hydrogen. This was the first instance of elements being transmuted by man, for what the Curies and others had studied was natural or spontaneous transmutation.

At that time there were three main centers of atomic research in the world; two of them were the preserves simply of a single outstanding scientist together with his students. It was Rutherford who put Cambridge University on the map, and Niels Bohr who did the same for Copenhagen. The third place, Göttingen, in Germany, had a somewhat more numerous group of physicists and mathematicians; its leaders were Max Born, James Franck, and David Hilbert. It was to Göttingen that J. Robert Oppenheimer as well as many other young American physicists were to come to get their main training.

At Copenhagen, Göttingen, and of course elsewhere, the responses to the findings in Cambridge were immediate. There was at once the recognition that the world of physics was on the brink of revolutionary and even potentially dangerous discoveries. Nothing of quite comparable importance happened during the 'twenties, which were really a decade of preparation for what was to come. In 1927, however, at Göttingen, the young Austrian Fritz Houtermans and the Englishman Geoffrey S. Atkinson postulated the theory which correctly attributed the energy of the sun and the stars to the fusion of the lighter atoms. This theory, which was later to lead to the hydrogen or thermonuclear bomb, was refined in the 'thirties by Hans Bethe to the now generally accepted concept that the energy of the sun proceeds from a whole cycle of nuclear changes involving carbon, nitrogen, hydrogen, and oxygen and leading eventually to the formation of helium, the name of which (derived from the Greek for "sun") incidentally reflects the fact that it was discovered spectroscopically in the corona of the sun before it was ever found on earth.

The next step of real consequence, though its importance was not immediately appreciated, was the discovery of the neutron. In 1930 W. Bothe and H. Becker in Germany found that if the alpha particles emitted by polonium were permitted to fall on certain light elements, specifically beryllium, boron, or lithium, an unusually penetrating radiation resulted. Two years later Irène Curie (the daughter of Marie) and her husband F. Joliot showed that if this radiation fell on hydrogen-containing compounds like paraffin, it ejected protons of very high energy. Apparently something more than gamma rays were involved. Later in 1932, James Chadwick, working in the Cavendish Laboratory in Cambridge, performed a series of experiments which enabled him to prove that the new radiation consisted of uncharged particles of approximately the same mass as the proton.

The neutron, which exists in the nuclei of all atoms other than ordinary hydrogen, and usually in more than twice the numbers of the protons in the same atom, was to provide the key to atomic fission, and for two reasons. First, the neutron, being without an electrical charge (unlike the alpha particle), is not repelled by the nuclei of atoms, all of which are positively charged. It thus provides a particle for the bombardment of nuclei which, unlike gamma rays or even beta rays (which are free electrons), has appreciable mass. Second, one of the effects of bombarding some nuclei with neutrons is the release of other free neutrons (all of which have great kinetic energy upon release); the neutron thus provides means for a "chain reaction."

As early as October, 1933, the idea occurred to the young Leo Szilard that "a chain reaction might be set up if an element could be found that would emit two neutrons when it swallows one neutron." He even began as early as 1935 to question his scientific colleagues about the advisability of refraining for the time being from publishing the results of their current researches! To his far-ranging mind the atomic developments would probably have appeared dangerous in any case, since this was the time of Hitler's Third Reich, from which Szilard himself, though Hungarian-born, was a refugee.

The accession of Hitler to power in January of 1933 was to have another effect besides that of producing the war that was to hasten the development of nuclear weapons. Hitler's special fanatic hatred of the Jews was to guarantee that the bomb would first be made in the United States and not in

Germany. For reasons which, considering the low total number of Jews in the world, a sociologist would find difficult to explain, an extraordinarily high proportion of the world's leading physicists at that time were Jews. At the time of the accession of Hitler, a very significant proportion of these were either German nationals or were in any case living in Germany. Besides men of an older generation, like Albert Einstein, their number included men like Max Born and James Franck—two-thirds of the great triumvirate at Göttingen—and others who were later to become famous to the outside world, like John von Neumann, Edward Teller, and Leo Szilard. In another part of the Rome-Berlin axis was Enrico Fermi, the leading Italian physicist, also a Jew. Niels Bohr in Copenhagen, later to be overrun by Germany, was half-Jewish. These and many others were to push the last stages of the developments which led to the bomb in the United States rather than in the lands which they had previously called home.

The next step of crucial importance was the discovery by Fermi and his collaborators, in Rome in 1934, that when certain metals were bombarded with neutrons the resulting radioactivity was likely to be a hundred times greater if the neutrons had previously been slowed down by water or paraffin. Here was the chance discovery of the "moderator" that was later to make the controlled chain-reacting pile possible. Fermi, who was systematically bombarding one element after another with the newly discovered neutron, made another startling find when he finally reached uranium, the last natural element in the periodic table. What he found made him believe that certain new "trans-uranic" elements had resulted from his bombardment. Perhaps they had, but there is now no doubt at all that he had spilt the uranium atom and was probably the first to do so.

During the same year, the hypothesis that the heavier elements could be broken down by bombardment with neutrons into isotopes of lighter known elements was advanced by Ida Noddack, on the distaff side of a husband-wife team of Czech physicists, but Fermi did not take her view seriously. He was convinced that, considering the tremendous binding energy of the nucleus, the neutron simply did not have the energy to accomplish so mighty a task. In this respect he was supported by Otto Hahn of the Kaiser Wilhelm Institute at Berlin, who was acknowledged as the leading expert in the world on radium. Hahn even refused to make reference to Ida Noddack's hypothesis in his own publications for fear, as he put it to her husband, of making her look ridiculous.

Next followed a kind of comedy of errors, in which important experiments by that other great woman physicist, Irène Joliot-Curie, were consistently discounted by still a third woman among leading physicists, Lise Meitner, who despite her "non-Aryan" blood was permitted for some time to continue work with her close collaborator Otto Hahn at the Kaiser Wilhelm Institute. Each of the protagonists had her supporters, and strong disagreement developed about the reliability of the experiments going on in Paris, where the claim was nothing less than that the bombardment of uranium atoms with neutrons was producing a new substance that resembled lanthanum, an element with an atomic number of 57 and an atomic weight of about 140. To accept the claim was, of course, to allow that the uranium atom was being split.

Finally, in 1938, on the publication of a third paper by Madame Joliot-Curie, which summarized and expanded her startling findings, Hahn was provoked by his new collaborator, F. Strassmann (Lise Meitner having meanwhile been forced to leave Germany), to repeat and check her experiments. Just before Christmas of that year he and Strassmann were finally able to send off for publication a paper which generally confirmed Mme. Joliot-Curie's results. However, from their more precise analysis (the amounts of the new element they were examining were of course submicroscopic) they were led to assert that the element concerned was barium rather than lanthanum. In all likelihood, both were present. Hahn later recounted that after he had posted the paper he wished he could recall it—its conclusions seemed too preposterous.

Deeply loyal to his former collaborator, Hahn immediately dispatched to Lise Meitner, now living in Stockholm, a complete account of his new work, not without some fear of her criticism of his results. However, Meitner knew too well the precision of her former partner's work to question its reliability. But as her penetrating mind pondered these results, she began to see something which had escaped even Hahn.

Now comes a deeply moving scene (described by Robert Jungk in his *Brighter Than a Thousand Suns,* to which we are heavily indebted in these pages) in the little village of Kungelv, near Göteborg, a seaside resort which is almost entirely lifeless in winter. Here Fräulein Meitner had come to spend her first Christmas in exile at a small family boarding house, and here she received the news from Hahn. Visiting her at the time was a nephew, O. R. Frisch, himself a physicist and a refugee from Germany, now working in the circle of Niels Bohr in Copenhagen. But he had come to Kungelv not to talk shop but to visit his aunt and enjoy some winter sports. He tried, as he himself later told it, literally to run away from her on a pair of skis as she ran alongside bombarding him with observations and questions. Simply because the ground was flat, she was able to keep up. Finally her ideas penetrated his indifference. Then followed the first of a series of inspired debates between the two, most of which took place in the lounge of the boarding house. In the course of the conversations they gradually worked out the process by which the uranium atom must undergo splitting.

As we have seen, the conviction of researchers up to that point that the kinetic energy of the neutron could not possibly overcome the binding energy holding together the positively charged protons, along with the neutrons, in the nucleus of the atom, had kept several great physicists from seeing the next step or from even reading their own results correctly. The clue to the answer for Meitner and Frisch was the fact that the uranium atom had split into nearly equal parts. Since the elements near the middle of the periodic table have much more binding energy per proton than those near the extremes (and are therefore more stable), one would have expected bombarding neutrons to have chipped off, at most, particles comparable to their own mass.

They concluded—no doubt drawing also upon Fermi's discovery that enhanced radioactivity resulted from bombarding metals with slowed down neutrons—that the shattering effects of the neutron on the uranium atom did not result simply from the kinetic energy of its impact but occurred, rather, because its intrusion into the uranium nucleus (or "capture") activated forces intrinsic to the nucleus which resulted in the splitting—that is, converted a stable into an unstable nucleus which resolved its instability by dividing. They pictured something comparable to the fission by which bacteria cells multiply, and it was this similarity to bacterial fission that prompted them to use the phrase "nuclear fission" in the publication of their conclusions, which appeared in *Nature* in February, 1939.

The authors were of course struck with the tremendous amount of energy released from this nuclear reaction, but as Frisch later acknowledged, he missed the really important question—whether more neutrons were liberated in the process. On this question hinged the all-important issue of whether a chain reaction was at all possible. Nevertheless, the Meitner-Frisch paper put two and two together in a way that enabled the community of physicists to understand the results they had achieved thus far and to set the stage for new discoveries.

## THE WARNING

We are now in the year in which World War II began, and there were physicists who had begun to fear the possible portent of their next discoveries. They recalled that Francis W. Aston, British Nobel-prize chemist, had warned mankind as early as 1922 against "tinkering with the angry atom." Einstein and Niels Bohr were convinced that practical exploitation of atomic fission would never be accomplished, but some of their colleagues were fearful lest the next discoveries would lift the last bars in a gate they preferred not to see opened. Chief among these was Leo Szilard, who had now arrived in the United States.

Szilard, accorded the use of the physics laboratory at Columbia University, borrowed money to obtain the use of a gram of radium with which to make some experiments. His first tests indicated the possibility that nuclear fission was attended by the emission of additional neutrons. His foresight, quickened by his exceptional sensitivity to political affairs, had already embraced the awful consequences of the possibility that there be enough neutron emission to sustain a chain reaction; and without waiting for the final evidence that this was so, he began to urge his scientific colleagues to consider a self-imposed secrecy concerning their future researches.

It seemed to him not altogether out of the question that Hitler's increasing boldness had some connection with the discoveries that had already been published, and in any case the possibility that Hitler might be the first among the political leaders of the world to see the military implications of nuclear fission in chain reaction was simply too terrifying to be borne. Despite the number of scientists pushed into exile (whose published work continued to be available from abroad), Germany probably still had the technological resources to develop a nuclear bomb if science pointed to its feasibility. At any rate, there was enough reason to be concerned with Hitler's winning the nuclear bomb race to justify security steps which in the scientific world were unprecedented and in the opinion of many were shocking.

The opposition to Szilard's proposal was based on two factors, only one of which was likely to be openly acknowledged. The sentiment which over the generations had developed in the scientific world concerning the free exchange of new scientific knowledge and discoveries had become an article of faith among scientists, and was deeply felt by most of them. Governments might keep secret, if they could, the new gadgetry which their military inventors had devised for their armed forces, but these almost invariably concerned merely engineering developments, having nothing at all to do with pure science. Where truly scientific questions were concerned, freedom of communication was not merely the rule but the elementary requirement of what had come to be regarded by most of its devoted adherents as a sacred profession.

Certainly that was the feeling that animated people like Enrico Fermi (now a fugitive from Fascist Italy and a guest at Columbia University) and Isidor Rabi (like Fermi a Nobel Laureate, and host for Columbia to both Szilard and Fermi), both of whom strongly opposed Szilard's proposal for secrecy. But there is another and less discussed side to the scientist's dislike for secrecy. The factor of personal rivalry cannot but affect some of them considerably, particularly since so much recognition is accorded the scientist who gets there first. There are reasons for the severe conventions which require due credit in scientific publications to the work of one's precursors.

One of the people to whom Szilard wrote his proposal was M. Joliot-Curie in Paris, who never replied for the very good reason that he, together with his collaborators (his famous wife had died), was just then on the verge of experimental realization of the chain reaction about which Szilard was so anxious. As Jungk puts it: "Joliot was determined not to be deprived, under any circumstances, of the credit for being the first in this field. When the experiment succeeded a month later, he did not entrust the account of it, as in the case of all his previous work, to a French periodical. He sent his report to the British magazine *Nature*. For the organ in question usually published the work sent in to it more quickly than any other journal concerned with natural science. To make assurance doubly sure that this important 'communication' should arrive in London without fail, in time for the next issue, Kowarski himself [one of Joliot's collaborators] travelled, on the 8th of March, to the airport of Le Bourget . . . and personally supervised the document's deposit in the London mailbag."

The publication of the paper of the Paris group increased the feeling among Szilard's American colleagues against his proposal for self-censorship. Rabi called on Szilard and informed him that if he did not yield on this issue he would probably have to forgo the hospitality of Columbia University. Szilard had no choice but to agree. But in the course of the controversy Eugene Wigner of Princeton made a proposal which was destined to have far-reaching consequences. He suggested that the American government be informed about the status of the uranium investigations and warned of what Hitler might do with such a development if he took it under his control. At this time the outbreak of World War II was only about five months away.

The first attempt to acquaint high-ranking representatives of the American government with the military implications of the recent discoveries failed utterly. Enrico Fermi called on an Admiral Hooper in the Navy Department, armed with letters of introduction, and tried to communicate his important message. Apparently he made little impression. Even a report in the *New York Times* the following month quoting Niels Bohr on the potentialities of a uranium-235 bomb failed to arouse any interest. Nor is this really surprising when one considers on the one hand the very limited state of knowledge at the time, and on the other hand the really stupendous conclusions that nonscientists were being asked to accept.

It happened that among the handful of leading scientists in agreement that the American government should be informed—which in addition to Szilard and Fermi and Eugene Wigner included Edward Teller and Alexander Weisskopf—not one was a native-born American, and only Wigner held U.S. citizenship. This was not going to make their job easier. Meanwhile they were receiving confidential —and true—reports that in Germany work was already in hand which reflected official government connection with the uranium problem. They did not know that the discussions in Germany had hardly mentioned a bomb but had been largely confined to the possible exploitation of atomic energy as a fuel for motor vehicles.

Dr. S. Flügge, a close collaborator of Hahn's, meanwhile wrote a detailed description of uranium chain reaction for the July, 1939, issue of *Naturwissenshaften,* and shortly thereafter there was published in the *Deutsche Allgemeine Zeitung* an interview with Flügge on the same subject addressed to laymen. These publications could hardly be reassuring to the band of fugitive scientists in America. Shortly thereafter came the dismaying news that the Germans had forbidden the export of uranium from Czechoslovakia, which they had recently occupied.

The Szilard group now conceived the idea of contacting Albert Einstein and enlisting his services, not only because his great name would carry weight with the United States government but also because he belonged to a group of highly gifted people, artists rather than scientists, whom the Queen-Mother Elizabeth of Belgium had especially befriended—and the Belgian government controlled in the Congo the only other known large source of uranium ore besides the mines of Czechoslovakia. Szilard and Wigner visited Einstein in July, 1939, and as a result of their interview it was agreed that a letter should be drafted to the Belgian government with a copy for the American State Department.

This device, Szilard realized, would not really solve the problem, so he enlisted the aid of the exceptionally well-informed and scholarly financier, Alexander Sachs, who enjoyed the confidence of President Roosevelt. Szilard and Teller now persuaded Einstein to draft and sign a letter for communication to the President, which would be put in Sachs' hands. It is noteworthy that the pacifist-minded Einstein later came to regret his action, especially when it became known after the war that the Germans had done substantially nothing to produce a bomb.

It was one of the essential accidents of the chain of events we are describing that Sachs himself, who until the moment of his enlistment in the cause knew nothing of nuclear physics, became ardently interested in his mission. He did not have an opportunity to talk to the President until ten weeks later, on October 11, 1939, and on that occasion the letter which he read and handed to Mr. Roosevelt, plus his own more comprehensive elucidation of the situation, had the effect only of wearying the President. He managed, however, to elicit an invitation to breakfast the next morning. That night Sachs did not sleep at all but paced his room, and also the walks of a park adjoining his Washington hotel, pondering how he might present his case in a manner best calculated to grip the President's imagination.

The device he finally hit upon was to tell the President the next morning a somewhat apocryphal story of how Robert Fulton had offered to build a fleet of steamships for Napoleon which, if the latter had seized the opportunity, would presumably have enabled him to invade and conquer England, so that the whole subsequent course of history would have been changed. Here is a nice example of the forensic merits of not being too accurate or discerning about one's historical facts, because nothing is less likely than that Fulton could have provided the Emperor with any such capability even if he had won full co-operation.

However, the President was deeply impressed with the story, treated Sachs and himself to some old French brandy from Napoleon's time, and called in his attaché, General "Pa" Wilson, to whom he addressed the historic words, while pointing to the documents Sachs had brought: "Pa, this requires action!"

It is not to be supposed, however, that such words could inaugurate intensive government efforts for the development of nuclear weapons. They were the *sine qua non* of further progress, but there was still enormous bureaucratic lethargy and disbelief to be overcome, plus the bare fact that no government funds could be made available for the project before July 1, 1940. The answer to the lethargy was the answer which is always most effective in such circumstances—word (whether true or false) to the effect that others, either allies or enemies, are going ahead with a similar project and making progress. In this case the critical information concerned British developments involving, among other things, some heavy water which had been shipped by Joliot-Curie to England while the Germans were descending upon Paris during the great offensive of May, 1940. The British achievements were later put entirely at

America's disposal, along with some of the British scientists involved. There had also been continuing reports of ominous German developments. The conviction gradually developed among those who had something to do with American nuclear-bomb development that the Germans had a dangerous start in the race, and that it would be all the Americans could do to catch up. This conviction was the key to the intensity of the whole subsequent effort.

## THE CHAIN-REACTION PROBLEM

By July 1, 1940, the following facts, among others, were generally known.

(1) That three elements—uranium, thorium, and protactinium—could be split by neutron bombardment into approximately equal fragments, and that these products were isotopes of elements along the middle of the periodic table, ranging from selenium (atomic number, 34) to lanthanum (atomic number, 57).

(2) That these isotopes were mostly "radioactive," decaying through the successive emission of beta particles (and often gamma rays) to various stable forms.

(3) That fission fragments had very great kinetic energy, the energy being derived from the transmutation of some mass, and that the total energy released per fission of a uranium nucleus was approximately 200 million electron volts.

(4) That while fission in thorium or protactinium could be caused only by very fast neutrons, fission in uranium could be caused by either fast or slow neutrons; specifically, that slow (or "thermal") neutrons could cause fission in U-235 but not in U-238, and moreover that in U-235 slow neutrons had a higher probability of causing fission than fast ones.

(5) That at certain neutron speeds there was a large "capture cross-section" in U-238 for producing the unstable U-239 but not fission, and that U-239 would change by successive beta emissions into the new elements neptunium 239 and then plutonium 239. The latter was rightly guessed to be fissionable like U-235.

This information was much, and yet it was also very little. There were many gaps in what had to be learned before the possibility of a bomb could be established as even feasible scientifically. The existing theory itself was full of unverified assumptions, and the necessary calculations were extremely difficult to make. The substances to be studied often existed only in submicroscopic quantities.

One of the fundamental questions still to be answered was whether a chain reaction was feasible. This depended not only on how many neutrons were generated per fission but also on what might subsequently happen to them. Generally, one of four things might happen to an emitted neutron:

(1) escape from the reacting mass
(2) non-fission capture by uranium
(3) capture by impurities
(4) fission capture

The chain reaction could occur only if the loss of neutrons by the first three events was less than the surplus of neutrons produced by the fourth. Thus, the fact that "one to three" neutrons were emitted per fission did not necessarily promise success.

It was also clear that only one isotope of uranium, U-235, tends to undergo fission whether bombarded by slow neutrons or fast, and that U-235 is found in nature only in a mixture with U-238, the latter comprising 99.3 per cent of the total (with negligible proportions of U-234). U-238 could be split only by very fast neutrons, yet even with these there was a considerable probability of inelastic collision which might effectively absorb neutrons without producing a nuclear reaction. Thus, U-238 was not an appropriate material for bomb manufacture.

The problem of the escape of neutrons from the reacting mass imposed the requirement of having a sufficient or "critical" mass. The critical mass can be defined as that amount in which the production of free neutrons by fission is just equal to their loss by escape and by non-fission capture. It is affected by such factors as geometry (a perfect sphere being the best form in a bomb), degree of compression (significant compression might bring the nuclei closer together, thus giving free neutrons a greater chance of collision with them), and the presence of impurities. Also, there might be "tampers" around the mass to reflect some neutrons back into it. Thus, "critical mass" is a variable, not a constant, though certain arbitrary standards might be adopted for describing it (like the "standard conditions" of air pressure under which water boils at 100° C.).

There was also the question whether, given that a chain reaction in a bomb could be initiated, it could be maintained long enough to permit a substantial proportion of the fissionable material available actually to undergo fission. The tremendous energy generated by the first fissioned atoms would begin to disrupt the process by causing the mass to fly apart. How many "generations" of fissions could be brought about? This involved the crucial problem of bomb efficiency. The inertia of the heavy atoms of uranium (or plutonium) could be counted upon to help; but nevertheless, in 1940 this question of efficiency was a huge unknown factor.

The chain reaction takes two drastically different forms. The first occurs in the fission bomb; it requires the very rapid assembly (to avoid predetonation) of a sufficient mass of either U-235 or Pu-239, or a combination of both, to be above the critical limit. This form of reaction depends upon fast neutrons, and while, as we have seen, U-235 is less likely to split with fast neutrons than with slow ones, we can have enough fast neutrons present to satisfy the high speed requirement. This is the "uncontrolled" nuclear reaction; it is uncontrolled in the sense that the whole of it is over in a matter of microseconds and that it terminates itself, by its very violence.

The other form of chain reaction is the controlled one that occurs in the so-called "pile." This has as its purpose the production not of explosive force but of either a continuing supply of energy in the form of heat, or of the production of the element plutonium, or of both. Here the problem is to build up the flow of neutrons to a level which can be both sustained and controlled.

In both the bomb and the pile, initiation of the reaction can be allowed to depend on stray neutrons deriving in part from cosmic rays but mostly from the fact that U-235, though relatively stable (i.e., possessing a long half-life) undergoes spontaneous fission at a certain statistical rate. However, while this phenomenon is sufficient to start a properly constructed pile functioning, the requirement of efficiency in the bomb makes desirable a very copious infusion of neutrons at the onset of reaction. And if one remembers the discovery of 1930-32 that neutrons could be produced by bringing certain elements into contact with each other (e.g., polonium and beryllium), one can begin to conceive of various possibilities for a bomb "initiator." For a bomb, the spontaneous fission of U-235 or plutonium is in fact a nuisance, because it creates the possibility of a premature explosion. Neutrons can be supplied on demand in other ways.

That the pile operates in a way fundamentally different from the bomb is attested by the fact that it introduces a "moderator." We noticed above that U-235 nuclei are much more likely to undergo fission if the neutrons bombarding them are slowed down from their initially great velocities to so-called "thermal" speeds. Of course, under such circumstances the U-238 nucleus will not undergo fission at all, but since the probability of its undergoing fission even from fast neutrons is rather low, one gets a better neutron pay-off, in any natural mixture of the two isotopes, by enhancing the chances for fission of the U-235, even though the U-238 is 140 times more abundant in nature. That is why the previous separation of the uranium isotopes is unnecessary for a pile but essential for a bomb.

Naturally one can also have "enriched" piles where the proportion of U-235 to U-238 is much greater than exists in nature, and these were later to be produced for the sake of getting considerable power from units of small dimensions (as in submarines); but in the initial work that we are describing, the object was to build a chain-reacting pile from uranium metal, or uranium oxide, which was chemically pure but not isotopically separated. For the sake of getting plutonium, U-238 must be present; and for starting the nuclear reaction which leads from U-238 to plutonium, the slowed-down neutron does at least as well as the very fast one.

It seemed obvious at an early stage that to construct a pile one must need a lattice in which small units of uranium metal, or oxide, were separated from each other by the moderating substance, so that neutrons emitted by fissioning U-235 nuclei would be highly likely to escape the small mass in which they were created and thus to traverse moderating material before encountering another mass of uranium atoms. The concept of critical mass still applied, but to the whole pile and not to the individual pieces of uranium within it. Also, a wholly different order of figures applied to critical mass in a pile as compared to critical mass in a bomb. The moderator, it was clear, had to be formed of atoms which are relatively light, so that much of the velocity of neutrons striking them could be imparted to them, and not given to the absorption of neutrons; the moderator also had to be a liquid or a solid (this let helium out of the running). Deuterium (heavy hydrogen) had obvious advantages as a moderator, which explains the early efforts to produce heavy water—its hydrogen atoms are of the deuterium type—but the cost-time factor, which incidentally let beryllium out, required the pursuit of an alternative; it turned out to be pure carbon in the form of graphite.

Why was it thought necessary to produce a pile at all, since what was wanted was a bomb and not a source of power? The answer is at least three-fold: First, until it was known that isotope-separation processes for uranium would give the desired results, the prospect of using the plutonium manufactured in the pile, and subject to chemical rather than isotopic separation from it, could certainly not be discarded. Second, from the construction and operation of a pile much could be learned that would be applicable to the design and construction of bombs. Third, it was desirable from the point of view of gaining the necessary support for the project to have some kind of chain reaction actually take place at as early a date as possible. As it later turned out, the first self-sustaining chain reaction was achieved on December 2, 1942, more than two and a half years before the first bomb, in a pile constructed under a portion of the football stadium at the University of Chicago.

## THE MANHATTAN PROJECT

In the year and a half following July 1, 1940, there were no such tangible results in the nuclear research as a chain re-action or the production of significant amounts of fission-able material, but there was a considerable gain in knowl-edge and a wholly different spirit of expectation. The third report (November 6, 1941) of the National Academy Com-mittee on the "Uranium Project" spoke of a U-235 fission bomb's being "as sure as any untried prediction based upon theory and experiment can be." It stated that the critical mass of U-235 could hardly be less than 2 kg. nor more than 100 kg., and predicted that between one and five per cent of the potential fission energy present could be re-leased. It also definitely predicted that the separation of the isotope U-235 could be accomplished in the necessary amounts, since of the several methods concurrently under development "at least two . . . seem definitely adequate and are approaching the stage of practical test. These are the methods of the centrifuge and of diffusion through porous barriers [gaseous diffusion]."

Until this time the organization of the project had been under the Uranium Section of the National Defense Re-search Committee (NDRC), which was in turn a part of the Office of Scientific Research and Development (OSRD) headed by Dr. Vannevar Bush. Dr. Bush proposed on No-vember 28, 1941, to set up the uranium program outside NDRC but still within OSRD. At a meeting of the relevant OSRD section (S-1) on December 6, Dr. J. B. Conant, speaking for Dr. Bush, proposed further reorganization of the group in order to produce an "all-out" effort. The next day the Japanese attack at Pearl Harbor brought the United States into the war.

Five months later, Conant in a memorandum to Bush

(May 14, 1942) was able to state that there were five separation or production methods which were about equally likely to succeed: the centrifuge, gaseous diffusion, and the electromagnetic method of separating U-235 from U-238; and the uranium-graphite and uranium-heavy-water pile methods of producing plutonium. All were considered about ready for pilot plant construction and perhaps even for preliminary design of production plants. Some of these methods were bound to prove better than others, but Conant recommended that all be pushed—entailing a commitment of half a billion dollars—because there were grounds for believing the Germans might be ahead of the United States in a similar program and no opportunities for overtaking them must be left unexploited.

Conant's observations and recommendations formed the basis for a report which was sent to the President on June 17, 1942, and which resulted in the formation on the next day, within the Corps of Engineers of the Army, of the famous Manhattan District Project. For security reasons it was named the "DSM Project" (Development of Substitute Materials). Three months later, on September 17, 1942, the Secretary of War placed the newly promoted Brigadier General Leslie R. Groves of the Corps of Engineers in charge of this project. General Groves, who was to see the project through to its close, was chosen not for any scientific qualifications but rather because he had had more experience in supervising building construction than any other officer in the Army, and had in particular directed the erection of the Pentagon. Groves was an officer of quite special and remarkable qualities, which included a tremendous confidence in his own judgment and a passion for "security" exceptional even in a military commander. His mark upon the course of the project was to be a striking and indelible one.

From this time onward the scientists became in a very real sense captives of the enterprise, or simply "scientific personnel," obliged to submit to military forms of control in most respects but especially with regard to secrecy. The degree of control and secrecy imposed is unprecedented in the annals of military technological development, and for the large group of outstanding theoretical physicists it was a wholly new and quite unwelcome way of life. They were of course aware of the need for secrecy; Szilard and his colleagues, as we have seen, had actually proposed it much earlier, on a voluntary basis, for publications. But the military people now in control of the project went far beyond anything the scientists could have dreamed possible. They erected barriers around each individual branch of research so that scarcely more than a dozen of the 150,000 people eventually employed in the Manhattan District Project had an overall view of what was going on, and relatively few more than that dozen even knew that the object was the development of an atomic bomb.

It is a revealing and somewhat wry commentary on the change to point out that it was Szilard himself who was one of the first to fall into difficulties with General Groves over censorship regulations. After the war Groves said about him: "Sure, we should never have had an atom-bomb if Szilard had not shown such determination during the first years of the war. But as soon as we got going, so far as I was concerned he might just as well have walked the plank!"

It is now well known how new centers of research and development were created, essentially isolated from the rest of humanity, and what steps were taken to keep secret the purpose of these new communities. The most famous was Los Alamos, created on what was previously an almost uninhabited mesa in New Mexico. This remote place, under the leadership of J. Robert Oppenheimer, quickly became the seat of a large group of outstanding physicists and other scientists such as had never before been gathered for any length of time. This, of course, is not to say that all the great names in physics and chemistry who were associated with the project were at Los Alamos, since such distinguished scientists as E. Fermi and J. Franck made their contributions at the "Metallurgical Laboratory" of the University of Chicago, and many others made theirs elsewhere.

A great deal of fundamental research in nuclear physics was done at Los Alamos, but the main purpose of the laboratory was to design and construct the bomb or bombs which would contain the fissionable materials produced elsewhere. These materials, as we have seen, could be and were derived in two ways. The first was the separation of U-235 from its sister isotope, the abundant U-238. The second was the production in the chain-reacting pile of plutonium-239, which could then be separated out by chemical means.

The separation of isotopes was deemed difficult enough where it involved separating deuterium from ordinary hydrogen, even though the former has twice the mass of the latter and even though one can exploit differences in behavior which could almost be described as chemical differences between the two. Thus, despite its excellent qualities for the purpose, deuterium was practically shelved as a moderator during the war, being used in only one pilot-model pile operated on an experimental basis.

The separation of the two isotopes of uranium, however, is very much more difficult, since it depends on differences in mass which, proportionately, are very much smaller. The differences are not simply between the two isotopes of uranium metal, but between the molecules of compounds which contain these isotopes. With uranium hexafluoride ($UF_6$), which was used in all the separation processes, the difference is not between 235 and 238 but between 349 and 352.

Nevertheless the leverage afforded by the difference in mass, slight as it is, was exploited successfully in what were actually four different methods. The first and perhaps most important was the gaseous-diffusion process, which depends on passing the gas uranium hexafluoride through an extremely long cascade of barriers involving literally thousands of stages, each of which tends to let the lighter molecule through rather easier than the heavier. The fluoride was chosen for the good reason that fluorine exists in only one isotope, though its extreme reactivity made for serious corrosion problems.

Another method which was to become important in production was chosen relatively late in the work of the project, namely electromagnetic separation. This consisted fundamentally of shooting a beam of ionized uranium particles across a very powerful electromagnetic field which would deflect the beam, deflecting the lighter ions more than the heavier ones. Thermal diffusion, the third method, was utilized for the purpose of enriching the uranium mixture which was subsequently fed into the electromagnetic separation process, thereby greatly improving the productivity of the latter. And, fourth, there was the "centerfuge process; it had earlier been considered very promising, but during the war it was carried only as far as a pilot-plan model and never used for production.

The production of U-235 by isotope separation was carried out in huge plants built in amazingly short time—and designed on the basis of amazingly little experimentally confirmed knowledge—at the Clinton Engineering Works at Clinton, Tennessee, which subsequently grew into the city of Oak Ridge. Incidentally, the word "tube-alloy" was for security purposes applied to the pure but unseparated uranium fed into these plants, and the product coming out (U-235) soon gained the designation "Oralloy," the first two letters deriving from Oak Ridge. The production of plutonium from graphite-moderator piles was carried out also at a huge plant at Hanford, Washington, daringly designed for the purpose after experiments with little more than microgram quantities of plutonium derived from the cyclotron at the University of California at Berkeley. Both Oak Ridge and Hanford were chosen because they were in areas remote from large population centers and yet close to huge sources of hydro-electric power, but the latter site also had the advantage of the cold, abundant waters of the Columbia River for the cooling of the reacting piles.

The story of these extraordinary accomplishments has been told in some detail in that excellent official report prepared by Professor Henry D. Smyth which was published immediately after the war, and republished by Princeton University Press as *Atomic Energy for Military Purposes: The Official Report on the Development of the Atomic Bomb under the Auspices of the United States Government,*

*1940-45.* We are indebted to it for our presentation here.

The Smyth Report revealed much concerning methods of producing fissionable material but little concerning the design and construction of the first bombs. The United States government waited until December, 1960, to release photographs of "The Little Boy," dropped at Hiroshima, and "The Fat Boy," dropped at Nagasaki, and even then did not clarify the difference between the two. It had been officially admitted in 1945 that the bomb dropped on Nagasaki was the more efficient and powerful. In the ensuing years popular magazines speculated about "gun-type" versus "implosion" bombs, implying that the Hiroshima type belonged to the former and the Nagasaki type to the latter, but there was no official release of the actual technology involved, even though it had clearly become obsolete. This curious phenomenon reflects the tendency for secrecy to remain tied in a disproportionate degree to military gadgetry rather than to associated phenomena.

Production figures have, of course, also been kept top secret, but it is now generally recognized that the stockpile must clearly be very large. It is interesting to remember, however, that at the time the Nagasaki bomb was dropped no others were available, which made its use one of the most successful military bluffs in history.

It is remarkable how many of the people who helped build the first A-bomb were confident that it would take the Soviet Union a long time to duplicate it. Certainly General Groves was of this opinion, and even J. R. Oppenheimer, who had led the research at Los Alamos, predicted a long time span. The Russians were reputed at the time to be very backward technologically, but they had at least two inducements which the Allied scientists had lacked in the beginning: the knowledge first that a successful atomic bomb could be produced, and second that a great rival nation had already done it.

Moreover, as the Smyth Report makes clear, even the subsidiary projects of the Allied scientists had usually turned out better than expected. The first graphite pile at the University of Chicago began to reach criticality considerably before the expected level of completion, as was true also of the first pile using a heavy-water moderator, which became chain-reacting when only three-fifths of the expected requirement of heavy water was poured in. Every one of the several methods pushed at least to the pilot-plant stage for isotope separation of U-235 was technologically successful, as was also the method projected for the manufacture of plutonium. Why, then, was it expected that the Russians would take many years to produce a bomb? Certainly it was a widespread miscalculation that points up a useful lesson, which is that underestimation of an opponent's talents may easily result from our being too pleased or too astonished at what we have ourselves accomplished.

## NUCLEAR DEVELOPMENTS AFTER WORLD WAR TWO

The important developments in nuclear weaponry in the seventeen years since the end of World War II might be listed under the following headings: (a) the end of the American enjoyment of monopoly possession, signalled by the Soviet explosion of a nuclear weapon in October, 1948; (b) the development of a successful hydrogen or thermonuclear bomb, accomplished by the United States with its successful test of November, 1952, apparently followed by a comparable Soviet accomplishment less than a year later; (c) the coming of "nuclear plenty" and of a great expansion in the "family of weapons" in the United States, and presumably also the Soviet Union, as a result of continuing production and research; (d) the accession of the United Kingdom and France to the "nuclear club," which framed the question which states would be next; and (e) the marriage of nuclear warheads to missiles capable of ranges up to five and six thousand miles and of fantastic accuracy at those ranges.

The ending of the American monopoly, which we have already commented upon, was in any case inevitable. More technically interesting and also of enormous military importance was the development of the thermonuclear bomb. The problem of producing such a bomb was that of holding hydrogen atoms together under enough pressure and enough heat (measured in millions of degrees, centigrade) for a long enough time to cause them to fuse into heavier atoms, presumably of helium. We have already noted that a related but "controlled" process goes on in the interiors of the sun and other stars, where the required heat and pressures are already provided. Comparable heats and pressures were unknown on earth until the advent of the fission bomb itself, but assuming that some way could be found to direct the heat and pressure of that bomb onto a mass of hydrogen atoms, the time interval allowed by the fission explosion seemed much too short to "ignite" the hydrogen.

Early research seems to have centered on the use of tritium as a means of reducing the time required for ignition. Tritium is that isotope of hydrogen which has a mass of 3 (1 proton and 2 neutrons), but unlike deuterium (mass, 2) it does not exist in nature. It would have to be manufactured by a difficult and costly reactive process comparable to the manufacture of plutonium. Thus, assuming even that a way could have been found to utilize it successfully, there might still be considerable question about the advantages derived from its use as against the use of very large fission bombs of U-235 and/or plutonium. There is, to be sure, an interesting theoretical advantage in the fusion of hydrogen, because a considerably larger proportion of the mass is transmuted into energy (in uranium fission only a tenth of one per cent of the mass of each fissioned atom is so transmuted); but unless a theoretical advantage can be translated into a real dollars-and-cents advantage it is not militarily interesting.

Naturally, the "secret" of the hydrogen bomb has never been officially revealed, but we know officially (from the publication of the hearings concerning the security review of J. R. Oppenheimer in 1954) that the basic idea was something which developed mostly in the mind of Edward Teller, and that its merit lay in its producing a bomb which was not only technically feasible but also relatively cheap, and therefore available for production in substantial numbers. One may presume that it made tritium either cheap to produce or altogether unnecessary. It is possible that the Soviet thermonuclear bomb resulted from a solution quite different from that of Dr. Teller, but one equally good—or at least good enough.

Since their initial appearance in 1952-53, thermonuclear bombs have apparently undergone an enormous diminution in overall weight, so that they are now available for use even in the smaller, intermediate-range ballistic missiles (IRBM). Inasmuch as the basic fissionable materials of nuclear weapons are quite stable (i.e., have long "half-lives"), or for that matter can easily be cleaned chemically after being "poisoned" over the years by their own slight radioactivity, the gradual accumulation of a stockpile was bound in time to convert a period of scarcity to one of plenty, with far-reaching effects upon military planning. However, certain notable events or developments have greatly hastened this process.

One was the continuing research on bomb geometry and technology, which has resulted in greatly increased efficiencies for any given amount of fissionable material. The step to thermonuclear weapons was in a sense only the most spectacular and most publicized of these jumps. Another influence was the Korean War, which caused the United States greatly to expand its rate of production. Up to that time a fairly conservative economic philosophy had prevailed at the Atomic Energy Commission. Production rates were supposed to be responses to military requirements indicated by the Joint Chiefs of Staff, but the arbitrary estimates of these requirements certainly did not develop in a vacuum. The conservatism was reflected in, among other things, an unwillingness to bid too high for raw materials. The fears created by the Korean War changed all this. Meanwhile, thanks to a great deal of prospecting for uranium ores, vast new resources were made available.

"Nuclear plenty" has, along with increased sophistication about bomb design, helped to encourage a considerable diversification of bomb types. When nuclear materials were scarce, they were considered suitable almost exclusively for strategic bombing. Considerations of bomb efficiency as well as dimensions of bomber bays and the payload-carrying capacities of the bombers (originally B-29's) helped determine the dimensions and weight of the early stockpile bombs, which for some years were very close to the size and weight of the Nagasaki bomb. Later, however, the desire to adapt nuclear bombs to light bombers and fighter bombers, and even large field guns, resulted in a considerable diversification of bomb sizes and shapes, mostly in the direction of lesser weights than the original standard bomb.

Then the development of thermonuclear weapons permitted great increases in power, so that one might say that the diversification of bomb types has proceeded dramatically in three different directions: (a) much greater power for the maximum-power bombs within the dimensions adaptable to the largest carriers, i.e., heavy bombers; (b) greater power for any given weight of bomb, which for many uses tends to encourage the design and adoption of relatively light bombs which are nevertheless very powerful; and (c) the adoption of very-small-yield types of bombs intended for specific tactical uses. These include antiaircraft missiles, submarine depth charges, and numerous others. In fact any ordnance requirement which previously called for bombs or gun shells is likely to be one for which nuclear weapons have been considered if not adopted.

The entrance of the United Kingdom and France into the nuclear club has emphasized what used to be called the "4th country problem" and is now called the "5th" or more usually the "$n$th country problem." It is clear that many countries besides the four possessing nuclear weapons enjoy sufficient resources in scientific talent and technological equipment to be able to develop such weapons by their own efforts, and other states might acquire them through some sort of lend-lease arrangement with stronger allies. This raises the nightmarish prospect of bombs falling into the hands of irresponsible governments, or extremely hostile ones like Communist China. The mere expansion in numbers of governments having the power to use nuclear weapons automatically increases the statistical chances that some of them will be poor risks for reliabiltiy.

This fear, which the Soviet Union seems to share with

us at least in part, has already had a considerable effect on disarmament proposals and certainly on bomb-testing moratoriums. It should be noted, incidentally, that several states who have the capability, like Sweden, have deliberately refrained from entering this deadly competition. In these countries councils have usually been divided into pro-nuclear and anti-nuclear parties; external developments could well cause a shift in national decision from being opposed to having the bombs to being eager for them. The reverse is conceivable but much less likely.

Finally, we must consider the effects of the marriage of nuclear weapons to missiles of all sizes. This has meant a military revolution distinctive from and almost comparable to the revolution introduced by the nuclear weapons themselves.

### STRATEGIC CONSEQUENCES OF THE NUCLEAR REVOLUTION

Inasmuch as the Japanese surrender in August, 1945, followed hard upon the dropping of the two nuclear bombs at Hiroshima and Nagasaki, these weapons have often been given the credit for ending the war or even for winning it. From what we now know about events in Japanese government circles at the time, it is fair to say that although the close connection in time between the dropping of the bombs and the surrender was something more than a coincidence, it should not be permitted to obscure the fact that even without those bombs Japan was in a military position her leaders knew to be hopeless.

However, we make this statement only for the purpose of keeping the historical record straight. It has nothing whatever to do with one's estimate of the strategic impact of the atomic bomb, which reasonable people at the outset conceded to be enormous for any future wars in which it might be used. Perhaps the most significant thing about their use against Japan was that the world was thereby granted a demonstration of their awesome power in the most arresting and sobering way possible.

Nuclear bombs made it clear first of all that there could

be no question among reasonable and objective men about the decisiveness of strategic bombing in future wars. The value of strategic bombing had been argued between airmen and members of the other military services ever since the last years of World War I. The Italian General Giulio Douhet had heightened the controversy by his writings on the subject in the 'twenties. One would have thought that World War II would have ended the debate for good, but it only made the problem more ambiguous.

The issues might have been debated interminably following World War II, but the nuclear bomb effectively quashed the question after a relatively brief flurry of argument. There was still—and continues to be, on constantly varying grounds—no end of debate on whether other kinds of military force ought also to be provided and in what strength, but the dominance of nuclear strategic bombing in any war in which it is used is hardly any longer in question.

Another somewhat more sophisticated conclusion, which supported the former, was that the effective range of strategic bombing was now enormously extended. Under World War II conditions, the weight of bombs carried per bomber on any one mission depended on the distance it had to fly, because the lifting capacity of the plane—after certain constants were taken care of, like the weight of crewmen and their gear—had to be divided between weight of bombs (payload) and weight of fuel. If the distance was great the plane might be able to reach the target, but without enough bombs to make the sortie worthwhile. Planes could be made larger, and thus capable of lifting appreciable bomb loads to considerable distances. This could mean, as it meant in World War II, raising effective bombing range from 600 miles to 1,200 miles.

The B-36 was originally developed to carry H.E. (high-explosive) bombs to considerably greater distances than 1,200 miles, but the B-36 was also very expensive to build and to operate. It is doubtful indeed that it could have been an effective bomber with H.E. bombs at the maximum ranges at which it was designed to operate. With nuclear weapons, on the other hand, any bomber was an extremely effective instrument at whatever range it could reach while carrying just one. With the bombers available from the end of World War II onward, this meant that all great nations, and specifically the United States and the Soviet Union, were within effective bombing range of each other.

The coming of nuclear weapons also put a premium on developing new types of carriers, because with so much more effectiveness in the bomb it was worth spending more on each carrier to get higher performance. The modern jet bomber would probably have been developed anyway, but it might very well have priced itself out of the market without waiting to be superseded by long-range ballistic missiles, which themselves would have been much too expensive to develop and build simply for the sake of delivering an H.E. warhead. That the Germans apparently found the V-2 worthwhile gives the measure of the change.

The relevant question could reasonably be put this way: What are the overall costs, including losses to defenses, in putting a certain weight of H.E. bombs on a given target, and do the military results justify the cost in view of alternative military uses of the same dollars and cents—i.e., of the same basic resources in materials and manpower?

Nuclear weapons also made defense against strategic bombing enormously more difficult and disheartening to the defender. The defense of London against the V-1 was considered effective, and yet in eighty days, 2,300 hit the city. The record bag was that of August 28, 1944, when out of 101 bombs approaching London 97 were shot down and only four got through. But if those four had been atomic bombs the record of defense would not have been considered good.

Naturally the attacker might not be able to afford such a rate of loss. Here the question we should ask is the following: How much does the defender have to spend to reduce the effectiveness of the enemy's strategic bombing from value x to value y? Even if the difference between the two can be made appreciable, there is not the slightest doubt that the defender is far worse off in such calculations than he was before the atomic era. It may also be that the best he can do even with very large expenditures is pitifully poor by World War II standards.

The coming of nuclear weapons has meant also that henceforward great wars would have to be fought almost entirely with existing military forces. In such wars, the expansion of war production and the mobilization of material resources that characterized the two world wars on both sides would be impossible. However, if wars continue to be fought as the Korean War was fought, the kind of wartime build-up we have known in the past would still obtain.

Finally, the atomic age has seen the first widespread questioning of the basic utility of war as an instrument of national policy. Clausewitz consistently preached that war makes no sense unless fought for a specific political objective, and that this objective should be allowed to determine the whole character of the fighting. This was an ideal approach which was sometimes catastrophically lost sight of, as in World War I, but the most imprudent nation, pursuing a conflict blindly and needlessly, could nevertheless rise from the ashes. With atomic weapons, the possibility of recovery in a reasonably short time has become dubious. Between opponents who possess substantial stores of atomic weapons and the means of delivering them there can no longer be positive objectives in war, only negative ones, like avoiding being overrun or overwhelmed.

What changes have the H-bombs wrought that were not already imposed by the A-bombs? The answer is perhaps few or none of basic consequence, for the A-bomb revolution was so drastic that no mere multiplication of the bomb's power, even by a thousand times, could compare with it in significance. Thermonuclear weapons have, however, forced home some conclusions that were insufficiently absorbed before. The revolution is now unambiguous and unchallengeable.

Nevertheless, thermonuclear weapons have brought changes in addition to reinforcing those of the original revolution. In discussing these, we may as well take up at the same time the implications of the long-range, or inter-continental, and the intermediate-range missiles (ICBM's and IRBM's), which followed hard upon the development of thermonuclear weapons. These missiles now have an accuracy that was not being predicted a few years ago, but even with this accuracy they remain expensive, one-shot weapons; they therefore make more sense carrying thermonuclear bombs than they ever could have with the pre-1952 fission bombs.

The post-war rockets have achieved "escape" velocities, that is to say, literally unlimited ranges, with payload capacities capable of covering an awesome array of warheads. They have reached such a degree of accuracy in their various guidance mechanisms that the limitations on accuracy tend to be found more in factors outside the rocket, including ignorance about the exact position of the target, than in factors inside it. Propellant fuels have progressed through a period of dependence on liquid oxygen, with its requirement for cooling, into one of use of solid fuels, as in Polaris. The limits of progress on the ballistic missile seem to be set more by what it is desirable to accomplish than by what is possible.

The combination of the thermonuclear bomb and ballistic missile has given a further excruciating twist to the problem of defense against strategic bombing. One is tempted to say that it has made really hopeless what was formerly only apparently so, but one must avoid saying this because there are always some defensive devices which are better than others and maybe even intrinsically worth pursuing, depending on what it is that we want to defend.

The following conclusions are not final or incontrovertible, but it seems reasonable to suppose that long-range missiles with thermonuclear warheads have three consequences: (a) They greatly reduce the efficacy of radar screens and other detecting devices, and also that of the "active defenses," which depend upon shooting down the attacking carriers. (b) For that reason they enhance the importance of "passive defenses," which depend on concealment, dispersion, armoring, mobility, and the like. (c) They enhance the importance of concentrating attention on defending the retaliatory force, especially since such defenses can hardly be applied to cities, and to only a limited extent to the populations within cities.

In defenses against thermonuclear weapons and missiles it is essential to concentrate on what is feasible and worthwhile and let the other things go. The retaliatory force must be defended at all cost; otherwise one has no defense at all, no dissuasion for the aggressive impulses or designs of the enemy. Fortunately this force can be defended, but by measures which are novel, and neither inexpensive nor easy to acquire. Such measures must put a minimum dependence upon warning, and an equally minimum dependence upon shooting down or otherwise destroying the attacking enemy forces. We must depend upon passive defenses which are always in operation.

One of the most significant new developments in this regard is the Polaris-firing nuclear-powered submarine. The first submarine designed and built with atomic power was the *Nautilus,* launched January 11, 1954. This was the first submarine capable of submergence for unlimited periods. There has never before been an instrument of such potential power which was also so invulnerable to detection. One great advantage of this excellent weapons system is that its relative invulnerability relieves us of much of the pressure in a crisis to "hit while the hitting is good."

Today the most important force that a great nation can have, the one indispensable force it *must* have, is its striking force, which is wholly offensive and not at all defensive except insofar as it succeeds in deterring war—or, possibly, succeeds in destroying the enemy before he can retaliate. The latter can be accomplished only if one side has not made his retaliatory force secure. If one or both sides fail to take the necessary and expensive precautions, the situation becomes highly unstable militarily. Where such circumstances obtain, one can hardly speak, as some do, of thermonuclear weapons having "abolished war." On the contrary, in some important respects they tend to make war more likely.

The tremendous effect of radioactive fallout, first revealed in its full dimensions in the March, 1954, H-bomb test, creates wholly new problems in the defense of populations. Until the facts about fallout were released, it was widely believed that while populations in large cities were likely to be destroyed during war, those in smaller towns and in rural areas would remain relatively safe. It is now common knowledge that fallout—the radioactive debris of the materials of the bomb—affects an extraordinarily large area, and that the fallout of many bombs can overlap and increase the intensity of the radiation. Serious students of the problem are now earnestly advocating the construction of nation-wide shelters for populations against fallout. They argue that even if the populations within large cities cannot be saved by shelters, the remainder of the nation's citizens can and therefore ought to be.

Finally, the recent developments in thermonuclear weapons and missiles have given new impetus to the necessity of limiting war. If contests cannot be avoided in some areas, it might be possible to limit them to a military action which is not all-destructive, and therefore absurd. The idea has developed that wars can be fought which avoid strategic bombing, and perhaps nuclear weapons, altogether. The old axiom that modern war is total war is now receiving some serious and long due reconsideration.

This problem is too complex to be discussed in any detail here, but we should repeat that much depends on whether or not the retaliatory forces of both sides are adequately defended. If they are, it is possible to fight limited wars, and in fact senseless to resort to any other kind. If they are not, the reverse is true. Then limited wars of any duration or magnitude become impossible to contain, because it is too dangerous to withhold that great striking force which is terribly powerful but also terribly vulnerable. The importance of protecting adequately the main retaliatory striking force of the nation is at this writing second to no other security question.

# 10. Operations and Systems Analysis, The Science of Strategic Choice

We have in the previous chapter considered some of the advances in military technology since World War II. These in effect have embraced several complete "revolutions," even under the most modest connotation of the term. The changes from nuclear scarcity to plenty, from fission to thermonuclear bombs, and from aircraft and guns to attack and defense missiles of all kinds, argue considerable problems of readjustment, and we are speaking only of the gross changes, not the refinements. When, for example, President Eisenhower announced during 1960 that all of the seven or eight Atlas missiles shot down a 5,000-mile range in the Atlantic had fallen within a circle of two miles diameter, he was not only publicizing a degree of accuracy in long-range missiles which would have been incredible a scant two years earlier, but was also, whether aware of it or not, describing a development which gravely affected the whole crucial problem of the defense of our retaliatory force.

In this development, incidentally, involving as it does the simultaneous perfecting of guidance and of propulsion, we see illustrated the importance of the fact that science and technology have been advancing along a multiplicity of fronts. Each weapons system is likely to become so complex that it must call on many separate fields of knowledge, and it matters much whether the state of the art has advanced adequately in only a few of these fields or in all of them. In recent years the stimulation and mutual assistance across fields has been enormous, and this accounts for much of the acceleration in the advance of science generally.

For one of the fronts on which science has advanced quietly but effectively we have reserved this next to last chapter. It is a fitting culmination because it deals with the application of scientific method not simply to the hardware designed for military purposes but to the whole field of military strategy and tactics itself. In view of some of the traditions inherent in the military art and in the profession which practices it, it is the most novel and possibly the most hopeful development of all.

Near the beginning of this book we quoted Captain B. H. Liddell Hart in a prophetic observation that the military problem had developed in complexity beyond the competence of the military profession. That was in 1935, before the atomic bomb, and even before World War II. No doubt Liddell Hart was right concerning the majority of senior officers of that time—some exalted names came toppling in 1940—but not concerning the best representatives of the profession. Today, however, we can say without hesitation and without animus that the military problem is, even in its stark outlines, not only beyond the competence of any one person or group of persons but beyond the competence of any one profession.

In the past we have had the kind of collaboration between scientists and soldiers which enabled the former to provide the latter with new hardware, which the latter could accept or reject as his insight and experience might indicate. In many instances, because of ignorance or stupidity, the system worked badly; but given reasonable and intelligent men it worked sufficiently well. One can argue that had systematic analysis rather than mere intuition been applied to the choice of certain weapons systems in the past, the results would have been better. It is likely, however, that the gain would have been marginal because the problems were relatively simple.

Today the situation is quite different. Now the soldier must make choices between weapons systems which do not yet exist but which may be developed within loosely predicted time periods according to his choice and support. Whenever he chooses something of certain predicted performance characteristics, he very likely has to give up something else with other predicted characteristics. Each item has its own family of inevitably related other items, all of which have to be bought in a package, and that is why we talk about weapons *systems*.

To take one of the least complicated examples, the soldier may be faced with a choice between two quite different types of bombers. If such a choice looks simple, the simplicity is deceptive. For one thing, the commitment is likely to involve colossal sums and a whole strategic position. But consider how much more difficult is the problem of knowing *whether* to replace a certain kind of bomber with a certain kind of missile—the performance characteristics are hardly comparable, and the advantages are by no means entirely on one side—*to what degree,* and *at what rate of changeover.* If one assumes simply that any missile is better than any airplane for any strategic purpose, and the sooner the changeover the better, one is bound to throw away a lot of money, and one may also end up with a very poor weapons system.

When the military officer was first plunged into involvement with nuclear weapons, he found himself obliged to master a new kind of scientific lore. It was not too troublesome at first, but as nuclear techniques rapidly developed, the problems of choice became serious and difficult. The new promise of missiles added to his difficulties. It was clear that the soldier needed assistance from people who, if not research scientists themselves, were at least trained in the appropriate sciences and able to act as advisors on critical issues of choice between systems. Besides being appropriately trained and talented, they had to be uncommitted, which is to say objective and dispassionate. Such people were indeed available to him within the normal service structure or on an intermittent consulting basis. But, for a variety of reasons, this was not going to help enough.

Meanwhile, however, a movement had begun to develop, of which the RAND Corporation of Santa Monica, California, is perhaps the prototype. The late General H. H. Arnold, as wartime Chief of Staff of the U.S.A.A.F., had concluded that all the scientists who had come to work for the Air Force during the war should not be completely lost to that service the moment peace was established. He was aware, however, that the existing civil service structure could not meet the needs. It was decided that an organization should be set up which would be administratively independent of the Air Force and of the government, but which would be supported by the Air Force and would work on problems relevant to its needs. Project RAND (for Research and Development) was first set up under the Douglas Aircraft Corporation on a cost-plus-one-dollar-fee basis. Within a few years the new organization separated from Douglas and became an independent, non-profit research body.

The other services followed suit, though in distinctively different ways, the Army with its O.R.O. (Operations Research Office) administered by Johns Hopkins University, and the Navy with its Operations Evaluation Group, administered by the Massachusetts Institute of Technology. At this writing, such organizations have proliferated; two notable ones are the Stanford Research Institute, which is independent of any single service, and the Institute of Defense Analysis, which works for the Joint Chiefs of Staff and the Secretary of Defense. All have in common the characteristics that they include people with a considerable range of skills in scientific analysis, that these people have access to classified materials, and that their results are intended for consumption primarily, and often exclusively, by agencies of the government responsible for national security.

What these organizations were able to contribute from the beginning was something called "operations analysis." Actually operations analysis had its roots in old-fashioned staff work and did not become something distinctive from the "my guess is better than yours" system until World War I, but then it began to be applied to strictly tactical problems. The father of operations analysis—if any one person deserves that distinction—is probably the British mathematician F. W. Lanchester, who wrote a ground-breaking treatise in 1916, *Aircraft in Warfare.*

It appears that operations analysis was first applied, as one might expect, to the hunting of submarines. A typical problem can be described as follows: A destroyer has pinpointed the position of an enemy U-boat by running out to the beginning of a wake left by a torpedo fired from the U-boat. By the time the destroyer gets there, however, the U-boat has moved somewhere else. The torpedo commander does not know the exact speed and direction of the U-boat, but he probably does know its top speed, and he also knows the time interval which has elapsed. Question: How should he maneuver in order to maximize his chances of re-establishing contact and making an effective depth-charge attack?

The solution of such a problem involved the application of what came later to be known as "game theory," which differed from probability theory in that it involved not an evaluation of chance but rather of the deliberate and responsive actions of two opponents. It was found that in problems like the one we have described there was usually one best way, and that often that best way was better by a good margin than other ways; it was also found that while the best way might look obvious after it was pointed out, it was not necessarily the one that might suggest itself to the intuition of even the most experienced commander. In this particular submarine problem, for example, it was found by analysis that far the best tactic was for the destroyer commander to make a circle around the beginning of the torpedo wake, the radius of this circle being determined by the assumption that the U-boat was moving in a straight line at its highest submerged speed. This particular tactic, it so happened, was *not* being employed by the destroyer commanders.

After World War II organizations like the RAND Corporation, as well as civilian and military persons of appropriate training within the services, began to work on numerous problems of choice, especially as they concerned choice between weapons systems. This work came to be called "systems analysis." The persons concerned had to be scientifically trained in order to understand thoroughly the state of the art in any of the weapons systems they were examining, and also to be able to evaluate independently the predictions and promises of various contractors. Also, the team involved on any one project had to embrace a range of skills which covered not only the development and production of a new weapons system but also its use and effectiveness under a variety of circumstances. These circumstances might involve political as well as strategic assumptions. With the passing of time a good deal of experience and new insight was gained, and a distinctive art as well as science began to develop.

One of the discoveries of systems analysis was the relevance of the dollar. The layman is apt to assume that in wartime dollars do not or should not count, which in certain limited circumstances may be true. But if we think of the dollar not as a value in itself but as a unit of account—a means of measuring as well as commanding resources—we see that it is of considerable importance even in wartime. In all peacetime preparedness efforts the dollar is of paramount importance, partly because it tells us, first of all, the limits of the total resources available to us. Within those limits, we buy one thing at the expense of another, so that the cost of the thing we buy can be measured in terms of the denial of something else, which is akin to what the economist calls "opportunity cost." One often hears the charges made that, with regard to a particular weapons choice, there has been too much concern with dollars. But the absence of a deep and constant concern with dollars in making choices between weapons systems would argue the grossest kind of incompetence.

Within the limits set by the technological environment, we can have anything we want given only enough time and dollars. Given enough dollars, we can even cut down to some degree on time, through crash programs, the outstanding case being the development of the atomic bomb. A lot of extra money was spent simply to telescope the time required to develop and produce a bomb, which that money did very effectively. By spending money appropriately we accelerate advances in the "state of the art" in any specific field. With dollars we can buy talent for defense purposes, winning it away from other pursuits by higher salaries; and given time and purpose we can also expand with dollars the total fund of talent by encouraging and assisting gifted young people to acquire the requisite training. The latter course the Soviet Union seems to be pursuing much more avidly than the United States.

In comparing weapons systems we need some common base of comparison. We can compare only systems which are intended to fulfill the same or similar functions, and the only basis for evaluating their relative efficiency is their respective money costs in accomplishing a fixed goal. This may seem an absurd idea—it was certainly a revolutionary one—until it is pointed out that money is the only common denominator.

As an example, we return to the relatively simple example of choosing between two kinds of strategic bombers. In bomber A the designers want to maximize range. They have therefore adopted a top speed somewhat below Mach 1 (the speed of sound) in a plane of fairly large size. The designers of bomber B, on the contrary, think it important to have a high dash speed over enemy territory, and propose a small, shorter-ranged plane capable of over Mach 2 speeds for portions of its flight. We assume that the latter plane, being smaller, costs only about two-thirds of the larger.

Even if we decide to buy both types—which is often a way of postponing decision until more experience is acquired—we should still have to determine which to buy in larger numbers. We therefore pick a number of representative targets in enemy territory, say two hundred, and specify the destruction of these targets as the job to be accomplished. We now ask which aircraft can do it cheaper; we do not yet ask which bomber can do the job more reliably, because reliability is also largely purchasable with dollars, usually by buying more units.

If bomber A has a range of 6,000 miles and bomber B of

4,000 miles, bomber A needs refueling only on its post-strike return journey, while bomber B needs it once in each direction. That affects the "time of arrival over target" issue, and may reduce or nullify the advantage of bomber B. What it certainly tells us is that bomber B requires a larger number of "compatible tankers" than bomber A. What looked before like the cheaper plane may now appear the more expensive. It is pointless, however, to compare merely procurement costs. One has to compare the operations costs of each system over a suitably long peacetime period, perhaps five years.

Now we have to consider as best we can how each of the two bombers will fare in combat. There is much experience and information available to reduce the area of sheer guesswork. We are interested especially in the survival expectancy of each type over enemy territory, and for the moment our concern with that question is confined to what it tells us about the number of planes we will need. What we have to find out is how much the greater speed of bomber B is worth in protection. If the enemy relies mostly on interceptors, the bomber's high speed may help a good deal; if he is depending heavily on guided missiles, it may help relatively little. Thus we consider not only his present but also his projected defenses. We will certainly not know as much as we want to, but we will probably know a good deal. We ought not to forget that our decision about bombers may affect his decisions about defenses, but we put aside that question for the moment.

If bomber A relies on a low-altitude approach to target—which its greater range capability may permit it to do—it may actually have a better survival expectation than its faster competitor. Penetration capability is enhanced also by increasing the number of bombers penetrating, or by using decoys to help confuse the enemy's radar and saturate his defenses. We may find that bomber B will outrun the cheap decoys we want to buy, which again reduces its survival expectancy relative to bomber A.

We do not wish to suggest that slower planes are usually better than faster ones, but we do want to make clear that what may look like an obvious advantage in performance characteristics can turn out to be illusory. This point is worth emphasizing because the bias of airmen in the absence of rigorous systems analysis—and sometimes despite it—is always for higher performance characteristics. There is nothing reprehensible about such a bias; it is better than a bias against change, but it must not be too rigid. Good and serviceable interceptors may at times have been phased out at costs of hundreds of millions of dollars in favor of newer models that had only slight performance advantages of marginal value. That is not merely a waste of money to the country; it is a loss of military value to the service concerned, which always operates within tighter budgets than it would like. Possibly the dislocations resulting from changeover have even wiped out the margins of advantage deriving from the performance differences.

We have described enough to show the outlines of a typical though simple problem in systems analysis. The central ideas are these: No weapon can be considered independently of the other weapons and commodities that have to be used with it; all are expected to endure through some period of time and thus require routine upkeep; all these items and considerations involve costs; and therefore relative costs of different systems considered against some common function are basic to the problem of choice between them. The problem naturally becomes harder as the common function becomes more elusive, as for example when we begin to compare long-range bombers with long-range missiles. Ultimately we fall back on informed intuition to settle some of our so-called "planning factors," but it is good to postpone the intervention of intuition as long as possible. This is not because we distrust intuition intrinsically but because the area in which it is obliged to operate for want of analytical foothold is quite large enough already. Intuition in the form of good sense—or perhaps bias—is at work even in those areas which we regard as analytical, and good intuition is priceless; but its reliability is inversely proportional to the burden we call upon it to bear.

It was inevitable that those who became skilled in the

arts of operations and systems analysis would want to broaden the scope of their work. Where they were content originally to consider a problem within the assumptions communicated to them by the relevant service or services, they were bound in time to begin questioning and sometimes remolding those assumptions. From being concerned with strictly tactical matters of a very precise nature, they were bound to become more and more interested in strategic issues of broad import.

The services have naturally looked upon this development with mixed feelings, glad for the assistance but alarmed at some of the conclusions reached—and withal aware of the fact that their status as unique possessors of an esoteric kind of knowledge is increasingly challenged. The response varies with the individual officer, depending upon his character. We should, incidentally, emphasize that we are talking about something that is thus far almost entirely an American phenomenon. Other countries, especially the United Kingdom, have had individual civilian commentators on military affairs, and sometimes very good ones (Capt. B. H. Liddell Hart, despite his military title, is an outstanding example), but only the United States has had large, officially sponsored organizations of scientifically trained civilians who make a life-long calling of the study of tactical and strategic problems. The military do and must retain ultimate control, with freedom to reject or accept any study prepared for them.

Lest the reader become too optimistic about the new gains of science in the field of decision, we have to remind him of certain dreary facts: First, even the best systems analyses are far from infallible, because they are perforce dealing with so many uncertainties; second, not all such analyses are well done, one reason being that talent is a limited commodity; third, even good analyses are often rejected by the military "clients" for reasons good and bad— like lack of funds, or bias. Fourth, and above all, scientific analysis is applicable to important problems, but usually not the most important. The profound issues of strategy and certainly of politics, those likely to affect most deeply the fates of nations and even of mankind, are precisely those which do not lend themselves to scientific analysis, usually because they are so laden with value judgments. Therefore they tend altogether to escape any kind of searching thought. It is also true that the complexity and difficulty of the problems with which we have had to deal have far outrun the development of our techniques for analyzing them.

There are some grounds for satisfaction, on the other hand, that the same kind of ruminating and objective thinking and research that produced the nuclear weapons and missiles which add so much to our own cares is now being directed to the consideration of what we do with them. It is the second best thing to not having those cares at all, but in this imperfect world it should not on that account be disdained.

Fig. 46. German V-2 Rocket, World War II

# 11. Recent Weaponry Changes
# (1962-1972)

In the decade or more since the publica-
tion of the first edition of this book there have been no
*scientific* revolutions in weaponry comparable to those
which produced the two major types of nuclear weapons,
first those of nuclear fission and later those of nuclear
fusion. This was indeed to be expected. The utilization of
nuclear energy, whether for bombs or for power plants,
was a secret long crying out to be discovered. Once it was
fathomed that that is how the stars yield their nearly limit-
less energy, it was not entirely fanciful to assume that a
way would ultimately be found to produce and harness
that form of energy on earth. At present there are no comparable "secrets," certainly none of comparable moment,
blinking their beacon lights seductively to the scientific
discoverer.

Naturally there has been continued improvement in nuclear weaponry, especially in the direction of continued
reduction of weight of the warhead and of continued
specialization of types, the former being important in the
multiple warhead missile and both being important in the
anti-missile missile; but in comparison with the nuclear
developments of the previous two decades, those of the last
decade have not been remarkable. The most interesting
developments in this field are political: the accession in
1964 of Communist China to the "nuclear club"; the agreement of 1963 against nuclear testing in the atmosphere,
signed by the United States, the Soviet Union, and Britain,

but not by France or China; and the Non-Proliferation Treaty of 1968. Equally interesting and significant were the Strategic Arms Limitation Agreements between the United States and the Soviet Union, signed in 1972.

However, in the area of *engineering* refinement based on known scientific principles, the area in which almost all the technological progress in weaponry has taken place through the ages, the last decade has been no less remarkable than preceding ones. The most striking developments have had to do with improvements in missile accuracy, in the design and application of radars, and in computers. Improvements in all three areas are combined in the first anti-ballistic missile system (ABM) alleged by its designers and by numerous other qualified people to be technologically suc- cessful, that is, the system known by the names "Sentinel" or "Safeguard." More recently we have had the so-called smart bombs, or guided conventional bombs, first used in 1972 in Vietnam.

The war in Vietnam, incidentally, unlike previous wars, probably resulted in a net slowing down in technological development in weaponry rather than the reverse. For the most part, refinements in weaponry did not seem to be high on the priority list for the needs of Vietnam—the guided bombs and the new types of underwater mines used in 1972 being exceptional and being also the product of development antedating our major involvement in Vietnam —and the absorption of money and of attention in Vietnam meant a reduced supply of both in the channels of normal weaponry development.

However, before we proceed with a description of these devices and of certain others, it might be well to take up a notable development in strategic thinking during the past decade which has profoundly affected weapons develop- ment. We are speaking of that modification in strategic thought which has resulted in renewed emphasis on the "conventional" weapons of war, inevitably at some cost to the emphasis that would otherwise have been placed on nuclear weapons and associated instruments.

## THE NEW SCHOOL OF CONVENTIONAL WAR THINKING

In the penultimate paragraph of Chapter 9 (p. 267) it was pointed out that "recent developments in thermonuclear weapons and missiles have given new impetus to the necessity of limiting war." The same paragraph talked about the long-overdue reconsideration then being given to "the old axiom that modern war is total war."

Even when that statement was written it was perhaps too lean a remark with which to refer to the considerable amount of thinking that had been going on at least since 1952 concerning the need to limit wars in such wise as to avoid use of nuclear weapons. However, the prevailing view of the authors was that this was a book about weapons and not about strategic thought, and there was no need to complicate things. That may have been a mistaken view even then, and it would be more so now. We could of course merely remark that technological development continues unabated in conventional weapons as well as in nuclear ones, but the reader would be entitled to ask, why? Nuclear weapons are certainly far more efficient engines of destruction than any other kind, and in previous eras that would have been enough to guarantee that they would displace all competing types. But, as some observers remarked when nuclear weapons first appeared, they are perhaps *too* efficient—and therefore hardly the weapons for all seasons. In any event, the quantity and the character of the relevant theorizing that has gone on since 1960 demands at least some brief recounting.

Even before the nuclear age began there had been some, notably the late Sir Basil Liddell Hart, who had cautioned against too great a preoccupation with total or unlimited war. However, these complaints by him and others did not get much attention. Then, the coming of nuclear weapons absorbed the attention of those who by inclination and self-training were competent to think about and to discuss *strategy,* as distinct from tactics and weaponry.

With the coming of thermonuclear weapons in 1952, all

that was changed. Even before the successful test of a thermonuclear device in November of that year, the knowledge that it was in the offing began to stimulate thinking among a few about the need to limit war, at which time it was realized that the ongoing conflict in Korea was an example of the kind of restraint needed. When Secretary of State John Foster Dulles made his famous "massive retaliation" speech in January, 1954, in which he threatened that the United States might choose to counter all aggressions regardless of magnitude with nuclear weapons, there had been enough thinking on the other side of the issue to enable some people to come forward with strong criticisms of the Dulles view. The latter, it might be noted, was simply an expression of President Dwight D. Eisenhower's conviction that the United States could not afford to maintain both a large nuclear capability and a large conventional capability. For one with that conviction, the choice would obviously have to be to develop the nuclear capability. In a world of nuclear weapons, a superpower could not choose not to have them in adequate supply, along with all the means of delivery.

The emphasis on nuclear power was in Eisenhower's eyes primarily an economy measure, fortified by the notion that a President tough-minded enough to threaten use of nuclear weapons whenever aggression reared its ugly head would be able to deter such aggression without having to resort to actual use of any force. Thus, a substantial conventional capability was superfluous. The critics of this view argued that this was unrealistic thinking, that aggressions like that which had so recently taken place in Korea would not necessarily be deterred, inasmuch as the potential aggressors would doubt the American readiness to resort to nuclear weapons in small-scale affairs. And they would be right, the argument went, because the United States under such circumstances ought not to use nuclear weapons.

However, for the time that he remained in office, Eisenhower's view prevailed among the military, where it was in fact applauded, especially by members of the Air Force. The United States Air Force essentially deprived itself of a conventional capability, removing from its bombers the bomb shackles for carrying conventional bombs. During the Matsu-Quemoy crisis of 1958 the U.S. Joint Chiefs informed the President that the United States had no capability to intervene effectively for the defense of Taiwan unless he granted permission to use nuclear weapons. Eisenhower indicated that he was not unequivocally opposed to intervention under such circumstances, but he preferred for the moment to go slow. As it turned out, our modest conventional intervention proved sufficient.

When John F. Kennedy became President in January, 1961, however, he brought into power with him an entirely different philosophy. A former member of the Senate Armed Services Committee, one who read books and articles on the subject of national defense, he had become familiar with the  contemporary thought opposed to the massive-retaliation doctrine. Among the books he had read was General Maxwell Taylor's *The Uncertain Trumpet* (1959), which had absorbed and restated a good deal of the thinking of the times in favor of enlarging conventional capabilities. Immediately after the disastrous Bay of Pigs affair, which occurred in April, 1961, shortly after he took office, President Kennedy brought General Taylor out of retirement to become his personal military adviser. A far more significant appointment, however, was that of Robert S. McNamara as his Secretary of Defense. President Kennedy, as one of the historians on his staff put it, wanted "to put the nuclear genie back into the bottle," and he found in his new Secretary of Defense a lieutenant with exactly the same wish.

Secretary McNamara at once appointed to his staff a group of civilians, mostly young, to assist him in his reforms. These included a contingent from the RAND Corporation who were skilled mostly in systems analysis but who had also developed to a novel degree the idea that the best way to avoid nuclear war was to build up large conventional capabilities. McNamara quickly made these ideas his own, and moved not only to impress the quite receptive President Kennedy with the need to build up American conventional forces, especially in the Army, but also to induce our NATO Allies to build up theirs as well.

It soon became evident that Secretary McNamara was interested not simply in having substantial conventional forces available to fight "brush fires" and to deal with local threats in Europe, especially around Berlin, but also in having a large enough army under NATO command to be able on a conventional basis alone to deal with a full-fledged, deliberate conventional attack by the whole Soviet field army acting with its Warsaw Pact allies. This plan envisaged not only bringing up NATO divisions on the central front to the number (thirty-two) stipulated by existing agreements but also fleshing them out considerably and providing munitions and other supplies sufficient for ninety days of fighting. The general idea was that only this kind of force would fill in a deterrence component otherwise missing. The advocates of this thinking held that nuclear weapons deterred only nuclear attack but not the conventional variety. They also held that if deterrence nevertheless failed there was a good chance, if we had the appropriate forces, of keeping the resulting war non-nuclear.

There was, however, much to be said on the other side. Even to some who had previously espoused the notion that we had to build up our conventional forces, the new thinking seemed to go to absurd extremes. Building up large conventional forces is extremely expensive, no less so than building up large nuclear forces, and requires a heavy dependence upon conscription. It is incumbent upon us always to scrutinize with great care any extra demands which we make upon our own resources and manpower; but we also had to recognize that we were asking allies to make very considerable additional sacrifices for ideas with which they did not agree, at a time when the Soviet threat in Europe seemed clearly to be diminishing.

It seemed also bizarre to assume that the Russians could make a deliberate attack on western Europe in the hope *and expectation* that nuclear weapons would not be used against them. There was no reason to encourage any such expectations on the part of the Russians, even if we could do so. Besides, it was like assuming they would commit themselves to a duel to the death while leaving the choice of weapons entirely to us. In short, we had on the basis of experience every reason to believe, contrary to the assumptions of the new school, that nuclear weapons in our possession, including over 7,000 tactical nuclear weapons situated in Europe, deterred not only a nuclear attack but *any* deliberate attack on the part of the Soviet Union against the NATO powers. Clearly our European allies thought so, too, because they contented themselves with giving some lip service to the new American ideas while stoutly refusing to implement them with additional forces and supplies. This refusal ultimately killed the plans for a large conventional buildup in Europe. However, the American buildup of our own conventional forces proceeded apace. It probably had much to do with our involvement in Vietnam. It is not irrelevant that when President Lyndon B. Johnson was considering whether to send in combat forces, such forces were in fact available, as they had not been only four years previously.

## NEW WEAPONS FOR NON-NUCLEAR WAR

Because of the time period we are dealing with, security classification covers much of the weaponry we should otherwise wish to describe. In fact, there has been a peculiarly high classification on much of the new weaponry designed for conventional warfare. However, the use of some of it in Vietnam resulted in the inevitable exposure.

Although some types of guided "glide bombs" were experimented with during World War II, the first truly successful guided bombs were dropped from American aircraft in 1972 over Vietnam. Actually, the novel elements were guidance systems in the form of nose and tail assemblies which could be fixed to ordinary 2,000 or 3,000 lb. bombs. The bombs remained gravity-fall weapons, dropped in the usual manner, but the small fins and flaps affixed to them made it possible to feed in small degrees of correction to what would otherwise be a free-fall ballistic trajectory. These were therefore distinct from fully guided bombs, which would have required some form of rocket power in the bomb itself, greatly adding to the latter's complexity and cost.

The guidance systems were developed during the 1960's,

and seem to have been available for some time before they were actually used in Vietnam. Two new major types of guidance systems were adopted. One uses a sensor, in the nose of the bomb, of the "electro-optical" or television type, which can be locked onto a target image. The other uses a sensor that responds to reflected laser-beam radiation.

The electro-optical system used in the Walleye I and Walleye II bombs operates somewhat as follows. The nose of the bomb has a tiny television camera that can be swiveled slightly. In the cockpit of the launching plane is a small television screen, with which the pilot or his radar-observer (in a two-place plane like the Phantom) fixes on the target. Through miniaturized computers on the plane the bomb's camera is turned on and focused on the same picture, and, when the bomb is within appropriate range of the target, it is automatically released. The bomb falls by gravity pull, but with the image of the target impressed upon its memory it manipulates flaps which keep it from straying off target. The plane that has dropped it is meanwhile free to maneuver to avoid ground fire.

The other major type of guided bomb is that which takes its guidance from a laser beam, projected either from the plane which drops the bomb or from another plane. When the laser beam hits the target, part of it is reflected upward, forming an upside-down cone of reflection. The laser-guided bomb locks onto the reflected impulse, guiding itself down that inverted cone to the apex. The laser-beam guidance system is more expensive than the electro-optical, but unlike the latter it can be used in poor weather where the target is acquired not visually but by radar means. Although the aircraft projecting the laser beam cannot leave during the drop, it can be circling at extremely high altitude, above the range of antiaircraft fire.

Both the laser and the TV guidance systems are called HOBOS, for Homing Bomb Systems. In Vietnam in 1972 the various forms of HOBOS enabled U.S. planes to strike effectively targets that had previously defied air attack. Important bridges, for example, were always heavily defended by antiaircraft guns and missiles, forcing attacking aircraft to high altitudes, where the target presented an extremely slender profile. Also, the construction of important bridges is such that they cannot be seriously damaged except by quite heavy bombs, which in turn reduces the number that can be dropped in the usual bombing pattern. With HOBOS, however, a single heavy bomb dropped from an altitude above the range of the defending fire can usually do the job. The bridge at Thanh Hoa, for example, became a challenge to U.S. pilots from 1965 onward. It was heavily defended and strongly built. It spanned a deep gorge and was a major choke-point for arms traffic to the south. With the renewal of the air offensive in 1972, however, this bridge, along with various others serving the same purpose, quickly fell victim to the HOBOS.

Another advantage in using guided bombs is that targets can be singled out for destruction which are situated in heavily populated areas, as are some electric power stations, where the desire to avoid large numbers of civilian casualties may inhibit the normal type of pattern bombing. Thus, the guided bomb is at once more effective in hitting the target and also in avoiding those objects that one does not want to hit. Obviously, the extra cost of the bomb is much more than made up for by the greater effectiveness.

A true guided missile, in the sense that it is self-propelled as well as guided during flight, is the U.S. Army TOW (tube-launched, optically tracked, wire-guided) missile, also unveiled in 1972, though the French had developed another, less effective model considerably earlier. Weighing but 54 pounds, the TOW missile can be fired from a jeep, tripod, or helicopter and can reach a target up to 3,000 meters away in 13 or 14 seconds. During its flight it unreels behind it two thin wires that carry impulses by which the direction of flight is corrected. An optical source on the missile is tracked by a sensor on the launcher. The operator needs only to keep the cross hairs of his gunsight on the target (unlike the earlier French model, where he had to guide the missile in its flight as he would fly an airplane). The sensor feeds course information into the computer, which measures the angle between the missile's direction and the operator's line of sight. The displacement between the two is converted by the computer into guidance commands, which are sent over the wires to activate flaps on the missile. This makes for a very accurate and easily fired weapon.

Originally designed as a surface-to-surface infantry weapon to be employed against tanks and other armored vehicles, the TOW came into its most dramatic use when fired from helicopters in Vietnam. According to Army reports in 1972, just two TOW-equipped helicopters operating in May and June of that year knocked out thirty-nine armored vehicles, artillery pieces, and trucks. The weakness of the TOW in helicopter use, however, is the fact that the highly vulnerable and exposed launching vehicle has to remain stationary for the quarter-minute or so of the missile's flight. The North Vietnamese were thought to have in the Soviet SS-7 rocket a hand-launched heat-seeking missile which could be especially dangerous to hovering helicopters.

In any case, whether used from ground launchers or helicopters, the TOW missile represents only the most recent and most effective of the weapons which may ultimately end the career of the tank. World War II anti-tank weapons were usually unwieldly and inaccurate. The bazooka, for example, required a three-man team situated within 100 yards of the target for firing its unguided missile. That missile (see p. 229) depended on the effect of its shaped charge simply to punch a hole in the armor and to cause the armor fragments to ricochet inside. The TOW missile also lacks the kinetic energy of the armor-piercing shell, but it brings a much larger charge to the target, and of course does so more accurately and over a much greater range. With the tank becoming ever more costly, the development of a relatively cheap weapon which can hit it accurately and destroy it at up to two miles distance does not augur well for its future. Previously the only weapon that could destroy it at such distances was the high velocity field gun (or tank-mounted gun) firing armor-piercing shells, but a moving tank is a difficult target for a gun; it is much less difficult for a guided missile.

A number of other weapons and instruments used in Vietnam are still considerably protected by secrecy. Among these are the various types of marine mines dropped at

Haiphong and other North Vietnamese harbors in May, 1972. It is significant that they were dropped from aircraft and that several mine fields were laid in a very short space of time. The use of aircraft rather than mine-laying ships suggests a rather lightweight mine designed to be laid in relatively shallow waters close to shore. These would be untethered mines resting on the bottom, perhaps designed to move up towards the ship's hull when activated, which activation could be by any combination of pressure, acoustic, and magnetic means. These mines would be virtually unsweepable, designed to be activated by preset timing and also deactivated in the same way, subject to being replaced if necessary. With such mines, effective fields could be laid at very short notice at any distances within the range of bomber aircraft.

There has also been a good deal of mention in the press of sensors dropped on the Ho Chi Minh trail and elsewhere to signal the passing of troops or motor vehicles. There is nothing intrinsically mysterious about such objects, because at night, when ambient temperatures are lower, human bodies radiate heat, and motor vehicles radiate a good deal of it. When we are talking about radiated heat we are talking about infrared rays. An enormous amount of work has gone into developing infrared sensors for guiding missiles and for other uses—such a sensor has been used for a long time, for example, in the Sidewinder air-to-air missile —and the only thing remarkable about sensors for trails would be the degree of sensitivity designed into them, the radio transmitter for sending out the signals, and the small size necessary for the total package in order to escape easy detection.

## NEW NAVAL WEAPONRY

Apart from the new types of naval mines mentioned above embodying new principles of mine laying, there have also been other major naval changes of great moment. These can be grouped under two main categories: (1) a far-reaching displacement of guns by guided missiles; and (2) the increasing use of nuclear power plants to propel both surface and submarine vessels, effecting in the latter a basic change in the strategic utility of the craft.

The final retirement of the battleship following World War II (except for one or two used for shore bombardment in the Korean War, and to a much lesser extent in the Vietnam War) signified not so much the passing of one distinctive type of warship, but rather the downgrading of all types of gun-firing ships as opposed to new types. The battleship was only the largest and most powerful—and therefore the most expensive—of the gun-firing ships. The distinctive characteristics of the battleship were determined by its primary function, beside which other functions, like shore bombardment, were decidedly minor. That primary and preemptive function of the battleship was to fight its like in enemy fleets, that is, to engage the most powerful fighting ships which the enemy might bring to bear, which were likely to be other battleships. The battleship went because a large gun was no longer necessary or even efficient for sinking an enemy battleship—and that meant that before long there would also be no enemy battleships. Bombs from aircraft and torpedoes from arcraft or submarines did as well or better. Except for one old Japanese battleship sunk by old American battleships in Suraigo Strait during the Battle for Leyte Gulf in October, 1944, all the Japanese battleships destroyed or disabled during that battle or subsequently fell to bombs or torpedoes delivered far beyond the ranges of American battleships.

When some twenty-four years later a shore battery near Alexandria sank the Israeli destroyer *Elath* with a single guided missile, we saw demonstrated how completely the naval gun had been outclassed by a weapon that had only begun to make its appearance during World War II. A destroyer carries no armor, but is highly compartmented. Though any gun shell can penetrate its sides, it would take a pretty large one to destroy it with one burst. The tactical guided missile of the kind that destroyed the *Elath* has a clear advantage over the naval gun, not only in range and in accuracy against a swiftly moving and maneuvering ship—especially if its terminal guidance be by some homing device, like a sensor of the infrared rays which a destroyer will radiate copiously—but it will also bring to the target a mass of explosive which only the largest naval guns can match. All this naturally depends on the size and character of the missile, but most of those which have displaced guns on the decks of modern fighting ships easily fit the above description.

Soviet cruisers carry the Shaddock surface-to-surface missile (SSM) with a range of up to 400 miles, and their destroyers carry the Strella SSM with a range of about 100 miles. The guided missiles mounted on U.S. cruisers, frigates, destroyers, and destroyer-escorts are the Tartar SSM, the Terrier and Talos surface-to-air missiles (SAM), and the Asroc and Subroc antisubmarine-warfare missiles (ASWM).

Nuclear power plants have been applied in the United States Navy to one cruiser, two frigates, and to one completed aircraft carrier (the new *Enterprise*). One is also being applied to another carrier now building, and it is unlikely that any U.S. aircraft carrier built henceforth will carry anything but nuclear power plants. However, it is in the large submarine vessel that the nuclear power plant has its most far-reaching effect, for it changes the whole character of the underwater ship. U.S. submarines equipped to fire the intermediate range ballistic missile (IRBM) of the Polaris or Poseidon type, of which there are forty-one (SSBN), are nuclear powered. So also are some fifty-three attack submarines.

The conventional submarine has always been, except for a few experimental models, an exceptionally slow vessel, certainly the slowest of the combatant types. For surface cruising, at which time it charges its storage batteries, it uses diesel engines, and inasmuch as it needs a good deal of range but has no great need for surface speed (though that speed would be useful if not too costly in other performance characteristics), it has been content to use engines of modest power, thereby conserving space and fuel. When submerged it could cruise only on its storage batteries (except for some experimental types built during World War II which, through use of a *Schnorkel*, operated on diesel engines even when submerged), and the primary consideration always has been to conserve the very limited supply of electrical energy stored in those batteries. Thus, submerged endurance has been limited to at most 18 to 24 hours, and for such duration the vessel would have to cruise at a speed of only three to four knots, scarcely more than enough to give it steering way. In World War II types top speed when submerged, which permitted but little endurance, was about 12 to 16 knots.

One somehow got the idea that any submerged vessel is necessarily limited to low speeds, no doubt because of the density of the medium through which it moves. Actually, the reverse is the case. Given a submarine of the same displacement and power thrust as a destroyer, the submerged vessel will move *faster* than the surface ship. The reason is that, especially at high speeds, the destroyer will inevitably waste much of its power making bow waves, and in other perturbations of the water. The submarine does not waste power in that fashion, and its own distinctive resistances will not be sufficient to offset that gain.

Nuclear energy provides the ideal power plant for the submerged vessel. Where the steam or the diesel engine requires large amounts of oxygen, the nuclear plant requires none. Also, where the standard submarine requires a dual power plant, the power plant which is nuclear will do for both surface and submerged cruising. Finally, the fantastically long life of the nuclear fuel supply makes it feasible to cruise at high speeds both on the surface and submerged. Actually, there is not much need for surface cruising. There is no requirement for charging batteries, and the oxygen necessary for the crew is easily supplied chemically or from storage tanks. Thus, the nuclear-powered submarine can stay submerged literally for months. The one considerable drawback is that in order to use nuclear power efficiently, the submarine must be a large and expensive vessel.

There may some day be a great breakthrough in the underwater detection of the submarine. If it could be spotted while submerged in the same way that the eye or optical instruments or radar can spot a surface ship or convoy, its day would no doubt swiftly pass. However, that day does not now appear close. Salt water being an electrolytic, underwater radar seems hopeless. Sound ranging or Sonar appears inherently limited in range and reliability, besides which it requires that the vessel using it proceed at relatively low speeds. The hydrophone has been marvelously improved in sensitivity, but the ocean is a noisy place. Meanwhile, the attack submarine has had the advantage of steadily improving homing torpedoes—which of course can be used against it if it is spotted in time. Also, by simply surfacing an antenna, it can be in radio communication with surface ships and shore stations monitoring reconnaissance satellites, from which convoys can scarcely stay long hidden.

The Polaris submarine devised for firing submarine-launched ballistic missiles (SLBM) represented an enormous imaginative thrust forward, because even the prototype, besides being nuclear powered, was designed to carry sixteen such missiles in an upright position ready for quick firing. This configuration has remained the model for all forty-one constructed thus far. Of these, eight have now been converted to fire the multi-warhead Poseidon, and the others carry the Polaris A-2 or A-3 missile. The forty-one vessels carry 656 missiles and several times that number of warheads. What was once regarded as a backstop to the land-based force of ICBMs seems likely, as the latter appear less secure, to become the main deterrent force. For the moment its missiles appear less accurate, but new advances in missile guidance, including the possibility of course correction by steller orientation, promise to make the SLBM as accurate as any missile.

### NEW STRATEGIC WEAPONS DEVELOPMENTS:
### THE MIRV AND ABM SYSTEMS

It is not for nothing that the thermonuclear bomb has been called the "absolute weapon." For, whatever one wants to do with such a bomb, there is little sense in making it much more powerful than it has already become. In 1961, when the Russians detonated a device which yielded some fifty *megatons* of explosive power, the United States did not even bother to follow suit. There is no question that Americans could duplicate the accomplishment if they wished. Neither was there any doubt that a device of such magnitude, even if it could be packaged in a form capable of being delivered as a bomb, had no conceivable utility that could not be equally well or better accomplished by one or more much smaller bombs, say of one to ten megaton yield, the latter being by any previous standard a horrendously powerful weapon.

The Soviet 50 MT device, incidentally, exploded "clean," that is, without the intense radioactive fallout that was so prominent a feature of the American "Bravo" shot of March, 1954, which caused some casualties on a Japanese fishing vessel in the area. The significance of its being clean was that the Russians could easily have made the same device yield perhaps twice the energy, which is to say about 100 MT, if they had been willing to explode it "dirty." That is because the fallout comes from fission fragments rather than from hydrogen fusion, and fission fragments are produced by having a "tamper" of ordinary uranium around the bomb, that is, uranium which is chemically clean but not isotopically separated. There is so copious a release of free neutrons in the thermonuclear fusion that a substantial proportion of any U-238 atoms present will be induced to fission, not to mention the more responsive U-235. One seeks in this case not a chain reaction among the uranium atoms but simply an augmentation of the yield from the fusion reaction, which is accomplished by having uranium atoms present to react to the neutrons that would otherwise be wasted. In the usually dirty thermonuclear bomb, as much or more of the energy yielded actually comes from fission as from fusion.

Anyway, granted that powerful thermonuclear bombs can be designed to be easily transported in a vehicle like a bomber aircraft or long-range missile, the emphasis in development inevitably shifts to the packaging and to associated improvements in the mode of transport. Reduction of the weight of the warhead for any given yield means (a) ability to use a smaller missile or aircraft to transport it, or (b) ability to mount several warheads in one missile or to carry a substantial number of them in one large bomber. Meaningful improvement is also gained by improving

ing the accuracy of the means of delivery, especially of the long-range ballistic missile. The layman normally assumes that with a weapon as powerful as the thermonuclear bomb, pinpoint accuracy is hardly necessary. That is certainly true if the target is a huge sprawling city, with building structures that are easily destroyed by modest blast overpressures (that is, instantaneous pressures over and above the normal atmospheric pressure). But if the target should be an enemy missile sitting in a hardened underground silo which is capable of withstanding an overpressure of perhaps 300 psi (pounds per square inch) or more, then accuracy becomes very important. In the latter instance it will make a quite considerable difference if the C.E.P. is one mile or if it is only a quarter of a mile (C.E.P. stands for "circular error probable," the radius of the circle within which will fall one-half of whatever kinds of bombs or missiles are aimed at its center).

We shall discuss first the matter of multiple warheads in a single missile, because that subject is more easily dispatched than the ABM. The multiple warhead systems are basically of two kinds: (a) that which lacks separate targeting for each warhead, and (b) the system known as MIRV (for multiple, independently-targetable, reentry vehicles).

The former system seems to have been passed over by the United States but developed by the Soviet Union. Even without independent targeting, if a number of warheads or RVs (reentry vehicles, capable of withstanding the heat of reentry into the earth's atmosphere in completing their trajectory) are sent towards a single target by one rocket booster, the advantages are at least twofold. For one thing, the attacker offers several targets rather than only one against whatever defensive ABM system the opponent has. Much money has gone into research on decoys, which are objects attending the warhead and meant to confuse the defender's radar so that he finds it difficult to judge which among the objects appearing on his radar screen he must fire at. If instead of decoys, or along with them, there are several real warheads, the problem for the defender is certainly augmented. Second, because of the cube-root law concerning dispersion of blast pressures—that is, the radius for any given blast pressure expands only according to the cube root of any increase in power of the bomb—one is likely to come closer to the target and thus gain much more effectiveness by having a spread-out pattern of warheads rather than only one, even if the total yield from the several amounts to substantially less than might be obtained from a single warhead.

However, especially if the targeting for each be sufficiently accurate, one can readily imagine the advantages of being able to aim separately each warhead of a multiple system. The principle involved is easily described. The missile upon separating from the booster is moving along a trajectory which, depending upon distortions produced by reentry, must terminate at a particular point on the earth's surface. If the missile is well aimed, this point will be at or near the initial target. One may, however, with little additional bursts of propulsion, have one or more predetermined shifts in the trajectory. If before each shift an RV containing a warhead separates from the main system, that RV will continue along the path or trajectory determined by the last previous course shift. By making these course shifts early in the flight, maximum dispersion is achieved from relatively modest propulsive impulses. That is the idea of MIRV—simplicity itself in conception, rather more difficult in execution.

According to press reports, undoubtedly sanctioned by Pentagon releases, the land-based Minuteman III is designed to have three independently targetable warheads, and the Poseidon missile launched from a submarine, the successor to the original Polaris, is designed to have ten to as many as fourteen. It is curious that the smaller and shorter-ranged missile should have the larger numbers of RVs, but one possible explanation would be that the RVs from the Poseidon have basically different kinds of targets and therefore require much smaller energy yields than the RVs from Minuteman II. The former, for example, might be intended primarily for counter-force targets, which would be mostly enemy missiles in their silos, while the latter could be intended mostly for counter-value targets, which could be cities of varying sizes or portions of cities.

The latter are soft targets as compared with the former, as the damage done at Hiroshima with only a 12 to 14 KT bomb will forever demonstrate.

We should note that while it is easy enough to count the rival nation's land-based missiles, because one's own reconnaissance satellites will pick up and locate exactly any silos under construction, and while it is also relatively easy to keep tab of the number of submarine-launched missiles available to that nation, it is essentially impossible to monitor the number of warheads within any missile. It is partly for that reason that MIRV and other forms of multiple warhead systems were omitted from consideration in the Strategic Arms Limitation Agreements of 1972. The MIRV also greatly affects the problem of ballistic missile defense. Any ABM system is more likely to suffer saturation if the attack against it is from missiles with multiple warheads. On the other hand, one can support the loss of many retaliatory missiles and still have a formidable second-strike capability if the surviving ones are of the MIRV type. In both respects the existence of MIRV would seem to depreciate the value of an ABM defense.

We turn now to the ABM (anti-ballistic missile) system as developed within the United States by the year 1972, a most complex and ingenious technological achievement.

Almost from the time it became known that an intercontinental ballistic missile (ICBM) was scientifically possible and therefore probably technologically feasible (calculations to prove as much were available by the time World War II ended), some venturesome souls began to consider using an anti-missile missile. To those who knew how difficult it was to devise an effective active defense against aircraft, whether with guns or self-propelled missiles, the idea of shooting down an ICBM moving at many times the speed of sound might seem impossibly difficult. And difficult it certainly was—and remains. But one should also notice that in two respects the problem is easier than that of shooting down aircraft.

First, an ICBM must inevitably have a trajectory with a pretty high maximum ordinate—on the order of several hundreds of miles. It is possible to vary the height of the trajectory for any given distance traversed, but even the lowest possible (or minimum energy) trajectory for that distance will still be considerably higher than that of any aircraft bound to the atmosphere. This means that the ICBM may be picked up by a radar while it is still hundreds of miles away. Second, though the flight of missiles can be somewhat altered—as we have seen, the MIRV depends on variations in course direction early in the missile's flight—the missile has nevertheless proved thus far an object of far more predetermined and therefore predictable course of flight than any aircraft. Thus, a missile which begins to be tracked as soon as radar picks it up, which may be while it is still hundreds of miles from its target, is already providing usable data for launching a missile against it. There has been talk of devising RVs which will be able to maneuver somewhat after reentry, but thus far they have not been perfected, and whether they will be or not depends partly on the progress made with the ABM.

However, let us not make it look too easy. First of all, one needs to develop a radar which is capable of picking up a pretty small object while it is still hundreds of miles away, and preferably also one which is capable at least to some degree of discriminating between the RV containing the warhead and other objects, the latter being either the booster, whole or fragmented, or a variety of decoys which are deployed along with the warhead. One also needs a radar which is capable of handling a good deal of incoming traffic at one time without becoming overloaded. Finally, it is necessary to have a radar which is not susceptible to being easily knocked out by the first of the weapons with which it is expected to cope. Insofar as we have the answer to these problems it has proved to be the "phased array" radar, the chief characteristic of which is that it scans electronically rather than mechanically. This means that its antenna rods may remain stationary. The antenna can thus be made sufficiently large to meet its requirements in sensitivity and discrimination, and its rods can be embedded in concrete to withstand enormous blast pressures.

One naturally needs also computers capable of performing at high speed a variety of tasks, which include accurately

tracking incoming missiles and from the data thereby acquired, firing and guiding the interceptor missiles. The
computers must also be capable of effecting discrimination,
and they too must be able to handle a large amount of traffic.

One also needs the appropriate interceptor missile or
family of missiles, and on this issue hangs a considerable
tale. Certainly one wants a missile which can intercept
while the incoming RV is still a considerable distance
from its target, perhaps three or four hundred miles away,
but this requirement raises a variety of problems, including
the question: by what means is the interceptor going to
destroy the incoming RV? We are talking about an interception above the atmosphere, where there can exist no
blast pressures, which would in any case have to be exceedingly high to do damage to or even knock appreciably off
course a vehicle that has to be constructed solidly enough
to withstand reentry. Thermal radiation will not do either,
unless the interception is exceedingly close.

Actually, this problem proved a stumbling block for
many years and resulted in a waning of interest in the whole
ABM problem, until in the late 1950's someone (reputed
to be Dr. Albert Latter, then of the Physics Division of the
RAND Corporation) discovered by studying some test data
in his files that the X-rays which form so large a proportion
of the energy released in any nuclear explosion will have
above the atmosphere an astonishingly wide kill radius,
and will of course move with the speed of light. The "fast"
or "hot" X-rays will impinge so copiously on the RV as to
cause an implosion on the surface affected. It was indeed
known before then that it would have to be X-rays which
did the lethal damage, but the new insight was that the kill
radii would be much broader than previously expected.
The nuclear explosion to produce the rays would have to
be a powerful one, and the weapon would have to be designed to maximize the emission of hot X-rays as compared
with other forms of energy normally released in nuclear
reactions. But we are now considering a reasonably wide
latitude for interception.

However, let us point out immediately two weaknesses
in this system of exo-atmospheric destruction. An incoming
vehicle designed for reentry of the atmosphere has to be

quite rugged anyway, but if it also has to encounter heavy doses of X-rays, it can be redesigned for additional ruggedness of the appropriate kind. It is conceivable that such redesign will reduce considerably the radius of destruction of a given interceptor missile. Second, even if the X-rays damage the incoming RV sufficiently to render it harmless, that fact may not be registered on the observing radar. The radar might register an interception close enough to warrant the assumption of a kill, but it would still be only an assumption, possibly erroneous. Would another interceptor missile have to be fired at the same RV?

We have thus far been describing strictly an exo-atmospheric intercept system, and such was already available in the Army's Nike-Zeus, first tested at the White Sands Missile Range in New Mexico in 1959. The Army pressed Congress and the Eisenhower administration to approve deployment of Nike-Zeus, and offered the estimate that it would succeed in bringing down about 25 per cent of any long-range missiles fired by the Soviet Union, which at that time was considered to be developing a strong ICBM capability. The 25 per cent estimate must not be taken too seriously. It is interesting only for underlining the relative modesty of the Army claims, despite which it wanted to go ahead with deployment. President Eisenhower, nearing the end of his term of office, decided to leave the decision to the incoming administration.

The new president, John F. Kennnedy, and his Secretary of Defense, Robert S. McNamara, soon decided that there was no "missile gap" with the Soviet Union to worry about, that there were other defense needs with higher priority than an ABM system, and that in any case Nike-Zeus was not a good enough system to warrant deployment. The Army was instructed to continue its R and D (research and development), and in late 1962 McNamara decided to reorient the development program from the Zeus concept to what became known in the following January as Nike-X. The Nike-X system differed from Zeus primarily in incorporating, in addition to the long-range Zeus intercept missile, the Sprint missile for close-in or intra-atmospheric interception. Meanwhile, in July, 1962, a Zeus missile fired from

Kwajalein Island successfully intercepted the warhead of an Atlas missile fired from Vandenburg AFB in California.

The purpose of adding a Sprint missile was twofold. First, it was considered desirable to be able to defend also against Soviet submarine-launched missiles, for which warning and response times would be minimal. Much more important, however, was the second idea, which was that with the development of decoys (upon which there had been considerable and costly R and D in the United States) there had to be a stronger emphasis on discrimination. Some rough discrimination might be achieved by use of very powerful radars while the incoming objects were still far out and well above the atmosphere, but with more sophisticated decoys it might be necessary to wait until those objects reentered the atmosphere. Upon reentry, which begins at about an altitude of eighty miles, each object, depending upon its mass and configuration, could be expected to show a distinctive behavior with respect to rates of deceleration and the like; and a properly programmed computer might be expected to distinguish between decoys and RVs with warheads, directing the firing of missiles only against the latter.

By this time, however, the warhead would be getting dangerously close to its target and it would therefore be necessary to fire a fast-reaction missile, one that would take off extremely fast and accelerate rapidly. Hence the term Sprint missile. As one would expect, it has a cone-like appearance with a relatively wide base for maximum initial thrust, and its two stages allow for quick separation of the initial booster. Inasmuch as its interception must take place within the atmosphere, which sharply limits the range of X-rays, the kill has to depend upon another feature of nuclear detonations, in this case the release of fast neutrons. These can be expected to incapacitate the electronics of the incoming warhead and perhaps also to predetonate its fissionable materials, causing enough heat to fuse the mass. For a variety of reasons, including the need for fast acceleration in Sprint, its likelihood of a close interception, and the fact that detonation would take place quite close to home, the nuclear warhead of the Sprint missile had to and could be much smaller than that of the long-range Zeus intercept missile. Again it would not be known at the observing radar whether a kill had actually been effected, but it would in any case be too late for further action.

In late 1965 a Sprint test missile was successfully launched from its underground silo, and at the same time it was decided to modify the long-range Zeus missile, giving it a larger second stage to improve payload and range. This became known as the Spartan missile. With its development all mention of Zeus either as a missile or as a system disappeared. Meanwhile, too, the mechanically scanning radar of the Zeus system had given way to a phased-array type. Computer development had also proceeded apace, no doubt assisted by the R and D devoted to the Apollo program for lunar exploration. By 1967 we already had the modern Nike-X system, named the "Sentinel" system by the Johnson administration and renamed "Safeguard" by President Nixon when he changed its basic mission from the defense of cities to the defense primarily of our own retaliatory forces.

The contemporary Safeguard system consists, as we have seen, of two kinds of missiles, the Spartan and the Sprint. The former is a large (54-foot long) three-stage missile, capable of boosting a powerful thermonuclear warhead and of reaching its maximum range of about 400 miles in one minute. Its costs have been stated to be between $2 and $4 million each without its nuclear warhead and without its silo housing. The Sprint, also a two-stage missile, is at 27 feet considerably smaller than the Spartan and carries a lighter nuclear warhead, but it is designed to accelerate at well over 100 g. during its initial scramble to altitude. It must also withstand temperatures of 6,000 F. during launch from its silo, because it is surrounded by the flaming gases which are causing its ejection. One must assume that it, too, with its silo housing, is not going to be cheap. Associated with these missiles are also two basic types of radar, the PAR, or perimeter acquisition radar, and the MSR, or missile site radar, both housed in enormous concrete structures. In the one American ABM installation building at this writing, that near Grand Forks AFB, North Dakota, there is a PAR structure which is 200 feet square at the base and towers up 120 feet. It contains one mammoth radar eye staring northward at a slope of 120° from the terrain ahead. The MSR, 36 miles away, is housed in a concrete structure 231 feet square at the base and 125 feet deep, of which 50 feet are underground. The MSR has four radar rings enabling it to look in all directions. Nearby is a "farm" of thirty Spartan missiles, and scattered about are smaller farms containing 68 Sprints. There is also a multi-function array radar (MAR), very large and powerful, and a reduced version of same called TACMAR, but these do not seem to be scheduled for deployment. It is possible that the scheduled PAR and MSR have taken over some of the functions of the MAR.

The function of the PAR is to pick up the incoming missile as far as 1,000 miles away, track it, and communicate its information to the MSR. The latter takes over the tracking as the RV comes closer in, triggers the firing of a Spartan or a Sprint missile, as appropriate, and guides the missile to interception. Each radar with its computers is engaged also in discrimination, especially the MSR, which has the delicate job of discriminating enemy objects by their atmospheric reentry patterns.

Secretary McNamara had always been dubious of the worth of an ABM system, and remained dubious even of the highly perfected Sentinel system which became available during his term of office. He felt that if an ABM could be devised with characteristics approaching that of a water-tight umbrella, the United States would be obliged to provide itself with one, at almost any cost. But inasmuch as no such near-perfect kill ratios could be expected, he was convinced that the system simply was not worth the very large sums of money—with unpredictable ceilings—that it was bound to cost. He did not think that major cities could be defended by such means, because the enemy needs in each case to get only one or two missiles past the defenses, and he thought that insofar as our retaliatory missiles might be threatened by the increasing accuracy of enemy missiles, there were probably better ways of meeting that threat.

However, during 1967 President Johnson, probably with an eye to the coming election year, appears to have put some pressure on his Secretary of Defense to approve a modest deployment of Sentinel. Secretary McNamara accordingly made the announcement in San Francisco in September, 1967, at the end of a speech which in the main outlined all the weaknesses of ABM, that the United States would nevertheless proceed to deploy a "thin" ABM defense of our major cities "against China only." This was described as a defense adequate against the very modest threat that China would presumably be capable of mounting within the next decade, but not adequate against the Soviet Union.

Mr. McNamara showed no inclination to defend the strange logic of his pronouncement (he was to retire from the office of Secretary of Defense within a few months), though others were ready to do it for him. However, this logic became moot early in 1969 when the new president, Richard Nixon, came out in strong support of the new ABM system, though with an entirely different mission from that announced by McNamara. The idea of defending cities was abandoned, except for Washington, which was the main command center of the nation. Instead the system, renamed Safeguard, was to be deployed to defend our own land-based retaliatory missiles.

This change in purpose was a wise one, for the following three basic reasons: (1) nuclear deterrence depends upon the safety of our retaliatory missiles against surprise atttack, and if their safety can be guaranteed the safety of our cities is also virtually assured; (2) the formerly formidable protection afforded our land-based missiles through "hardening," that is, through emplacement in underground concrete silos surmounted by heavy steel trap doors, was threatened with decay by the increasing accuracy of missile guidance; and (3) "hard point" targets, like missiles in concrete silos, are much more effectively defended by ABM means than large, sprawling, soft targets, like cities. Only the latter point needs explanation. The reasons are basically twofold: (a) only enemy RVs that appear to be coming close to their individual hard-point targets need to be intercepted, which means that many can be simply ignored; and (b) the kill ratio does not need to be nearly so favorable to the defender in order to provide a highly effective defense. If, for example, the defender can count on shooting down two out of every three incoming RVs, that may mean little or nothing so far as defense of major cities is concerned, but it may be quite meaningful for the defense of a retaliatory force. The enemy actually does not know before an attack how many of his missiles will get through the defenses, but if he thinks it may be only about one in three, with not all of those getting through doing effective damage, he is hardly likely to find himself with a superiority great enough to warrant such attack.

However, what we are saying here is that *if* the ABM make sense at all, it makes sense mostly as a defense of one's own land-based missiles. That does not itself argue, however, that the ABM is definitely superior to various alternative ways of meeting the allegedly growing threat to our ICBMs. One alternative way already exists in the submarine-launched missiles of the Polaris/Poseidon type, and some would hold that the bomber, with its capability for early take-off and airborne alert, is another way. McNamara felt that building an ABM would only make the enemy increase the number of his missiles, and that the cost trade-offs favored such a tactic.

In any case, the whole ABM question touched off so intense and emotional a debate in this country as to be virtually without precedent on any issue of weaponry. There had also been an emotional debate of some intensity about 1960-1961 on the fallout-shelter issue, but it was as nothing compared to this one. The hawks, those who suspected and feared the aggressive designs of the Soviet Union, thought we now had an effective ABM system and should deploy it. The doves, who felt that our fears of the Soviet Union were perennially exaggerated, felt also that the Safeguard system was just not sufficiently reliable to be worth its huge cost. Senator Frank Church of Idaho called the new system "potentially the most expensive sieve in history." There was no doubt that the bitter U.S. experience in Vietnam had much to do with the general skepticism of Pentagon planning and the surfeit with cost over-runs, and all sorts of newly apparent domestic problems were inciting talk about "straightening out our national priorities." The vote in the Senate in 1969 for authorization of the project passed by only a single-vote majority, and if the margin was better in succeeding years, it was partly because the Administration supported its case in large measure by arguing the alleged bargaining leverage that a favorable vote would give in the ongoing negotiations known as SALT (Strategic Arms Limitation Talks).

We shall not attempt here the impossible task, impossible especially in a few brief pages, of weighing the case on its merits. Highly knowledgeable and specifically informed people could be found on both sides of the argument. Scientists, engineers, and others disagreed with each other about the reliability or basic workability of the system. The amount of obvious bias on each side was often wondrous to behold. In May, 1972, however, this debate suddenly became moot, as a result of the treaty signed in Moscow during President Nixon's visit there. This treaty severely limited the ABM deployments on both sides. It limited the Russians with their Galosh system to essentially the deployment they had already achieved for the defense of Moscow. The United States was limited to two ABM sites, comprising a total of 200 intercept missiles. One site is that of Grand Forks AFB already mentioned. The other site specified was to be for the defense of Washington. At this writing it seems unlikely that the latter deployment will ever take place.

## THE PROBLEM OF MOUNTING COSTS

As weaponry increases in complexity and sophistication, it is natural that it should become more expensive. But the kind of steep ascent in costs that we have been witnessing over the last decade or two, a rise which seems exponential rather than simply arithmetic, poses quite special problems of its own. One of the problems is to determine in each case whether it goes beyond anything that can be rationally justified.

One of the notions we should dispose of at once is the idea that only a large strategic nuclear capability is expensive, that the weapons called "conventional" are not. The contract for the F-14 aircraft, for example, a strictly conventional fighter designed for the Navy to be used on aircraft carriers, called for a price of something over $12 million per plane, which was about four times the price of the preceding F-4 or Phantom plane. However, during the building of the first 86 of these planes the Grumman Aircraft Corporation announced that it would be unable to fulfill its contract for over 300 of them unless the price were renegotiated. The price fixed upon for the next portion of the original order was $16.8 million per plane. Meanwhile the cost of the nuclear-powered aircraft carrier itself was already going well over the $1 billion mark. Thus, carrier-borne aviation was indeed becoming extremely costly. It was becoming more costly not only intrinsically but also in comparison with other means of doing its job.

The F-14 is indeed a remarkable aircraft, with quite ingenious navigational characteristics. It can now also drop "smart bombs" rather than the unguided variety, and thus have an increased effectiveness that almost justifies its increased cost. We say "almost," because after all the Phantoms can drop guided bombs too. As technology advances, it proceeds on so many different fronts that the opportunities for designing in new performance characteristics for any vehicle tend to outrun our ability to evaluate the utility of those characteristics. It is always possible to show that these new features help. It is not always possible to demonstrate that they are worth their additional cost. After all, the debate about the ABM, whether Sentinel or Safeguard, concerned almost exclusively the question: will it be worth its cost?

It is a military question as well as an economic one. The country can hardly be expected to increase steadily the proportion of the GNP (gross national product) devoted to defense if the international political environment is not clearly worsening. The GNP steadily advances, which means that a stable proportion of it accounts for an increasing amount—though not increasing as fast as the unit costs of new weaponry. Moreover, we are not certain the country will or should continue to support a stable though high proportion of GNP for defense. Thus, mounting unit costs will usually eventually mean diminished numbers. Will the Navy continue to have fifteen carriers in its fleet if the cost of each carrier mounts to three or four times the cost of only a few years ago (and 200 times the cost of the *Enterprise* of World War II fame, which was $19 million) and if the cost of each aircraft operating from that carrier mounts at an even steeper rate? Similarly, if on land the tank becomes obsolete, it will not be simply because of the appearance of an inexpensive TOW missile which was able to destroy it but rather because the TOW appeared *while the tank kept steadily rising in cost*. The battleship became obsolete before the cruiser did, even though the battleship in its final form could do everything the cruiser could do, including propelling itself at high speed. It simply cost a good deal more per unit. The cruiser, too, may soon be obsolete, but it will have taken a little longer.

If there is any single trend that seems to dominate in weaponry, it is for missiles of all kinds to become more accurate and more destructive. Therefore, building more size and more protection into any military vehicle, which always means more cost, becomes at critical moments a step in the wrong direction. As in law, general rules do not determine specific cases. Each question must be decided on its specific merits. However, we quite literally cannot afford to forget that increasing unit costs in all kinds of weaponry constitute an increasing military problem. Secretary McNamara was often charged with being too sensitive to this problem, with being too much enchanted with systems analysis as a means of getting the most for one's money. His successor in the Nixon administration, Melvin R. Laird, may prove to have been too little concerned with it.

It is pleasant to sit back and speculate about the new kinds of devices that advancing techolnogy may make possible. To do so profitably, however, has always required the ingredient of discipline, which means among other things awareness of the importance of costs. Naturally, an even more basic question is the purpose or necessity for any given military posture, let alone any proposed military action.

# Bibliography

Baxter, James Phinney. *The Introduction of the Ironclad Warship*. Cambridge: Harvard University Press, 1933.
———. *Scientists Against Time*. Boston: Little, Brown and Co., 1946.
Blackmore, H. *Guns and Rifles of the World*. London: Botsford, 1965.
Brodie, Bernard. *Sea Power in the Machine Age*. Princeton: Princeton University Press, 2d ed., 1944. Reissued by Greenwood Press, 1969.
———. *A Guide to Naval Strategy*. Princeton: Princeton University Press, 4th ed., 1958. Reissued by Praeger, 1965.
———. *Strategy in the Missile Age*. Princeton: Princeton University Press, 2d ed., 1965.
———. *Escalation and the Nuclear Option*. Princeton: Princeton University Press, 1966.
———. *War and Politics*. New York: Macmillan, 1973.
Chayes, Abram, and Wiesner, Jerome B., eds. *ABM: An Evaluation of the Decision to Deploy an Antiballistic Missile System*. New York: Harper and Row, 1969.
Chinn, G. M. *Encyclopedia of American Handarms*. Huntington, W. Va.: Standard Printing and Publishing Co., 1942.
Churchill, Winston S. *A History of the English-Speaking Peoples*. 4 vols. New York: Dodd, Mead and Co., 1956-58.
Clagett, Marshall. *Greek Science in Antiquity*. New York: Abelard, 1955.

Clark, George. *Early Modern Europe from about 1450 to about 1720*. London: Oxford University Press, 1957.

_____. *War and Society in the Seventeenth Century*. Cambridge: Cambridge University Press, 1958.

Coffey, Joseph I. *Strategic Power and National Security*. Pittsburgh: University of Pittsburgh Press, 1971.

Conant, James B. *On Understanding Science*. New Haven: Yale University Press, 1947.

Crowther, J. G. *The Social Relations of Science*. New York: Macmillan, 1941.

Forbes, R. J. *Man the Maker, a History of Technology and Engineering*. London: Constable, 1958.

Fuller, John Frederick Charles. *Armament and History*. New York: Charles Scribner's Sons, 1945.

_____. *Military History of the Western World*. 3 vols. New York: Funk and Wagnalls, 1955.

Gibbs-Smith, Charles H. *The Invention of the Aeroplane, 1799-1909*. New York: Taplinger, 1965.

Gimpel, Herbert J. *The United States Nuclear Navy*. New York: F. Watts, 1965.

Hall, Alfred Rupert. *Ballistics in the 17th Century, a study in the relations of science and war with reference principally to England*. Cambridge: Cambridge University Press, 1952.

_____. *The Scientific Revolution, 1500-1800, the formation of the modern scientific attitude*. London: Longmans Green, 1954.

Hezlet, Vice Admiral Sir Arthur. *The Submarine and Sea Power*. London: P. Davies, 1967.

Hoffschmidt, E. J. H., and Tantum, W. H. *German Tank and Antitank in World War II*. Greenwich, Conn.: W. E., Inc., 1968.

Holst, Johan J., and Schneider, William, Jr., eds. *Why ABM? Policy Issues in the Missile Defense Controversy*. New York: Pergamon Press, 1969.

Howard, Michael. *The Franco-Prussian War, 1870–71*. New York: Macmillan, 1961.

Jackson, Herbert J. *European Hand Firearms, 16th to 18th Centuries*. 2d ed., London: Holland Press, 1959.

Jameson, Rear Admiral William. *The Most Formidable*

*Thing: The Story of the Submarine from Its Earliest Days to the End of World War I.* London: R. Hart-Davis, 1969.

Johnson, Melvin M., and Haven, Charles T. *Automatic Arms, Their History, Development and Use.* New York: William Morrow, 1941.

Jungk, Robert. *Brighter than a Thousand Suns.* London: Pelican, 1958.

Liddell Hart, B. H. *Thoughts on War.* London: Faber and Faber, 1944.

——. *The Revolution in Warfare.* New Haven: Yale University Press, 1947.

——. *Strategy, the Indirect Approach.* New York: Praeger, 1954.

Koller, Larry. *The Fireside Book of Guns.* New York: Simon and Schuster, 1959.

Kranberg, Melvin, and Pursell, Caroll W., Jr., eds. *Technology in Western Civilization.* 2 vols. New York: Oxford University Press, 1967.

Leithäuser, Joachim G. *Inventors' Progress.* New York: World Publishing Co., 1959.

Mattingly, Garrett. *The Armada.* Boston: Houghton Mifflin, 1959.

Montgomery of Alamein. *A History of Warfare.* New York: World Publishing Co., 1968.

Montross, Lynn. *War Through the Ages.* New York: Harper and Bros., 1944.

Mumford, Lewis. *Technics and Civilization.* New York: Harcourt, Brace, 1934.

Needham, Joseph, and Pagel, Walter, eds. *Background to Modern Science.* New York: Macmillan, 1940.

Nef, John U. *War and Human Progress.* Cambridge: Harvard University Press, 1950.

Newman, James R. *The Tools of War.* Garden City, N.Y.: Doubleday, Doran, 1942.

Oliver, John W. *History of American Technology.* New York: Ronald Press, 1956.

Oman, Charles. *A History of the Art of War, the Middle Ages from the Fourth to the Fourteenth Century.* London, 1898.

Penrose, Boies. *Travel and Discovery in the Renaissance, 1420-1620*. Cambridge: Harvard University Press, 1952.

*A Pictorial History of Science and Engineering*. By the editors of *Year*. New York, 1957.

Roberts, Michael. *Gustavus Adolphus, a History of Sweden, 1611-1632*. London: Longmans Green, 1953.

Rolt, L. T. C. *The Aeronauts: A History of Ballooning, 1783-1903*. London: Longmans Green, 1966.

Ropp, Theodore. *War in the Modern World*. Durham, N.C.: Duke University Press, 1959.

Sarton, George. *Six Wings, Men of Science in the Renaissance*. Bloomington: Indiana University Press, 1957.

Singer, Charles; Holmyard, E. J.; Hall, A. R.; and Williams, Trevor I. *A History of Technology*. London: Oxford University Press, 1956.

Smyth, Henry D. *Atomic Energy for Military Purposes*. Princeton: Princeton University Press, 1945.

Swinton, Ernest D. *Eyewitness to the Genesis of Tanks*. New York: Doubleday, 1933.

Thomas, Thomas H. "Armies and the Railway Revolution," in J. D. Clarkson and T. C. Cochran, eds., *War as a Social Institution*. New York: Columbia Universtiy Press, 1941.

Tunis, Edwin. *Weapons, a Pictorial History*. Cleveland: World Publishing Co., 1954.

Waitt, Brigadier-General Alden H. "Gas Warfare, the Chemical Weapon." *Infantry Journal* (Washington, D.C.), 1943.

Wedgwood, C. V. *The Thirty Years War*. New Haven: Yale University Press, 1949.

Wilson, Mitchell. *American Science and Invention, A Pictorial History*. New York: Simon and Schuster, 1954.

White, Lynn. *Medieval Technology and Social Change*. New York and London: Oxford University Press, 1963.

Wood, Derek, and Dempster, Derek. *The Narrow Margin: The Battle of Britain and the Rise of Air Power, 1930-40*. New York: McGraw-Hill, 1961.

# Name and Weapon Index

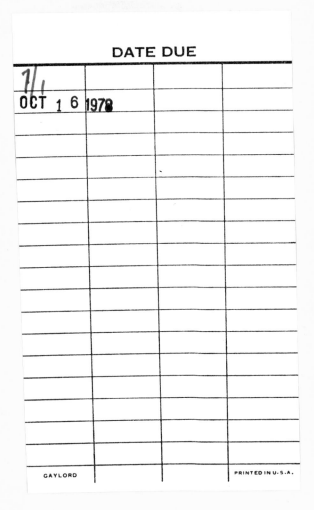

# DATE DUE

OCT 1 6 1978

GAYLORD       PRINTED IN U.S.A.